T0313819

THE MYSTERY OF
THE KIBBUTZ

THE PRINCETON ECONOMIC HISTORY OF THE WESTERN WORLD
JOEL MOKYR, SERIES EDITOR

A list of titles in this series appears at the back of the book.

THE MYSTERY OF
THE KIBBUTZ

Egalitarian Principles in a Capitalist World

————————————————

RAN ABRAMITZKY

PRINCETON UNIVERSITY PRESS
PRINCETON AND OXFORD

Contents

THE MYSTERY OF THE KIBBUTZ

To my wife Noya and our boys,
Roee, Ido, and Tom

INTRODUCTION

The kibbutz puzzle

THE ARGUMENT WITH MY UNCLE

I grew up in Jerusalem, but a central part of my life has always been the kibbutz, a place a few miles from the city and a world away. My grandmother was a founder of Kibbutz Negba in the South of Israel and remained a proud member for fifty-five years; my mother was born and raised in Negba; my aunt and uncle still live in Kibbutz Heftziba in the North; and my brother and his family are members of Kibbutz Ramat HaKovesh near the city of Kfar Saba.

As a child, I admired kibbutzim (plural of kibbutz). My younger brother[1] and I loved the freedom to wander around the kibbutz and to disappear for long hours—something our parents didn't mind because the kibbutz was so peaceful and safe. We used to walk barefoot all day in its green and spacious paths. We spent our days playing tennis, table tennis, soccer, and basketball. We loved swimming in the large pool, but we also enjoyed just getting wet in the shallower but warmer kid's pool. At noon ("and don't be late, kids!"), we lined up with all the kibbutzniks (nickname for kibbutz members) and guests

---

[1] My brother Gil is a year and a half younger than I am, and he was always a more natural fit for the kibbutz than I was. He could stay outside forever, his feet were tougher, and he could run barefoot on the hot concrete and on all surfaces, just like the other kibbutz kids. Indeed, he later married a kibbutz member (from Ramat HaKovesh) and moved to her kibbutz, where he is like a horse in a meadow.

in the communal dining hall, filled our plates with as much food and drink as we wanted ("Is it really all free, Mom?"), and joined other kibbutzniks at one of the long communal dining tables.

As a young teenager, I became even more charmed by kibbutzim. Not only was I having so much fun in Kibbutz Negba (and, less frequently, Kibbutz Heftziba), but the kibbutz principle of completely equal sharing seemed appealing, and the kibbutz way of life idyllic. A community in which everyone was provided for by the kibbutz according to her needs struck me as fair and virtuous.

But as I grew older, I began asking myself questions I couldn't easily answer. Why didn't our beloved family friend A., who always held high positions in the kibbutz and was so smart, talented, and hard-working, earn more than others who weren't as talented and didn't work as hard? Why didn't the kibbutz reward his talent and efforts? And why didn't he move with his family to Jerusalem or Tel Aviv, where he surely could earn more money and afford a higher quality of life? Why did A. agree to get paid for his esteemed job the same wage as the member who milked the cows or worked in the kibbutz kitchen?

And why did my Uncle U. work so hard at the irrigation factory, getting home late every night, when he would have earned exactly the same regardless of how hard or how long he worked? No one forced him to work hard; in fact, he had always been proud that there were no bosses at the factory and that everyone held the same rank. He liked his job, but I knew he always wished he could spend more time with his family. Why didn't he, since his earnings would have remained the same?

As I studied hard and stressed over exams, I wondered whether my cousins and friends in the kibbutz had weaker incentives to excel in school; after all, in a classic kibbutz, a high school dropout and a computer engineer with a PhD would earn exactly the same wage. I could not help but think that living in a kibbutz seemed a particularly great deal for lazy people or those lacking talent. What could be better for such people than sharing the incomes of brighter and harder-working people like A. and U.?

In time, I realized that I was not the first to ask such questions: many people became skeptical of the kibbutz economy as they grew

older. As the cliché goes, any man under thirty who is not a socialist has no heart, but any man over thirty who is still a socialist has
no brains.[2]

I remember distinctly one particular day in the late 1990s: I was
in my twenties and pursuing my undergraduate degree in economics. My whole family was enjoying lunch at my aunt and uncle's
house in Kibbutz Heftziba. By that time, it was acceptable and common for kibbutzniks to have meals at home when they had guests
(and even when they didn't). Heftziba was no longer thriving economically and socially, and the atmosphere in the kibbutz was less
upbeat than it had been a few years earlier. Heftziba was deeply in
debt to the banks, as were many other kibbutzim at the time. Kibbutz members were discussing reforms to waste fewer resources and
increase productivity, including radical ideas such as hiring outside
managers to run the kibbutz factories and businesses. We sat on the
sunny grass overlooking the kibbutz houses and paths, listening to
the crickets chirping in the orange trees and greeting kibbutz members returning from lunch at the communal dining hall.

My uncle described the latest path-breaking innovation his plant
had made to improve irrigation systems, and mentioned that the
kibbutz plant was among the best in the country. I decided to provoke him. I told him that, according to economic theory, the kibbutz plant shouldn't be that good. In fact it, and the entire kibbutz
itself, should not even exist. I pointed out that kibbutz members
had strong incentives to shirk on their jobs. After all, why would
anyone work hard if all she got was an equal share of the output?
I told him the term I'd learned for this problem in my economics
lectures: the free-rider problem. I also pointed out that the most
educated and skilled members have strong incentives to leave the
kibbutz—the problem of "brain drain"—so why would they choose
to stay in a place that forced them to share their incomes with less
skilled members? Surely they could earn higher wages in a nearby
city such as Afula or Hadera.

[2] There are many versions of this aphorism, with varying ages and political
labels, but the essence is always the same: the young lean left, but they typically
become more conservative as they age. E.g., http://quoteinvestigator.com/2014
/02/24/heart-head/.

I continued my (admittedly annoying) speech, adding that lazier and lower-skilled people have strong incentives to enter a kibbutz. Wouldn't it be great for someone who struggles to make a living in the city to enter a kibbutz and get subsidized by its more ambitious members? I had learned in intermediate microeconomics that this problem was called adverse selection, but knowing there was a term for it didn't convince my uncle.

He grew upset. Maybe economists are just too cynical, he said—wrongly believing that all people are selfish. In fact, he continued, everyone familiar with kibbutz history knows that the founders of kibbutzim were anything but selfish: they were idealists who wanted to create a "new human being" who, contrary to economists' traditional views of human nature, cared more about the collective than about himself.[3] Besides, he said, if economists are so smart, how did kibbutzim survive for so long despite all these incentive problems?

His arguments made sense to me, and they made me think: Did kibbutzniks respond to incentives, or did economic principles end at the kibbutz gate? How did kibbutzim survive, given the disincentives equal sharing created for talented people to join, work hard, and acquire skills? Did the kibbutz experience disprove the claims of the economists I had been studying as an undergrad?

A couple of years later, as I plunged into the world of economic research, I decided to focus my research efforts on these questions and to research the various perspectives behind kibbutzim's long persistence. I also wanted to understand why many kibbutzim had recently shifted away from income equality. I collected data on almost two hundred kibbutzim spanning the last seventy years: how many members they had; how many people left and how many entered—I was especially looking forward to finding my mother, who left the kibbutz in 1970, in the records; the degree of equality within the kibbutz; and which kibbutzim shifted away from equal sharing and when. I analyzed these data and wrote my PhD dissertation in economics on the kibbutz. My uncle was not wrong,

---

[3] This view of human nature is part of the notion of "*Homo economicus*," which views humans as narrowly and rationally pursuing their self-interest. Creating a new ideal human being is a notion often associated with utopias in general and utopian socialism in particular (discussed further in chapter 11).

but I also learned that kibbutzim were not immune to the economic principles I had studied as an undergraduate. Socialist ideals founded the kibbutzim and played an ongoing role in their functioning, but economics also has a great deal to say about how they had survived and flourished for so long.

I continued studying the kibbutzim after I completed my PhD, extending the data collection to learn about the choices and behavior of kibbutz members, and delving into the questions of how kibbutzim sustained income equality and why they eventually shifted away from equal sharing. While the book focuses on kibbutzim, it aims to address bigger questions about equality and inequality in a manner that is easily accessible to the nonspecialist: Can we create a society in which people have equal incomes? What are the costs of doing so?

WHAT THE KIBBUTZ EXPERIMENT TEACHES US ABOUT INCOME EQUALITY AND VOLUNTARY SOCIALISM

I quickly learned that the debate my uncle and I had was as old as the concept of the kibbutz itself. My uncle presented an idealistic view, which emphasized the role of idealism and ideology, in the survival of the kibbutz. The founders of kibbutzim were migrants from Eastern Europe who rejected capitalism. They wanted to establish a society based on voluntary socialism, adopting the elements that they liked from socialism but maintaining the freedom of members to leave if they chose so. I, in contrast, repeated to my uncle the most cynical economics view: an equal-sharing arrangement won't last because inherent and severe incentive problems will undermine it from the beginning.

This book brings an economic perspective to the study of kibbutzim. It addresses the following questions: How did kibbutzim maintain equal sharing for so long despite the inherent incentive problems? How did the voluntary egalitarian kibbutzim deal with the challenge of having a more capitalist world right outside their gates? What level of equality can be sustained within a kibbutz and under what conditions? What is the role of economic forces in the behavior of kibbutzim and in members' decisions? The premise of the book is that kibbutzim are fascinating social experiments to study the survival of egalitarian principles.

Think about it: If people were given a choice to live in a society where all incomes and resources were shared equally, who would choose that option? And would their society thrive? What rules and norms would they choose to govern their society? These questions are hard to address, because people are not typically given such choice of where to live. Former communist countries can't help us answer these questions because their citizens couldn't exit at will and couldn't vote against socialism. Liberal socialist countries like Sweden and Denmark offer more individual choice—and I discuss them later—but their egalitarian and socialist principles are more difficult to disentangle from other factors. Kibbutzim, in contrast, offer a laboratory with which to address these questions.

This book suggests that under the right circumstances, it is possible to create a viable egalitarian society. Equality worked in the kibbutzim for many decades, and it still does in a handful of them today. To be sure, economic theory did not stop at the kibbutz gate. Shirking was always an issue, and the best workers were the first to leave. But these problems were not nearly as devastating as naive economic logic would suggest. For example, kibbutz members have always had relatively high levels of schooling, even in periods when full equal sharing was practiced and kibbutzim offered no monetary returns to schooling. Kibbutz children did invest more in their schooling once their kibbutz shifted away from full equal sharing, but this effect was relatively small in magnitude and concentrated among children with less-educated parents. Overall, kibbutzim survived, and many of them thrived, for almost a century.

How did kibbutzim survive? Income equality provided much-needed insurance to kibbutzniks in the early days. Idealism, team spirit, and culture helped to sustain equality, as did homogeneity of preferences and abilities among members. Governmental support also helped. But members did not rely on idealism, goodwill, and external support alone. Social sanctions against shirkers were effective because the communities were small with limited privacy;

communal property served as a bond, and training in kibbutz-specific education and skills helped retain productive members; and screening and trial periods were used to regulate the quality of entrants. Kibbutzim effectively mitigated these challenges, but at the cost of individual privacy, which is a price that many were unwilling to pay. The decline in commitment of kibbutz values among younger generations, however, made these challenges increasingly difficult to solve. As practical considerations took over ideological ones, many productive members left, and the kibbutzim not only lost talented workers but also faced the question of who would take care of the aging founding generation.

Being rich helped. Rich kibbutzim could attain equal sharing through high levels of redistribution, without losing all their most-skilled members, whereas poorer kibbutzim could not. Once a financial crisis forced many kibbutzim to reduce living standards, their most-educated and highest-skilled members left, and these kibbutzim shifted away from equal sharing to improve economic incentives and retain talent.

A WORD ON THE ECONOMIC PERSPECTIVE USED IN THIS BOOK

The economic perspective offers insights that extend beyond kibbutzim. Any society, country, or firm that wishes to increase economic equality, even if it does not reach full equality, must deal with challenges such as free-riding and adverse selection described in this book. These issues are key to understanding the feasibility and desirability of equality from an economic perspective. In this sense, kibbutzim are an important social experiment from which all societies striving to increase equality can learn.

Although naive economic logic might seem at odds with the past success of kibbutzim, in fact a broader economic perspective that borrows insights from other disciplines can go a long way toward explaining why kibbutzim were created, what form they took, how they thrived for so long, and why they eventually declined. Thus, while the book focuses on economics, it also incorporates insights from history, sociology, and psychology. When it comes to quantitative sources, however, the sources are biased toward the more recent period, so that the empirical evidence on earlier periods is less systematic. Moreover, by taking a primarily economic perspective, this book misses out or touches only briefly on several important aspects of kibbutzim, such as identity, culture, politics, and social structure. For example, it only briefly mentions the topics of gender and ethnic inequality in the kibbutz, family and social arrangements, the internal politics of the kibbutz movements, the complex political involvement of the kibbutz movement with Zionist and labor politics, and issues of identity formation. These topics are explored thoroughly elsewhere.

Kibbutzim are not the first such social experiments. There have been many attempts to create communities that share a vision and follow alternative lifestyles. Such "intentional communities" are often labeled "utopian" by those who believe they are doomed to fail. Intentional communities ranging from cooperatives to communes to monasteries often strive for cooperation and mutual aid and are motivated by a common vision and a desire for a thoughtful alternative lifestyle. There is a large literature on intentional communities, which I touch only briefly in this book when I discuss other communes in chapter 11. Similarly, I do not discuss in detail the intellectual history of socialism or key figures in that intellectual tradition, such as Henri de Saint-Simon, Charles Fourier, Robert Owen, and Karl Marx.[4] Their insights and the experience of other intentional communities, however, surely influenced my thinking.

As even the most idealist members of the most sincere utopia, kibbutzniks too are not angels, and they are motivated by diverse motives, including economic and noneconomic considerations. For example, getting satisfaction from being appreciated by the social group is a substitute for getting a higher income. While I discuss these other motives throughout the book, my economics training may tempt me to discuss economic considerations in greater detail. Let me thus emphasize from the beginning that a kibbutz is a social unit and not merely an economic organization; culture, and

---

[4] See also Skinner's utopian novel *Walden Two* (1974).

specifically pride in being a kibbutznik, is an important glue, and human behavior is complex and diverse.

In a number of ways, kibbutzim offer an exceptional environment to examine the potential tradeoff between equality and incentives. Unlike members of many other communally based living arrangements, kibbutzniks were never at the margin of society. They have always interacted with the rest of the population and played an important role in Israeli society. In fact, kibbutzniks were once considered elites, and they were over-represented in leadership positions in both the government and the military. They thus had good opportunities outside the kibbutz, and the option to leave. This lies in contrast to many other communes, whose members have often been more marginal and isolated from the outside world. In this sense, the study of kibbutzim teaches us more about economic organizations than does the study of other communes.

In general, people might tolerate the existing social order if they are unaware that there are better alternatives, which could explain why many communes tend to keep members unaware of the world outside. Communist countries often restricted news media and printing presses, imposed import restrictions, blocked Internet access, and tightly controlled international travel and emigration.[5] In contrast, kibbutz members interact with nonmembers through Israel's mandatory military service, not to mention that many kibbutz members (especially since the 1980s) study and work outside their kibbutzim.

At the same time, the trade-off between equality and incentives is not specific to kibbutzim. In fact, this trade-off lies at the heart of modern economics and emerges in seemingly diverse settings, such as insurance, executive compensation, taxes, extended families, and immigration policies. Kibbutzim used mechanisms such as abolishing private property to limit brain drain, screening to regulate the quality of entrants, and social sanctions to limit shirking. Similar mechanisms have been used by a number of other organizations

---

[5] Isabelle Sin and I showed how former communist countries in Eastern Europe restricted the translation of Western books and how, following the collapse of communism, book translations increased dramatically and translation rates converged to Western Europe's translation rates (Abramitzky and Sin 2014).

and communities, ranging from professional partnerships, cooperatives, and academic departments, to village economies in developing countries, communist countries, and welfare states. However, such measures must typically be used in extreme ways if a community strives for full income equality because members receive zero monetary returns from working hard. In the case of kibbutzim, this meant, among other things, not allowing members to have any of their own savings, and taking away most of their privacy; in the case of many communist countries, individuals were often forbidden to leave. Such tough measures might explain why societies based on income equality are so rare.

BOOK STRUCTURE AND CHAPTER DESCRIPTION

The book has three parts. The first is about the rise of the kibbutz. Chapter 1 introduces the kibbutz way of life and early history through the lens of the personal story of my family—how my grandparents moved from Poland to Palestine and helped found one kibbutz, how they lived there in early days, and what my mother and her generation's life in the kibbutz looked like. I also continue to tell my family history in separate interludes and in the epilogue. It is the contrast between my economic knowledge and my personal experience with kibbutzim that triggered my interest and curiosity in studying them. I am well aware that including personal details about the author in a scholarly book is not standard, and some scholars might even find it outrageous. I invite such scholars to skip chapter 1 and the interludes and go straight to the analysis. However, I felt that my book, which mostly uses economic logic and systematic data analysis of almost two hundred kibbutzim, would be incomplete without also introducing the beautiful humanity underlying this unique experiment of kibbutzim.

My hope is that the personal history illustrates some of the concepts in the book, provides content, and adds warmth to the models and statistics. I also realize that while my family's story is close to my heart, there are thousands of similar stories and many different ones as well. In this sense, my family history is not intended to provide an exhaustive and accurate history of the kibbutz movement.

Rather, it tells the story of three generations of one family—my family—in one kibbutz. You can think about my family history as one anecdote. Like all anecdotes, it was not chosen at random. But, unlike most anecdotes, here the reader knows exactly how I chose that one. Similarly, even objective scholars (and I strive to be one) come with their unconscious personal bias to any topic. Sharing my family history should allow readers to evaluate any potential bias I might bring to the analysis.

In chapter 2, I present a brief bird's-eye view of the history of kibbutzim before a financial crisis hit them in the mid-1980s. The population of kibbutzim grew dramatically before the 1980s, although the percentage of kibbutz members in the Jewish population constantly declined. Dozens of new kibbutzim, each with up to a few hundred members, were established. Members' quality of life increased substantially over this period. These demographic and economic developments of kibbutzim during this period raise a number of puzzles that the rest of the book aims to explain: How were small and struggling egalitarian communities able to grow from a dozen members to many thousands and offer members living standards higher than the country's average? Why did only a small share of the Jewish population choose to live in a kibbutz? How were kibbutzim able to retain many kibbutz-born individuals? Who chose to leave their kibbutz? Why not create one large kibbutz instead of dozens of small ones? And how did kibbutzim thrive within the broader Israeli society despite the incentive problems that were arguably inherent to full income equality?

This book is not intended to be a complete and exhaustive history of the kibbutz movement, which is done ably elsewhere in a large literature on which I draw. Four books proved particularly useful—the impressive two volumes on the history of the kibbutz movement by Near (1992, 1997), and the books by Gavron (2000) and Mort and Brenner (2003) that beautifully tell the in-depth story of a number of kibbutzim. Together with my conversations with dozens of members over many years, these helped me better understand kibbutzim beyond the statistics and models.

In chapter 3, I discuss the economic issues involved in creating a kibbutz. I first discuss the attraction of equal sharing for a society.

In the early days of kibbutzim, equal sharing was appealing not just for ideological reasons but also for economic reasons: it provided a safety net, insurance against the many risks that life could bring. I then imagine a conversation between the founders of kibbutzim and an economist from the same era. If the economist had the sensibilities of my undergraduate self, she would probably tell the founders that their idea for a kibbutz was flawed. But if she had foresight on how economics would develop over the next century, and the humility to borrow insights from other social sciences, she might actually advise them to create a kibbutz with exactly the same rules and norms that they chose without any expert advice. A classic kibbutz with its initial rules and norms was a great way to enable a group of people to enjoy the insurance and ideological benefits of equal sharing, while fighting the incentive problems of free-riding (lack of incentive to work hard), adverse selection (the tendency of less-productive workers to enter), brain drain (the tendency of the most productive members to exit), and underinvestment in human capital (lack of incentive to study hard).

The second part of the book focuses on the survival of egalitarian kibbutzim. After a short interlude on how the kibbutz provided a safety net to my grandmother and why my mother decided to leave, I discuss in chapter 4 the way in which the driving force behind kibbutzim evolved over time. The idealistic zeal of kibbutz founders, coupled with favorable historical circumstances, sparked the creation of kibbutzim. But idealism and favorable circumstance declined over subsequent generations, and practical considerations took over as the dominant force behind members' behaviors and decisions. Kibbutzim survived in part because they set up their rules and norms so that they could survive long after the idealism and favorable circumstances of their inception had faded.

In the next few chapters, I discuss the various incentive problems and how kibbutzim dealt with them during this equal-sharing period: chapter 5 covers the free-rider problem, chapter 6 adverse selection and brain drain, and chapter 7 underinvestment in human capital. In each of these chapters, I first explain the economics of the problem. I then use census data on kibbutz members to empirically test the extent to which the problem was present in kibbutzim during this period. Finally, I explain how kibbutzim dealt with the problem. The bottom line is that these problems were all present in kibbutzim, but they could have been much worse if kibbutzim hadn't abolished private property, screened entrants, and encouraged social sanctions. I suggest that the norms and rules that helped kibbutzim deal with these incentive problems could also explain why kibbutzim were small, why many Israeli Jews did not find living in a kibbutz attractive, and ultimately how kibbutzim survived for many years despite the incentive problems.

Did the founders of the kibbutz actively think through the economic rationale and intentionally design their kibbutz to avoid incentive problems? It's possible. It's equally likely, however, that kibbutz members might have behaved as if they were trying to solve incentive problems even though this was not their main objective.[6] Whether or not this was their intention, the society that kibbutz members designed was remarkably successful at fighting incentive problems.

The third part of the book moves on to the decline of egalitarian kibbutzim. Chapter 8 starts by explaining why kibbutzim shifted away from equal sharing and why this didn't occur until the 1990s. Winds of change started to be felt in kibbutzim as early as the 1970s. Until that time, kibbutz children slept outside their parents' homes in special residences; beginning in the 1970s, many kibbutzim abolished these communal sleeping arrangements and moved children into their parents' homes. In 1977, a right-wing government was elected in Israel for the first time, and kibbutzim could no longer expect the explicit and implicit support they were accustomed to. This political development was followed in the late 1980s by an upheaval known as "the kibbutz crisis." A number of elements of kibbutz life came under stress: many kibbutzim had

---

[6] And note that the fact that they didn't have an explicit economic model in mind doesn't mean they didn't act as if they did. To give an analogy, the expert billiard player doesn't need to know the laws of physics to be a great champion, but the laws of physics still apply on the billiard table (Friedman and Savage 1948). The expert billiard player acts as if he knows the rules of physics, hitting the ball at a certain angle and taking friction into account as he attempts to land the ball in the pocket at the corner of the table.

borrowed heavily and then experienced financial difficulty when interest rates rose; the development of a high-tech economy in Israel offered potentially larger rewards for high-ability workers; and all the while, ideological commitment to the socialist aspect of kibbutz life continued to wane.

I then document the shift away from equal sharing that has been taking place in kibbutzim over the last twenty years. Kibbutzim have introduced various degrees of reforms, ranging from small deviations from equal sharing to substantial ones wherein a member's budget is mostly based on her earnings.[7] As of 2011, about 25 percent of kibbutzim still maintained completely equal sharing between members,[8] but the majority of kibbutzim had adopted a "safety net" model, whereby members keep some fraction of their earnings and share the rest with their fellow members. Despite the large deviation from the original model, the language used to describe reformed kibbutzim conveys that even kibbutzim that have shifted away from equal sharing still provide a safety net to members in need, revealing the importance of insurance and mutual support in kibbutzim's ongoing mission. To be sure, the safety net was a compromise—a way to achieve the majority required in a vote for the "capitalistic" reform that rescued the kibbutz. Moreover, as is often the case, those who stood to lose from the reforms—here the elderly and the less skilled workers— had an obvious interest in a generous safety net and they had the ability to impose it. The end result, however, is that insurance and mutual support remain important principles of the kibbutz. In a brief interlude, I return to the final chapter of my family's story: the lives today of my brother and his wife and children in a reformed kibbutz.

In chapter 9, I explain how these recent developments in kibbutzim allowed me to test an economic theory of the limits of equality. The financial crisis of the 1980s and the Israeli high-tech boom of the 1990s in particular exacerbated the brain-drain problem, and

[7] The information on kibbutzim's degree of equality was collected by Shlomo Getz of the Institute for Kibbutz Research based on kibbutzim's self-reported degree of income equality.

[8] Sixty-three out of 266 in Getz (2011).

can explain the degree to which different kibbutzim shifted away from equal sharing. Economic theory predicts that wealthier kibbutzim would experience lower exit rates, would be able to retain most of their talented workers, and would choose more equal sharing. Less wealthy kibbutzim, on the other hand, would experience higher exit rates, lose talented workers in greater numbers, and would thus shift away from equal sharing in order to retain the most talented workers. The fact that the financial crisis hit some kibbutzim harder than others created differences in the wealth and living standards of kibbutzim that enabled me to test these predictions.

I continue by analyzing my findings of why some kibbutzim remained egalitarian and others did not, and why kibbutzim have shifted away from equal sharing to different degrees since the late 1990s. I first describe the kibbutz-level data I collected, which includes such information as kibbutzim's wealth, financial circumstances, size, age distribution, exit rates, ideological affiliation, and voting in national elections, and whether they shifted away from equal sharing. I then present the empirical findings and discuss what they tell us about the roles of communal wealth, group size, age distribution, and ideology in maintaining equal sharing.

Chapter 10 moves forward in time and considers the consequences of the rising income inequality in kibbutzim. The shift away from equal sharing increased the return to education of kibbutz members. Economic theory predicts that people will invest more in their educations when the return is higher. To test this prediction, Victor Lavy and I collected data on kibbutz students and their high school and post-secondary schooling outcomes before and after the reforms. We find that kibbutz students took high school more seriously and invested more in their education once their kibbutz shifted away from equal sharing, especially men and those whose parents were less educated. Besides improving education, I also present empirical evidence that the recent shift away from equal sharing, by increasing the monetary cost of raising children, discouraged members from having as many children as previously. There is also some suggestive evidence that the shift away from equal sharing improved work ethic in kibbutzim, but might have come at the cost of decreased happiness.

In chapter 11, I compare the experience of kibbutzim with other communes. Similarly to kibbutzim, nineteenth-century communes in the United States designed their societies to mitigate incentive problems by facilitating social sanctions, enhancing commitment, loyalty, and cooperation, and creating lock-in devices. Ideology, especially when religion-based, helped fight incentive problems. As ideology declined and outside opportunities for members improved, incentive problems worsened and communes' stability was threatened. To survive, communes used one of two opposite strategies. Kibbutzim, as we saw, shifted away from equal sharing and became more like the world around them. Communal groups such as the Hutterites, in contrast, increased their isolation, fighting brain drain by reducing members' knowledge of what the outside world had to offer.

Chapter 12 concludes and suggests, in light of the analysis in the book, an economic reinterpretation of the rise, survival, and decline of kibbutzim. The kibbutz experience suggests that income equality does not come for free. What you gain in a safety net, you lose in individual incentives; but if you raise incentives, inequality follows. Still, even under equal sharing, incentive problems were not nearly as severe as would be suggested by a naive economic logic. Even in the absence of monetary returns, kibbutzniks worked long hours and acquired education and skill, while talented members who could earn more outside often stayed in their kibbutz, allowing many kibbutzim to thrive. Even kibbutzim that shifted away from equal sharing continue to provide a safety net to weak members and maintain mutual assistance as a building block of the kibbutz. This chapter and the epilogue also discuss the broader lessons from the book for organizations and societies that wish to be more supportive and equal.

In the final account, it is impossible to know exactly how much of kibbutzim's success in maintaining equality stemmed from the ways in which they were able to successfully overcome various problems, and how much came from the support they received from the state of Israel (and the pre-state Jewish Yishuv). Both were crucial. I show that aspects of kibbutzim's community design and their responses to changes in their internal and external environments were critical to their survival. At the same time, I discuss how the fact that kibbutzim were heavily subsidized in various ways and for many years aided their success. These subsidies included transfer of land and other factors of production to kibbutzim, subsidies to the farming sector in the form of water and capital investments, subsidies for the consumption of farm goods in the state of Israel, and reduced competition by allocating production quotas and preventing the importation of food and industrial goods produced by the kibbutzim. This approach of subsidies and protectionism was not unique for the kibbutzim, but they surely enjoyed it. However, state support is not the whole story. For example, governmental support does not prevent kibbutz members from shirking and does not help kibbutzim with solving adverse selection in entry. Similarly, while the fact that the political environment became less friendly to the kibbutzim starting in the mid-1970s can partially explain why kibbutzim got into economic trouble and subsequently began to abandon socialism, it cannot explain why some kibbutzim remained fully egalitarian even in the absence of political support or why some kibbutzim remained equal and others did not.

At the end of the book, you will find a brief timeline of some of the key events in the history of kibbutzim. On my website,[9] you will find a list of all kibbutzim with information on each of them: the year they were established, movement affiliation, group size, economic circumstances following the financial crisis, and whether and when they shifted away from equal sharing.

[9] See https://people.stanford.edu/ranabr/the-mystery-of-the-kibbutz.

PART I

THE RISE

CHAPTER 1

How my grandparents helped
create a kibbutz

My grandmother, Breindel, was born on June 1, 1910, in Poryck, a small town in Eastern Europe located on a lake.[1] More than half of the town's two thousand inhabitants were Jewish and the rest were Polish or Ukrainian. Jews had been present in town since at least the sixteenth century; most worked in commerce and manufacturing, and owned little shops and plants. The town had a synagogue, a Hebrew school (called Tarbut, Hebrew for "culture"), and a Hebrew library; it seems the Jewish residents coexisted peacefully with the non-Jewish residents. At the end of the nineteenth century, more restrictions on Jews and Jewish settlements were introduced, and by the outbreak of the First World War, Poryck was a town in decline. Poryck's Jews found themselves in a dismal situation, suffering from pogroms and persecution.

Breindel's father, Mordechai Brezner, was a prosperous pharmacist in Poryck, and the family was relatively wealthy. My grandmother even told us they had a pony she loved to ride. Like some other Jews in Poryck, the Brezner family was Zionist. Breindel was among the founders of her town's branch of the Ha'shomer Ha'tzair movement, and she was active in the local group's cultural

[1] The city of Poryck, now located in Northern Ukraine, belonged to Russia following the division of Poland, and to Poland between the two world wars.

and social life. Ha'shomer Ha'tzair, which translates as "The Youth Guard," was a Socialist-Zionist Jewish movement that believed that the Jewish youth could be liberated by making aliyah.[2] Members of Ha'shomer Ha'tzair would later settle in Palestine,[3] found a number of kibbutzim, and, in 1927, form the Kibbutz Artzi Federation.

With friends from Ha'shomer Ha'tzair, Breindel moved to the nearby city of Lvov[4] to study in hopes of becoming a Hebrew teacher. Lvov, located in what is now Ukraine, had a population of over 300,000 and was home to one of the largest Jewish communities in Poland. In 1933, when she was twenty-three years old, her studies were interrupted when her friends decided to make aliyah and continue their training in Israel. We don't know why the group decided to leave right then, rather than waiting until graduation. But the alarming rise in anti-Semitism during the 1930s in Lvov must have been a contributing factor: anti-Semitism had moved beyond social exclusion and economic discrimination to include physical assaults on Jews.

My grandmother decided not to join her friends in making aliyah. Life in Poland was quite comfortable for her, and the Zionist idea of *hafrachat hamidbar* (Hebrew for "making the desert bloom") in the hot and humid Middle East sounded better in theory than in practice. She was also very close to her family; as an only daughter with three older brothers, she had always been coddled by her parents and siblings. For reasons that are not entirely clear, she said goodbye to her friends, wished them good luck, and returned to her hometown and family.

The decision to not join her friends and make aliyah must have been difficult, especially since her high school sweetheart, Baruch

[2] Aliyah, Hebrew for "ascension," was a term used by the Jewish people to describe the migration of a Jew from anywhere in the world to the promised land (Palestine), and in particular to live in a kibbutz. Ha'shomer Ha'tzair resulted from the merger of the Zionist defense organization Ha'shomer ("The Guard") whose purpose was to guard the Jewish settlements, and the Zionist and Socialist Ze'irei Zion ("The Youth of Zion").

[3] Palestine was then under the British mandate, authorized by the League of Nations, the purpose of which was to give the territory that was not self-governed a temporary trust that would ensure the well-being of the local population.

[4] Lvov is now called Lviv.

"Buzik" Honig decided to not stay with her and joined the rest of the group in Palestine. Buzik and some of his friends from Ha'shomer Ha'tzair had been training for a number of years to become agricultural workers in Palestine and to live a communal life there in a kibbutz of the type that had recently begun springing up in that region.

Buzik was more committed to making aliyah and joining a kibbutz than his girlfriend Breindel. His childhood friend Dov recalled years later that Buzik was "among the founders of Ha'shomer Ha'tzair in town, and he devoted all his energy to the educational activities [of the group] and to training youths in self-fulfillment and making aliyah to Israel,"[5] and that "at the gathering point he was the driving force. With his good humor, he influenced all the members, and, from the first moment, a strong tie between him and the rest of [those who would later become] the kibbutz members was formed."[6]

But, like Breindel, Buzik was the youngest son. His parents "could not accept the idea that their beloved youngest son would leave them, and they were opposed to his aliyah."[7] They did everything they could to stop him. Dov recalled that "one afternoon he escaped from home and went out of town to the gathering point of those who planned to immigrate to Palestine, but his family came and brought him back home. Buzik didn't give up his plan and after a short while escaped again, only this time he was successful."

---

[5] The full paragraph from the eulogy of his childhood friend Dov Melamed, who had been with him through his aliyah and until Buzik's death: "In the *Cheder* [a traditional elementary school that teaches Hebrew and Judaism] and later in the Hebrew school in town [Poryck], he absorbed a love for the homeland and its people. [Buzik] was among the founders of *Ha'shomer Ha'tzair* in town, and he devoted all his energy to the educational activities [of the group] and to training youths in self-fulfillment and making aliyah to Israel. He himself exemplified it."

[6] Dov also referred to him on that occasion as: "Buzik, the youngest son in his big family, beloved by everyone, who never stops laughing. Among the best students at school, beloved by both the teachers and students, full of talents. Always the one organizing the celebrations and parties at school and for the [Ha'shomer Ha'tzair] group. Performing himself with huge talents in reading texts and acting."

[7] Dov Melamed's eulogy.

Buzik and his group were fascinated by the social experiment of kibbutzim. In July 1939, they decided to establish their own kibbutz, called Negba, in the northern Negev. The land belonged to the Jewish National Fund, which had bought and developed land for Jewish Settlement, and was the southernmost Jewish settlement at the time. Their effort was part of the "tower-and-stockade enterprise," a settlement method used by Zionist settlers during the 1936–39 Arab revolt, in which dozens of kibbutzim and several moshavim were established throughout Palestine. Palestine at the time was under British mandate, and the British authorities had placed legal restrictions on the establishment of new Jewish settlements. However, Ottoman law, which was still in effect, provided a loophole: even an illegal building or settlement cannot be demolished once the roof has been completed. Hence, the Jews would build an entire settlement in the middle of the night, and by the time morning came it would be complete and couldn't be demolished. This tower-and-stockade enterprise was tolerated by British authorities as a means of countering the Arab revolt.[8] Like kibbutzim, moshavim were established as cooperative agricultural communities; but unlike the kibbutz, farms in the moshav were individually rather than collectively owned.

In the summer of 1939, Buzik fulfilled his dream and became a proud founder of Kibbutz Negba. The creation of Kibbutz Negba is described in Negba's archives (my translation):

> In terms of security, the place was very dangerous and the tower-and-stockade system addressed this problem very well. At the time this settlement point was established, we had to watch out for both the Arabs and the English who ruled the

---

[8] The tower-and-stockade system was introduced during the Arab Revolt and was meant to defend the new settlement against Arab attacks. The whole settlement with the stockade and observation tower was prefabricated and it was erected on the spot within twelve hours with the support of volunteers from the neighboring kibbutzim, Haganah members, Solel Boneh (a pre-state enterprise for construction and public work) workers, etc. The British authorities, who were themselves often fighting against the Arab revolt, usually disregarded these operations.

land at the time. All the buildings required were constructed and prepared at the center of the country and the operation of settlement on the land took place during the night. About 40 trucks arrived at dawn at the designated point (near the Arab villages of Beit Afa and Iraq-Suweidan), and through the hectic work of hundreds of people, the settlement was standing on the ground before 10am. The entire settlement was inside the wall, and in the middle stood a tower with a strong spotlight to overlook the area day and night. That same day, we decided on the name "Negba" [southward], because the tower served as a landmark for other settlements towards the south and the desert. We developed a successful agricultural farm and we made our living from vegetables, milk, wheat and fruits that our farm produced. Another source of livelihood was working at establishing military camps for the English in the region with the onset of the Second World War in Europe at the time. We tried to have a good neighborly relationship with the Arabs in the nearby villages. They were impressed by our mechanized and advanced agriculture, and tried to learn from us, and it looked like we would live in peace for a long time.

Buzik and his friends were motivated, driven, and hard-working,[9] even though nobody was supervising.[10] Cooperation was viewed as key. Kibbutz members were required to give the collective all their private property, including clothing and other personal items. All decisions were made collectively, from small things like what the members should wear and when they could get new shoes, all the way to what food the members would eat in the dining hall, what

[9] Buzik was a Socialist Zionist, but he did notice his kibbutz's imperfections. "He told me about his experience in writing skits and reading them in kibbutz parties. He saw imperfections in the community life but never judged them harshly, always tried to find justifications for them," said Dov in his eulogy.

[10] Asher, Buzik's friend, wrote in 1953 after Buzik died: "Here I remember Buzik from the times of the construction group, which built its first buildings. . . . [H]e was considered among the strongest workers and very capable in mixing concrete and running with wheelbarrows. Nobody was holding a whip, but the work continued in tempo, and there was always a smile on his face and he always had an encouraging word for his working friends."

tasks and jobs the members would perform, and whether and what the members could study outside the kibbutz. Even the showers were communal (separate for men and women).

However, Buzik's happiness was not complete. His love was still in the diaspora—in Poryck—and Buzik missed her greatly. To make matters worse, members of Kibbutz Negba became increasingly aware that war was approaching the borders of Poland, and they worried greatly about anti-Semitism and persecution in Europe. Shika, a childhood friend of my grandparents and a fellow settler of Kibbutz Negba, travelled to Europe on a mission on behalf of the kibbutz to bring members of their shtetl (Yiddish for a small town with large Jewish population in prewar Eastern Europe) back to Palestine. One day early in 1939, Shika knocked on the door of the Brezner family. Buzik had asked him to do everything he possibly could to bring Breindel to Negba.

In a rare moment of sharing, my grandmother later told her daughters (my mother and aunt) that her first reaction was "absolutely not." There was no way she was leaving her beloved family behind, and she knew they were not going to join her. Her plan had always been to take care of her parents as they got older, and she couldn't just go. At the same time, the war was getting closer to Poland, and Breindel must have already felt that making aliyah was a smart move. What's more, Shika presented a pessimistic picture: he said his friends and the members of his kibbutz all agreed that joining him and making aliyah was the only way possible for Jews in Europe to survive.

In the toughest decision my grandmother ever had to make, she decided to join Shika—Palestine's borders at the time were almost closed to aliyah—and the two decided to take no risks. They fictitiously married so Breindel could enter Palestine without trouble.

When Shika came to take my grandmother to Palestine, did the Brezner family suspect a German invasion was imminent? Did they have any inkling that later that year, Poland would be partitioned between Germany and the Soviets? Did they suspect that Jews would no longer be allowed to leave and that many of them would become refugees or would die? Unfortunately, we don't know the answers to these questions. We suspect that the Brezner family must have felt increasingly pressured and unwelcome in Poland. During the 1930s, with bad economic conditions in Poland, the Polish government increasingly promoted anti-Semitic policies that restricted Jews in the labor market and encouraged them to leave the country. At the same time, however, Jewish cultural and political activities thrived, so it hard to know how they weighed the good against the bad.

Did my grandmother try to convince her parents and brothers to join her to Palestine? Did she get their blessings or did she leave against their will? Did she know she would never see them again? Did she feel guilty for leaving her family behind? My family members asked ourselves these questions many times, but we never dared to ask my grandmother because we knew she wouldn't talk about her past and that these topics were off-limits. What we do know is that only several years after my grandmother left with Shika to reunite with her boyfriend in Kibbutz Negba, her parents and brothers all perished in the Holocaust, along with six million other European Jews.

In Negba, Breindel joined her high school boyfriend Buzik, who "felt he was the happiest person in the world."[11] Negba's kibbutz members helped Breindel cope with the loss of her beloved birth family in Europe. This would not be the last time in her life the kibbutz assisted her through tough events and provided her with tremendous support.

After Breindel was officially divorced from her fictitious marriage to Shika, in 1942 my grandparents finally married. When I look at their marriage certificate today, I can almost feel how proud they were to report "merchant" as the occupations of their parents and "worker" as their own occupations and the occupations of their two witnesses. They were now part of Socialist Zionism (Labor Zionism), a movement that believed that the Jewish state could only be created once Jews started to work again in "productive occupations," as laborers and peasants, rather than as merchants and professionals, professions to which Jews were driven in the diaspora. Of course, most economists today would dismiss this notion that

---

[11] From Dov's eulogy.

merchants and professionals are not productive occupations. In any case, Labor Zionism held that a Jewish state should be established through the Jewish working class settling in Palestine and creating kibbutzim and moshavim.[12]

The ideology of kibbutzim was Socialist Zionism, but socialism and Zionism didn't always coexist harmoniously. Arab workers were fellows under the socialist ideology but often enemies under the Zionist ideology. The attitudes toward new Jewish immigrants who arrived from Middle Eastern countries, discussed in the next chapter, also illustrate the tension between the socialist and Zionist missions of kibbutzim.

Buzik had left his old world behind him. He lost his parents and most of his siblings in the Holocaust, and it seems as though he didn't think there was room in Negba for whatever remained from his old world. This became clear when his older brother, Yosef, was about to visit him in Negba in the early 1940s. The two brothers were very close, and yet Yosef had moved to the United States and Buzik to Palestine.[13] Buzik was concerned about how the kibbutz members would treat his brother and whether he would get along with them. His fellow members could be rather critical about Jews who worked as professionals, let alone ones who chose to move to the United States rather than make aliyah. Regardless, Negba members were very hospitable toward Yosef and he became a friend of the kibbutz.

---

[12] In the words of A. D. Gordon, a key thinker of the Labor Zionist movement who made aliyah in 1904 and whose thinking (along with Ber Borochov's and that of others) motivated the establishment in 1909 of Degania, and soon after many other kibbutzim: "The Jewish people have been completely cut off from nature and imprisoned within city walls these two thousand years. We have been accustomed to every form of life, except a life of labor—of labor done at our behest and for its own sake. It will require the greatest effort of will for such a people to become normal again. We lack the principal ingredient for national life. We lack the habit of labor . . . [T]his kind of labor binds a people to its soil and to its national culture, which in its turn is an outgrowth of the people's toil and the people's labor." (Gordon, "Our Tasks Ahead," quoted in Glatzer 1982, p. 679.)

[13] This raises the more general question of why some Polish Jews would choose Palestine and others would choose the United States. More research is needed to answer this question.

FIGURE 1.1: The Honig family, ca. 1952: my grandparents, aunt, and mother. Source: Family collection.

Soon after my grandparents married, their first daughter Naomi (my aunt) was born in 1943. Reuniting with one another and having a healthy and smart daughter of their own, my grandparents must have been hopeful for a great future.[14]

The 1948 Arab-Israeli War changed everything. In May 1948, following the Israeli Declaration of Independence, the Egyptian army captured a number of Arab villages near the kibbutz, as well as Iraq-Suweidan, a police fort constructed during the British mandate that controlled the route to the Negev. The Egyptians bombed Kibbutz Negba from the air and ground, and Egyptian tanks made it to the gates of Negba in June and July of 1948. The battle of Negba was fierce and left many Egyptians and Israelis dead, including forty kibbutz members (about a tenth of the entire kibbutz population).

My grandfather served as a wireless operator, in charge of Kibbutz Negba's connection with the outside world, a skill that the kibbutz had sent him to acquire in a course run by the Haganah, the Jewish military organization that later became the Israeli Defense

---

[14] "He started to build his home, was so happy when his first daughter was born," recalled Dov Melamed in his eulogy.

FIGURE 1.2: Kibbutz members in 1948 rebuilding houses that were destroyed by the Egyptian air attack in Negba. Source: Robert Capa photos, © International Center of Photography.

Force.[15] Dov recalled, "As always, Buzik gave all his heart to acquire the skill, he never knew a limit, always gave his all."

Much property and many buildings in Negba were destroyed in the heavy fighting. In November 1948, Israel captured the police fort, thus saving Negba. An Egyptian tank and the old kibbutz water tower, full of bullet holes, stand in Negba to this day as a testimony to the battle, along with a Monument to the Negba Defenders that features an Israeli soldier, a kibbutz pioneer, and a nurse holding hands.[16]

During the war, my grandmother was pregnant with my mother, Bracha (born in June 1948). Otherwise, she might have been expected to participate in the war effort herself. Like other kibbutzim,

[15] The elite fighting units of Haganah, called Palmach, were often hosted in kibbutzim.

[16] The monument was built by Nathan Rapoport, a Jewish sculptor who was born in Warsaw, Poland, and in 1939 escaped the Nazi occupation of Poland, spending the war years in the Soviet Union.

FIGURE 1.3: Rebuilding Negba, 1948. Source: Robert Capa photos, © International Center of Photography.

FIGURE 1.4: The old water tower with the bullet holes. Source: Mashka Litvak, a family friend.

FIGURE 1.5: The monument for
Negba defenders: a soldier, a pioneer,
and a nurse. Source: Mashka Litvak,
a family friend.

FIGURE 1.6: Negba in 1948; the walls are still damaged from the Arab-
Israeli War. My grandfather Buzik is at far left. Source: Robert Capa
photos, © International Center of Photography.

Negba strove for gender equality, meaning that women were ex-pected to work in the same jobs as men, wear similar clothing, and take a role similar to that of men in raising their children. During wartime, the women fought too. It was decided by Negba's gen-eral assembly that only one spouse from each family would fight in Negba, while the other would be taken away from the kibbutz "so as to prevent the possibility of both spouses getting hit and, heaven forbid, leaving orphans with neither mother nor father."[17] They decided it made more sense for Buzik to stay and fight and for Breindel to go to a safer place outside the kibbutz.

A few years later, in 1953, during army practice at an officers' course, Buzik injured his leg. Nobody alive today knows exactly what the injury was or how it occurred, only that my grandfather later died in the hospital from complications. He was forty-two. I remember one time in the 1980s when we visited my grandmother and someone raised the topic. The room fell silent. Tears welled in my grandmother's eyes, and then she snapped with atypical anger that his nurses at the hospital were terrible and would not listen to her, that Buzik was not supposed to die that day, and why didn't we get back to eating our cookies and stop talking about it. In any event, in 1953, Breindel was left a single mother with two daugh-ters, aged five and ten.

That was a rare mention of my grandfather. My grandmother wouldn't talk about him much, a well-known coping strategy of Jews of her generation. Only years after my grandmother's death, when I delved into family history in my research for this book, did my mother and aunt take out my grandmother's dusty old suitcase containing some old documents that shed light on Buzik as a per-son and a kibbutz member.

My grandmother was a simple seamstress, mainly mending clothes and doing alternations but sometimes sewing clothes from scratch. In the early days, everyone wore similar outfits, and Negba was self-sustaining to the point of even making and mending their own clothes. She enjoyed the company of her friends and co-workers, especially in the early days when only kibbutz members worked in

---

[17] From Negba's pamphlet (1948).

the kibbutz and no outside labor was used in the factories or fields. But her work in the sewing shop itself was routine. When clothing became really cheap and members could get their clothing from outside, my grandmother's skills became largely obsolete. Despite the low demand for her services, she continued to work long hours and didn't miss a single day of work in thirty years. In the official kibbutz obituary, they wrote: "Work was, for Breindel, a way of life, and with devotion and perseverance and during many years, she woke up early in the morning to go to her work at the kibbutz sewing shop." I speculate it was also her way of thanking the kibbutz for everything.

Breindel loved the kibbutz. She lived the simple and meaningful life and worked hard. In return, the kibbutz supported her and her daughters and provided them with good educations. Still, the melodies she sang to herself in her pleasant soprano voice as she walked the kibbutz paths were always European melodies, from a faraway time and place.[18] It was clear that part of her still felt more European than Israeli.[19]

Despite the revolutionary nature of establishing the kibbutz, daily life in Negba was mundane. Like other members, Breindel would wake up very early, have breakfast in the communal dining hall, work, eat a communal lunch, and return to work.[20] On days

[18] Breindel was a singer in the kibbutz orchestra, and she performed with the kibbutz orchestra on holidays, and in regional and national kibbutz conferences.

[19] Like other Eastern European immigrants to Israel, Breindel's mother tongues were Polish and Yiddish, although she did speak Hebrew. The revival of the Hebrew language that took place at the time in Europe and Palestine meant that Hebrew was now used as a spoken language rather than just as the sacred language of Judaism. The revival of Hebrew as a spoken language became strongly associated with Zionism in Israel. Hebrew was the language my grandmother and other immigrants to kibbutzim spoke when they moved to Palestine and the kibbutz (although Yiddish was always my grandmother's favorite language, especially when she was trying to be funny).

[20] A typical day for Breindel as a young woman went something like this: She woke up at 5:00 am in her small one-bedroom apartment (or "room," as it was called in the kibbutz), and walked or biked straight to breakfast in the communal dining hall with the rest of the kibbutz, where she filled a plate with food, and ate at the communal dining table among friends. They talked about their day at work, the coming holiday, or their children. Then, she sewed clothes in the sewing workshop until noon, when she returned to the kibbutz dining hall for lunch.

FIGURE 1.7: My grandmother Breindel sewing in the kibbutz factory. Source: Family collection.

בריינדל הוניג

בת מרדכי חזיה

נולדה בפרויצק, פולין ב - 1.6.1910, כ"ג באייר תר"ע
נפטרה ב - 26.3.1994, י"ד בניסן תשנ"ד
בת 84 במותה

FIGURE 1.8: My grandmother Breindel. Source: Family collection.

when it was her turn (*toranut*) to work in the kibbutz kitchen, she would eat with the rest of her shift afterwards. Between 4:00 pm and dinnertime was the special time of the day when her daughters Naomi and Bracha would come for a visit and talk about their day.

Some days she then worked for a couple more hours before walking back to her room for her daughters' daily visit. They might tell her their experiences from the previous twenty-four hours at the children's residences—whom they played with, whether they slept well at night, and how things went at school. At 6:00 pm, my grandmother stepped outside her room and chatted with her neighbor Hanna, and they might walk to the kibbutz cultural center to listen to music or sing in the kibbutz choir. On their way, they passed the communal laundry room, where they dropped off their dirty clothes and sheets or picked up fresh ones (the high frequency may actually reflect free-riding behavior—people who don't have to do their own laundry might want to have their clothes washed more often than if they had to do it themselves). They walked by the swimming pool and the basketball court, past the little petting zoo, and then by the dairy barn and milk production plant, as well as by the pride of the kibbutz: Tzalaf, the factory that produced packages of food products to be shipped all over the country. Breindel then took her evening meal with her fellow kibbutz members in the dining hall, and finally returned to her room.

Children in Negba, as in other kibbutzim, slept communally (*lina meshutefet*) in special children's residences (*batei yeladim*) rather than in their parents' homes. This unique sleeping arrangement, which started as a temporary improvisation by members of Kibbutz Kfar Giladi around 1920, was soon after adopted by almost all kibbutzim and became a key principle. The communal sleeping arrangement had a number of attractive features: it echoed the idea that the children belonged to the community as a whole and not just to their parents, and it allowed kibbutzim to train children to live communally and to equip them with equal opportunities.[21]

My mother actually liked the communal sleeping and the independence she had there, but my grandmother hated having her children so far away. After all, my grandmother grew up in a close nuclear family and her parents would probably never have considered having their young daughter live outside their home. Indeed, the impact of communal sleeping on children and parents is complex, and not purely good or purely bad as many imagine (Golan 2012). However, some children and parents hated the system of children growing up outside their parents' homes, and it might have even caused psychological and social problems later on in some.[22] My mother (and the literature) talks about the "communal nanny" (*metapelet*) who was firm but pleasant and enforced a strict routine that included a fixed schedule for when the children had to eat, read, take a shower, go to the bathroom(!), and sleep. The overall goal was to convey equality and communal values. She also talks

[21] Recent research in the US (Cappelen et al. 2016) compared children who, at 3–4 years old, were randomized into a full-time preschool, a parenting program with incentives, or a control group. They found that early childhood education had a strong causal impact on social preferences several years after the intervention: attending preschool made children more egalitarian in their fairness view and the parenting program enhanced the importance children placed on efficiency relative to fairness.

[22] It appears that some children who were easygoing, very social, and very popular actually loved the independence of living away from parents. Others who were more sensitive hated it. Similarly, some parents tolerated the system and others hated it. The literature criticizing the communal sleeping arrangement describes emotional deprivation, pressure to conform, and lack of warmth. E.g., Leshem (1991), Lamdan (2009), also see the classic novel by Batya Gur (1995) and the 2006 satirical dramatic film *Sweet Mud*.

about the occasional child who ran away to his parents' room in the evening, only to be returned to the children's residence.

The communal sleeping arrangement, at least in principle, also promoted gender equality by freeing women from their traditional role in society of raising the children. During the second wave of immigration, in the kvutzot (literally "groups"—small and early versions of kibbutzim) such as Degania, women were a small minority. They were responsible for child care, and they were generally employed in traditional "women's jobs" in services rather than in agriculture. However, they strove for gender equality and established early on their right to work in agricultural and defense jobs, and kibbutzim established the communal responsibility for child care.

Gender equality in kibbutzim was more important in theory than in practice, however, and the nannies in kibbutzim were all women. Similarly, other occupations in kibbutzim followed the stereotypical gender divide: women were more often in charge of cooking, doing the laundry, and educating the children; and men worked in the fields and were in charge of the economy. Women were also underrepresented in kibbutz leadership, and they tended to be more quiet in general meetings.

As in other kibbutzim, Negba held a general assembly every Saturday after dinner, where all members would gather to elect officials and committees and to discuss and vote on kibbutz matters.[23] Such matters might include who should become manager of the kibbutz factory, whether the factory should extend its exports or extend its lines of production, whether the kibbutz should open another agricultural branch, whether the kibbutz should let someone study at a university a field that was not perceived as directly necessary in the kibbutz, who should be entitled to use the few

[23] As kibbutzim grew larger and their economies became more complex, committees replaced the direct democracy of the general meeting in various tasks. The general meeting elected the kibbutz secretary, treasurer, farm manager, and other officials—as well as committee members for various matters, such as event planning, education, and personnel issues. The committees would make decisions on small daily issues, and on large matters would make recommendations to the general assembly, where the matter would be discussed and voted on by all members.

cars owned by the kibbutz, and whether and when there should be a travel budget for members. Over the years, it would also decide on major issues such as whether to abolish the communal sleeping arrangement for children, whether kibbutz members should be allowed to work outside the kibbutz, and whether the kibbutz should support Russia or the United States during the Cold War.

When my grandmother died in 1994, a close family friend noted during the funeral that "work for her was not just a value, but a way of life, the essence of life." My mother had similar reflections at the funeral: "[L]ooking back, you raised all by yourself, two happy daughters. You gave us everything, always the best. . . . I remember that work always came first; it was the holiest thing. That's how it was in the sewing workshop and that's how it was at home."[24] My mother used to joke that my grandmother decided to die on Passover night, so that the shiva, the week-long mourning period in Judaism, would take place during a holiday and no one in the family would have to miss work.

[24] Similarly, members of Negba recalled in the kibbutz's official eulogy that "Breindel was able to keep her mental strength and her clear foresight, and she devoted herself entirely to educating her young daughters and to cultivating her humble world, which was full of human warmth and gentleness." Her longtime neighbor read these lines: "I did not come to tell the story of Breindel's life. I feel the need to note a period of good neighboring, of simple and human relationship, of mutual assistance, in times of happiness, sickness, and distress, each according to her way, approach and understanding."

CHAPTER 2

A bird's-eye view

K ibbutzim are thought-provoking. They reflect a genuine attempt to create an alternative society. Kibbutzim engaged in
full equality in the distribution of incomes among members and
collective ownership of all property, while promoting mutual assistance and cooperation.

However, the problems of free-riding, adverse selection, brain
drain, and underinvestment in human capital create a trade-off between equality and incentives: as equality rises, incentives fall. The
equality-incentives trade-off suggests that egalitarian societies are
doomed to fail. To be clear, the idea that there is a contradiction between equity and efficiency at the macroeconomic level is no longer
a consensus; new research argues that countries with higher rates
of inequality have slower rates of growth.[1] However, most economists would agree that full equality in the distribution of incomes
is doomed to fail. Yet kibbutzim survived successfully for most of
the twentieth century and are considered one of the most successful
experiments in voluntary socialism.

The first chapter told the story of the creation of one kibbutz,
Negba. In many ways, the stories of other kibbutzim are similar.
In some ways, they are different—some kibbutz founders came
from rich backgrounds, while others came from less well-off

---

[1] For example, see Stiglitz (2012); Alesina and Rodrik (1994).

backgrounds. Some people (like my grandfather) were willing to give up their high standard of living in order to accomplish their ideals and others (like my grandmother) came because life for Jews in Europe came under pressure. Some kibbutzniks settled in remote sites in the north of the country, not far from the Syrian or Lebanese border; others in the far south; some in the center; and some near the sea. The land of some kibbutzim is now worth a fortune. No one story fits all kibbutzim, or even fits all people in one kibbutz. In this chapter, I move from the "micro" level of describing one kibbutz in detail to the "macro"—bird's-eye view—level of describing some general patterns of the early developments of the kibbutz movement. To minimize repetition, I mention only briefly, if at all, topics and developments that were described in the previous chapter or will be discussed in the next ones.

This chapter is not strictly chronological. The goal is not to write an exhaustive history, but rather to survey the historical, demographic, economic, and social developments that are important for the remainder of this book. I include a timeline of events at the end of the book.

TOUGH EARLY DAYS

It was not always clear that kibbutz members would enjoy a high quality of life, and that kibbutzim would survive for so long. The beginning was not easy and the founding generation faced many hardships: employment opportunities were scarce, work was physical and hard, members often got sick, the neighboring Arab villages were frequently hostile, and many kibbutzim were geographically isolated. "The body is crushed, the legs fail, the head hurts, the sun burns and weakens," said one of the pioneers.[2] Idealism and a pioneering spirit were necessary to compensate for the harsh physical environment.

Material conditions and the work environment were not the only difficulties. Members also had to sacrifice their privacy. Others could make crucial decisions about their lives, including personal decisions such as whether and what they could study, what they

---

[2] Quoted in Gavron (2000), p. 21.

would do for work, and when their children could visit them. Such a way of life was difficult, and it was intolerable for individualists and for sensitive people. Even members who admired the kibbutz way of life often left, not because they were not devoted to kibbutz ideals, but because daily life was too difficult. Some left because after living several years in a kibbutz, they realized that they could not relinquish their privacy any longer. Others left because they wanted to study at a university, and the financial conditions of the kibbutz, or the community sentiment, were such that there was no chance for this dream to be fulfilled in the foreseeable future. Scruples over abandoning the kibbutz ideals prevented many people from leaving for a long time, and those who did leave often felt guilty about their decision.

Kibbutzniks were held in high esteem in Israeli society, both before and after the establishment of the state. They had high economic, social, and military status, and had a disproportionate impact on the ideological, political, and military leadership of Israel. They produced some of Israel's elite—from famous generals such as Yigal Alon and Ehud Barak, to famous musicians such as Shalom Hanoch and Meir Ariel. While always home to only a small percentage of the Jewish population, kibbutzim had a huge impact on the rest of the Israeli society. The unique combination of the socialist and Zionist ideology produced an ideal of the kibbutznik as a pioneer-warrior. This kibbutznik image, the classic Israeli *tzabar* (Hebrew for the cactus fruit), who was rough on the outside but soft on the inside, stood in sharp contrast to the image of the diaspora Jew who studied the Torah and avoided physical work. The kibbutznik, before 1948 and in the early State of Israel, had a mythical image within Israel, enhanced by the major role kibbutzim played in state-building, and this image spread to the rest of the world.

COMFORTABLE MIDDLE YEARS

By the 1970s, however, kibbutzim offered an idyllic, comfortable, and secure life to tens of thousands of members who were fit for this kind of life. As economic conditions improved, kibbutzim started to supply additional public goods. Each kibbutz looked

like a picturesque village in the countryside: small apartments surrounded by lush, green walking paths, a swimming pool, tennis
courts, basketball stadiums, cultural centers, and a modern communal dining hall. Kibbutzim appeared as living proof that socialism and equal sharing could succeed.

How did small and struggling egalitarian communities grow
from a dozen members to many thousands and provide living standards that were higher than the country's average? Before I address this question, let me start here by outlining some of the main
developments that took place between the early days, when living
standards were low, and the eve of the financial crisis, when living
standards were high (as we'll see later, probably higher than kibbutzim could afford).

The next chapter suggests that economic considerations such as
insurance were an important and understudied benefit of living in a
kibbutz, but a kibbutz was much more than that. The kibbutz was
a way of life, a social unit that was created to fulfill a wide array of
ideals—building a Jewish nation, creating a socially just society, and
being part of a community that promotes equality and mutual assistance. Specifically, the young idealists who founded kibbutzim were
pioneers, often members of Zionist-socialist youth movements in
Europe such as my grandparents' Ha'shomer Ha'tzair, whose goal
was to come to the Land of Israel in order to accomplish the dream
of national revival of the Jewish people and build a new society that
would be productive and just. The kibbutz life was for many of them
a natural continuation of the many years they had spent together as
a cohesive group whose members knew each other well.

In an era in which one could not just buy a small piece of land
for himself in an isolated location—because of Arab attacks, lack of
capital, lack of basic facilities, and the need for official permits—a
group of people was required to establish a settlement. The kibbutz
way of life had several advantages over alternative systems: it offered
strong social ties, mutual interests, and a shared destiny. A kibbutz
was also a cheap and effective way to provide services. The kibbutz
supplied many household services such as cooking, laundry, child
care, libraries, and culture. Such services feature what economists
call "increasing return to scale" (or "economies of scale"), meaning

that providing them to many people is cheaper per person than providing them to few.[3] Once the kibbutz built its dining hall, laundry room, children's residences, and cultural center, all members could enjoy those services at very low additional cost for the kibbutz. For example, women were released from most traditional household works and were able to work (although most of them were employed in these services). As another example, a kibbutz was an effective way to exploit military economies of scale in the hostile environment in Palestine. Equality in a kibbutz setting made sense because it ensured everyone was strongly motivated to serve. In this sense, even in early days, kibbutzim (or kvutzot) did not just stem from socialist and Zionist ideologies. Rather, they were a better solution than other settlement forms to deal with the harsh conditions and to work the land.[4]

The principles of communal life and equality were regarded not as a burden but as a sacred objective. Prior to 1948, kibbutzim served many national tasks. They occupied the land and extended the Jewish settlements, which eventually determined the borders of the Jewish state; hosted the Palmach units; and hid illegal weapons. All these were the seeds of the defense army, which helped Israel in the 1948 Arab-Israeli war. After the State of Israel was established in 1948, and especially after the Six-Day War of 1967, the importance of kibbutzim in nation-building was diminished.

Even in the heyday of the kibbutz movement, equality was not absolute. In each kibbutz, there were always position holders like the kibbutz secretary, the farm manager, the treasurer, and others who were sent to the main cities to serve in the central organizations of the kibbutz movements or the parties. Such position holders enjoyed benefits like a private car, a flexible expense budget, and even the ability to stay in the city for part of the week. Since in Hebrew the same word is used for "equal" and for "worth," there is a famous pun, saying that "In the kibbutz everybody was equal but some were worth more." Furthermore, even in early days, the

---

[3] To clarify, not every production or service good has the increasing return to scale property, but these goods do.

[4] See Near (1992, chap. 1), for earlier settlement attempts before the first kibbutzim.

degree of equality varied among kibbutzim. Some kibbutzim were more literal in their interpretation of equality and had all clothes except underwear commonly shared by members. Other kibbutzim allowed private clothing, and equality meant that the kibbutz supplied an equal quota of clothes to each member. Similarly, kibbutzim varied in their approach to issues ranging from outside gifts to the use of hired labor. Generally speaking, kibbutzim that belonged to the "Kibbutz Artzi" movement were more committed to their ideology and opposed "exploitation" of outside hired workers. Other kibbutz movements tolerated hired workers much more. And yet, it is fair to say that kibbutzim were all committed to equality—members enjoyed the same material living standards, they had the same access to goods and services, and all property belonged to the entire community.

FROM A DOZEN TO OVER 100,000 MEMBERS

Table 2.1 and Figure 2.1 below show the evolution of the number of kibbutzim and the number of kibbutz members since 1910. Degania was established southwest of the Sea of Galilee in 1910 by a dozen Russian and Eastern European Jewish immigrants. They had to deal with a tough climate, unfavorable conditions for agriculture, and uncertainty about the future. But they were young, driven, full of dreams, and still childless, and they created a seemingly simple society—"a closely knit egalitarian community where all, conferring together, decided the fate of each, and each bore responsibility for all."[5]

The scale of this social experiment quickly grew larger and more complex. Ten years later, there were already 800 members living in twelve kibbutzim. The founders of early kibbutzim mostly came to Israel in what are called the second and third waves of immigration (aliyah) in 1904–1914 and 1919–1923, respectively.[6] Pogroms such as the Kishinev pogrom and other outbreaks of anti-Semitism

---

[5] Near (1992).

[6] The first wave of immigration (First Aliyah), started in 1882 and consisted of Eastern Europeans. These immigrants mostly established *moshavot*, Jewish settlements with privately owned land, rather than kibbutzim. These five immigration

TABLE 2.1: Kibbutzim Population, 1910–2000

Year	Number of kibbutzim	Kibbutz population	% of Rural Jewish population	% of Jewish population	% of Israeli population
1910	1				
1920	12	805			
1930	29	3,877			
1940	82	26,554			
1950	214	66,708			
1952		69,089	20.9	4.7	4.2
1960	229	77,955			
1961	228	77,153	25.9	3.8	3.5
1970	229	85,100			
1972	227	89,700	33.9	3.3	2.8
1980	255	111,200			
1983	267	115,500	35.1	3.4	2.8
1987	268	127,000			
1990	270	125,100			
1994	269	124,600	29.4	2.9	2.3
2000	268	115,300	25.1	2.3	1.8

Note: The three right columns represent the kibbutz population as share of the rural Jewish population, Jewish population, and Israeli population respectively. Source: Pavin (2002).

triggered the Second Aliyah, which drove about 40,000 immigrants from Russia and Poland to Palestine, and even greater numbers to the US. Among those who came in the second Aliyah were young pioneers (halutzim) who established the first kibbutzim based on a synthesis of global socialism and nationalist Zionism. The Third Aliyah was, in part, a continuation of the Second Aliyah, which had been interrupted by the war. Over its five years, another 40,000 immigrants came from the Russian Empire. This migration was driven by a combination of push factors, such as the war, pogroms, and the Russian Revolution; and pull factors, such as the hope of establishing a home for the Jewish people within Palestine. This home was to be created through a British mandate in Palestine and the Balfour Declaration, which stated the support of the British

waves each tell a fascinating story about Jewish migration to Palestine and they are the subject of many books. Here I only mention them very briefly.

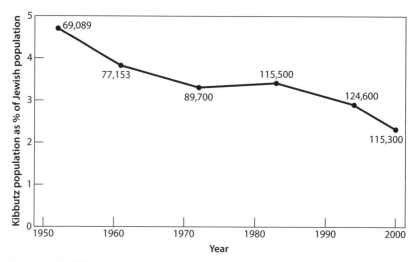

FIGURE 2.1: The population of kibbutzim: This figure shows the total population of kibbutzim as a percentage of the Jewish population in Israel. The values given by the points are the total number of kibbutz members. Source: Pavin (2002).

government for the Zionist plan. As with the Second Aliyah, many immigrants were ideological halutzim with agricultural training who were instrumental to the development of kibbutzim.[7]

The founders of kibbutzim belonged to the "practical Zionism," a stream that believed settling in the land of Israel was the only hope for Jewish nation-building. Kibbutzim's commitment to nation-building had a practical benefit—it ensured they were backed by the Zionist authorities. The implicit contract was that kibbutzim would lead the settlement effort, help protect the Jewish settlements, and provide a devoted workforce and manpower; and in return, the Zionist agencies would provide financial and political support.

The majority of kibbutzim were established in the 1930s and 1940s, shortly before the creation of the State of Israel. The borders

[7] The narrative that they aimed to create a "new human being" who cared about the group more than about himself, a *Homo sociologicus* who would challenge the selfish *Homo economicus*, is exaggerated, but ideology was important at the outset.

of the new state in many places traced the location of kibbutzim. Most founders of kibbutzim in this period came during the fourth and fifth waves of immigration, which occurred between 1924 and 1930 and during the 1930s. The fourth and fifth waves occurred after the closure of US borders; the rise of Nazi Germany during the fifth wave turned the trickle of migration into a flood. During the fourth wave, the two main kibbutz movements were formed: the Kibbutz Meuhad, which was more practical, and the Kibbutz Artzi (of Ha'shomer Ha'tzair), which was more ideological.

The source of kibbutz population growth changed over the years. Early population growth was often from new members joining from outside the kibbutz, many through the five waves of migration. After the Zionist youth movements in Palestine extended their activity, their graduates founded kibbutzim or joined existing ones. Among the first kibbutzim that were founded by members of Ha'shomer Ha'tzair from both Palestine and Galicia was Kibbutz Tel Amal (later renamed Kibbutz Nir David), one of the first settlements of the tower-and-stockade enterprise. Since the establishment of the State of Israel, the main source of kibbutz population growth has been internal, namely kibbutz-born individuals staying in their kibbutz. Many kibbutz-born people did leave, however, and many of the new arrivals to Israel chose to not live in a kibbutz. This shift in the kibbutz population from immigrants who left their family in the diaspora to Israeli-born people whose family lived a few miles away from their kibbutz and visited often brought about new challenges, such as how to retain members in the kibbutz and whether to allow members to receive gifts from their non-kibbutz family.

By the end of the 1970s, about 100,000 people lived in 255 kibbutzim; in 1995, there were 268 kibbutzim in Israel, with about 120,000 members. Kibbutzim were located all over the land of Israel (see figure 2.2). Kibbutzim also contribute significantly to the Israeli economy. Kibbutzniks today represent less than 2 percent of the Israeli population, but their contribution to the economy is disproportionately high. Whether growing produce or making plastics and rubber, kibbutzim supply more than 9 percent of the country's industrial sales and 34 percent of agriculture, and they export abroad almost two-thirds of their industrial products.

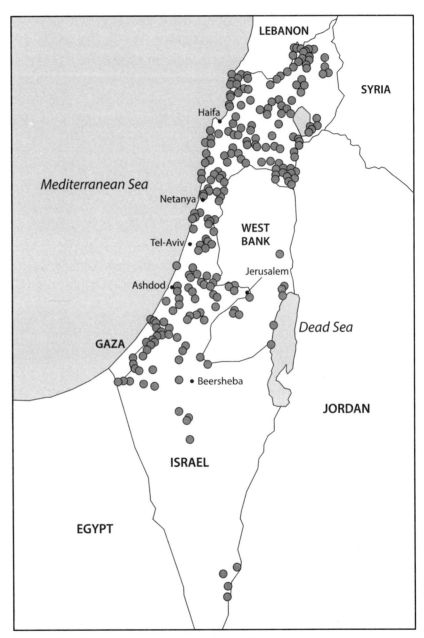

FIGURE 2.2: Kibbutzim are located all over Israel

While the kibbutz population was constantly growing, the share of kibbutz members in the general population has been in decline since the Second World War. The share of kibbutz members is believed to have reached its peak at 6.7 percent of the Jewish population in the early 1940s, just before the creation of the state.[8] It then fell steadily from about 5 percent of the population in 1952 to less than 2.5 percent in 2000.

Kibbutzim have always been relatively small. They vary in size from about 100 to just over 1,000 members, with an average of 440 members (as of 1995). The majority of kibbutzim have between 200 and 600 members. Why are kibbutzim so small? Why not create a single kibbutz with 100,000 members that would be more self-sufficient instead of many small ones? Kibbutzim have struggled with the issue of size from the very beginning, recognizing the trade-off between returns to scale, on the one hand, and the strong social ties and idealistic core, on the other. Degania was small at the outset, and its founder refused to expand it, at one early point suggesting a limit of twenty families (see figure 2.3). Its neighbor, Kibbutz Kinneret, was bigger and kept expanding, which became the more common strategy among kibbutzim. The kibbutz movements varied in their attitudes toward the size of the kibbutz. Those in favor of limiting size thought that sixty families was the optimal size that would facilitate deep relationships, which is an important feature for the sustainability of the kibbutz, as will be discussed later. Chapter 4 will further explore the issue of size and its role in kibbutzim's success.

FROM FARMERS TO BOURGEOIS

The economy of kibbutzim grew over the years. By the end of the 1950s, kibbutzim were one of the most prosperous sectors of the Israeli economy (Near 1997). In the 1950s, agriculture in kibbutzim flourished. In the early 1950s, kibbutzim mainly produced foodstuffs such as vegetables, poultry, and dairy products, which were in high demand. In the late-1950s, heavy machinery entered the

[8] See Barkai (1977), p. 3.

FIGURE 2.3: The first kibbutz,
Degania, (a) when established in
1910 and (b) as it appeared in 2009.
Source: (a) wooden shack at Umm
Juni (wikipedia page of Degania
Alef); (b) courtesy of Degania A
Tourism.

country following the reparation agreement with West Germany.
Unlike most private farms, kibbutzim were large enough to purchase and profitably use the new machinery. Their ideological op-
position to employing hired labor also encouraged their adoption
of the new technology. They gradually moved away from labor- and
toward capital-intensive crops, and they increasingly started to export some of their produce. They added field crops such as cotton
and sugar beet, and fruit trees such as citrus and avocados (see figure 2.4). They also raised poultry and cows. The government of the
newly established state contributed to the success of kibbutz agriculture. The government provided credit, subsidized agricultural
produce, and provided cheap water that enabled irrigation.

Kibbutzim during the 1950s did not just improve their agriculture, they also started to industrialize. They set up factories for
food processing, furniture manufacture, and later other industries
including plastic products, rubber, metal, and electronic equipment. Government was helpful here as well, providing credit and

FIGURE 2.4: Cotton fields in Kibbutz Shamir, ca. 1958. Source: Kibbutz value in Wikiwand (http://www.wikiwand.com/en/Kibbutz).

capital. By 1960, kibbutz factories numbered around one hundred; by the late 1970s, most kibbutzim had at least one factory and many had two or three (Barkai 1977, Near 1997). Kibbutz Negba, for example, built a factory in 1971 that produced plastic packaging for some of the main snack brands in Israel, which turned out to be quite successful and was key to Negba's economic success. Many other kibbutz factories were highly successful and provided kibbutzniks with high living standards. Mort and Brenner (2003, pp. 124–125) told the story of how Kibbutz Gan Shmuel became rich: "the factory, which earns about $80 million a year in exports, began during World War II when the kibbutz, unable to export its oranges, began producing orange concentrate. The kibbutz annual income is approximately NIS [New Israeli Shekels] 1.52 billion, plus they have the real estate assets." There are many other such examples, some of which I will discuss in chapter 8.

Established kibbutzim helped new ones to make their agricultural sectors profitable. Kibbutzim took out loans and bought equipment jointly to take advantage of their size and save money, and they also established regional enterprises that were owned jointly by a number of kibbutzim.

FIGURE 2.5: Kibbutz Ein Harod's dining hall in the 1920s. Source: http://farm4.static.flickr.com/3126/2577949529_15bb7fc802.jpg.

By the late 1970s, most kibbutzim were thriving, and kibbutz members enjoyed living standards higher than the country's average. Members lived in small but well-equipped apartments (*cheder*), each with a bedroom, small kitchen, and shower, surrounded by lawns, footpaths, gardens, and large, modern dining halls (see figure 2.5). Kibbutzniks were no longer mostly farmers, instead working in diverse occupations and industries, described in detail in chapter 6. Kibbutzim were "becoming bourgeois" (Near 1997, p. 249).

CRISES AND REFORMS

It wasn't that kibbutzim didn't face crises. There were some economic difficulties, but most were ideological or social: economic hardships in the early days; the creation of moshavim in 1921; the high exit rate of the 1930s; the crisis of faith surrounding whether kibbutzim should support the Soviet Union, which led to a split of the Kibbutz Meuhad movement into two groups in the early 1950s, resulting in many kibbutzim splitting into two separate entities;[9] the debate over whether to accept Holocaust reparations

---

[9] The history of kibbutzim's affiliations into movements reflects differences and changes in their ideological and political affiliations. Kibbutz Artzi

and whether kibbutz members who received reparations were entitled to keep them; a decline in commitment to kibbutz values among later generations, who wanted less conformism and collectivism and more individualism, increasingly wanted the ability to make their own choices of what to study, and wanted more privacy; a decline in kibbutzim's reputation among Israelis, especially following the Six-Day War of 1967, which saw the rise of a non-kibbutz military elite; and the election of a right-wing government in 1977 that was less favorable for kibbutzim.

One particularly challenging development was the use of hired labor in kibbutzim. Under kibbutz ideology, only members worked on the kibbutz, because hiring workers from the outside was considered exploitation. However, industrialization created manpower shortages, and Prime Minister Ben-Gurion asked kibbutzim to accommodate new arrivals from Middle Eastern countries following the creation of the state. The new immigrants, located in transition camps near kibbutzim, needed work and the kibbutzim needed labor. It made economic sense and hiring the new arrivals would also have helped the Zionist cause, but employing outsiders went against the socialist ideology. Kibbutzim eventually relented and began to hire nonmembers. By 1958, 19 percent of the kibbutz labor force was outside workers (Barkai 1977, Near 1997). Kibbutzim struggled with this issue and always aimed to eliminate it, but

---

Federation, established in 1927, was a Socialist-Zionist movement that was associated with Ha'shomer Ha'tzair and the Marxist-Zionist political party Mapam (ancestor of the modern-day Meretz political party). The Kibbutz Meuhad was also formed in 1927 by the union of several kibbutz bodies and was aligned with the Poale Zion, a Marxist-Zionist movement, and later Ahdut Ha'Avoda, a labor party (an ancestor of the modern-day Israeli Labor Party). In 1951, Ihud Ha'Kvutzot Veha'Kibbutzim was formed by the union of two smaller strands: Hever Ha'Kvutzot and Ihud Ha'Kibbutzim) and included kibbutzim that had left the Kibbutz Meuhad for ideological reasons. Ihud Ha'Kvutzot Veha'Kibbutzim was aligned with the Labor Party. In 1981, the Kibbutz Meuhad and Ihud Ha'Kvutzot Veha'Kibbutzim merged into the United Kibbutz Movement (HaTenua'a HaKibbutzit HaMeuhedet). In 1999, the Kibbutz Artzi Federation and the United Kibbutz Movement merged. While kibbutzim are largely secular, one minority is the Religious Kibbutz Movement, Kibbutz Dati, founded in 1935, which is an organization of the sixteen orthodox kibbutzim.

economic realities and Zionist goals won over socialist ideology.[10] "A number of kibbutzim resisted the idea of 'exploiting' outside labor and creating a 'master-servant' relationship, but the majority bowed to national imperative," writes Gavron (2000, p. 5). In part because of their resistance to outside labor, kibbutzim were perceived as elitists by many of the new arrivals, who felt that their labor was welcome but not their company. They said that "we are welcome in the kibbutz fields but not in its swimming pool" (Gavron 2000, p. 5). Most kibbutzniks were Ashkenazi Jews, who often viewed themselves as the ones that established Israel, and some viewed themselves as more culturally educated. Kibbutzniks were increasingly perceived as a privileged minority, especially in the 1960s, when the ethnic divide between Sephardic and Ashkenazi Jews began playing an increasing role in the political arena.

Another big development was the abolition of the communal children's residences (see figure 2.6). The existing system of communal child-raising imposed emotional costs on children and parents.[11] The younger generation increasingly resisted the idea of children's communal sleeping (*lina meshutefet*). Parents wanted their children to live with them. After heated discussions, kibbutzim voted to abolish the communal sleeping arrangement in favor of what was called a "family sleeping" arrangement (*lina mishpachtit*), which simply meant children would live with their parents. To accommodate the move of children from the special communal residences into their parents' homes, kibbutzim needed

---

[10] Simons and Ingram (1997) study the topic of hired labor in kibbutzim from an organizational theory perspective. They showed that kibbutzim that belonged to the Artzi movement, which was the most ideologically opposed to using hired labor, were most successful in resisting it during the 1950s and 1960s. The efforts of kibbutzim more generally to stay close to the principle of internal labor showed fruits: between 1969 and 1977 the use of hired labor declined substantially, leading some to view the 1970s as one of the most ideological decades (Satt and Schaefer 1994; Simons and Ingram 1997). See also Satt (1991) and Satt and Ginzburg (1992) for more theory and evidence on the topic of hired labor and the internal-labor principle in kibbutzim.

[11] The evidence on this point was mixed: some kibbutz children reported positive experiences, while others reported developing psychological complexes as adults (Spiro and Spiro 1958; Lieblich 1981).

FIGURE 2.6A AND B: Communal child care in the kibbutz. Source: Family collection.

to enlarge members' homes. To do so, many kibbutzim borrowed large sums.

A seemingly mundane development that ended up having far-reaching consequences was the introduction of personal budgets. Kibbutzniks refrained from using cash for many years.[12] The kibbutz officials of course used money to buy and sell products in the Israeli economy, but kibbutzniks had no bank accounts, and they only used money on rare occasions when they needed to buy something outside the kibbutz on their own.[13] In later years, kibbutzniks

[12] Indeed, when Angela Merkel visited a kibbutz in 2008, she asked "Do you get salaries here? How do you manage with money at the kibbutz?" (Roni Sofer, "Merkel Shows Interest in Kibbutz Life," Ynetnews.com, March 16, 2008, http://www.ynetnews.com/articles/0,7340,L-3519821,00.html).

[13] Golan (2012, chap. 5) describes what it was like to grow up in a world with no money. She describes how she and her fellow kibbutz children never heard terms like "livelihood," "economic situation," "profit," employer-employee," and instead used terms like "good and bad," "responsibly," "manual work," and "same for everyone." She describes how she first discovered money when her father took her to Tel Aviv and she approached one of the stands in the market and grabbed some grapes and was about to walk away. Her father told her that they needed to pay for them. She didn't understand why, and told her father that the man had so many and she would share hers if she had any. Her father explained why they needed to pay, but also looked down at these "bourgeois" ideas and felt kibbutz values were superior. In other spheres, kibbutzniks developed language

would use coupons or a point system to buy the likes of candy and cigarettes from the small general stores that opened in kibbutzim. Cash was not used in these stores, but each member had a personal "budget" that he could spend at the stores. As Inbari (2009, p. 192; my translation) put it in the context of Kibbutz Afikim: "in practice, when voting in favor of printing coupons the members introduced the most crucial reform in the history of the kibbutz. They became customers. Customers who had an annual personal budget that they were allowed to spend or accumulate from year to year." Personal budgets were later similarly used to buy items such as clothing, furniture, and personal items. These allowed members more freedom to buy according to their tastes but also introduced private property on a small scale in kibbutzim.

Each of these crises led some members to announce that the kibbutz idea was coming to an end. That kibbutzim survived all of these crises was a sign of their strength. Along the way, they demonstrated flexibility through relaxing some of their ideological principles: applying a less puritan interpretation of equality by allowing small outside gifts; allowing members to receive reparations from Germany; hiring outside labor; and moving children to their parents' homes. Nevertheless, kibbutzim stuck to their most fundamental principle: full income equality among members.

It is perhaps easier to imagine how a simple society of idealist farmers might choose to lead communal life, but how did kibbutzim survive as complex, industrialized societies, where members worked in a wide variety of occupations and produced a wide variety of products? These are some of the questions this book will address.

From the mid-1980s, however, kibbutzim faced challenges that were bigger than ever before. Members of the second and third generations no longer believed in kibbutz ideals as their parents had, governmental support declined, the opportunities of high-earner kibbutz members outside kibbutzim improved, and a severe

---

consistent with their socialist ideology. For instance, manager is a "capitalist" term. In a kibbutz there were no managers, but there were people who did the same as managers, but had a different name like coordinator (*merakez*).

FIGURE 2.7 A kibbutz in the North. Source: Laura Ratner, "Kibbutzim and Communism," *Life Examinations* blog, April 16, 2011 (https://lifeexaminations .wordpress.com/2011/04/16 /kibbutzim-and-communism/).

financial crisis hit many kibbutzim and left them with huge debts and lower living standards.

Common sense (and economic theory) suggest that these major upheavals would worsen the incentive problems facing kibbutzim, making equal sharing increasingly difficult to sustain. Did kibbutz members respond to these worsened economic incentives by leaving their kibbutzim? Chapter 5 addresses this question.

More specifically, the goal of maintaining an egalitarian society in capitalist surroundings became more challenging from the 1970s due to external and internal reasons. Externally, the economic environment became more tempting on one hand and more hostile on the other. Opportunities outside the kibbutz improved, especially for the most-skilled members, and standards of living rose faster in Israeli cities than in the kibbutzim. After the dramatic change in political regime from left to right that took place in May 1977, the attitude toward kibbutzim became increasingly negative. They lost their access to cheap credit, and instead of being appreciated they were blamed and slandered. Internally, kibbutzniks' ideological enthusiasm declined. The kibbutz education system did not succeed in instilling the second and third generations with the same ideological commitment that characterized the first generation. These factors, which are described and discussed in detail throughout this book, worsened the problem of free-riding and brain drain. Consequently, the economic situation in many kibbutzim deteriorated and the communal and social texture began to disintegrate, as I describe in detail in part 3 of this book.

A few years later, starting in the late 1990s, many kibbutzim introduced major reforms, such as abolishing the traditional dining hall and hiring outside managers to run the kibbutz. Most strikingly, many kibbutzim abandoned full income equality, their most fundamental principle. Even Degania introduced major reforms and shifted away from the full equal-sharing model. The degree of reform varied across kibbutzim, from small deviations from full equality to dramatic changes that essentially transformed some of the kibbutzim into capitalist neighborhoods. Most kibbutzim chose something in between, a "safety net" arrangement whereby if the member earns more than a certain amount, she gets to keep some fraction of her income and the rest is shared equally across members. As kibbutzim privatized and introduced differential salaries, they experienced a social and an economic revival—members stopped leaving, shirking stopped and kibbutz-born people who left came back, even if the sense of community and equity was not the same. Many kibbutzim also built new neighborhoods just outside the kibbutz to absorb kibbutz children and others who wanted to live in the kibbutz surroundings without necessarily becoming kibbutz members, and who were happy to pay for kibbutz services. I look at these issues more closely in part 3.

The coming chapters examine these developments in more detail. I discuss the extent to which a kibbutz was an efficient way to organize a society striving for income equality. I delve into the rules and norms that helped kibbutzim survive—including their ideology, their size, the communal ownership of property, the education system, the social sanctions and rewards, and the screening of entrants. I examine the processes that undermined kibbutzim, including how the financial crisis was the final straw that triggered the major reforms—the "privatization" of kibbutzim. I analyze conceptually and empirically why some kibbutzim shifted away from equal sharing while others did not, and identify the consequences of the recent rise in inequality. Along the way, I highlight general lessons from kibbutzim for societies striving to reduce inequality.

CHAPTER 3

Why an economist might create a kibbutz

WHY INCOME EQUALITY?

Idealism and Ideology

Why create an egalitarian kibbutz? Socialist ideology was an important and explicit motive for kibbutz founders, many of whom were socialist idealists committed to equality. They rejected capitalism and wanted to create an egalitarian society based on the Marxist principle "from each according to ability, to each according to his needs." While the emphasis on socialism has declined, with each generation becoming less committed than its predecessor (more on this later), some degree of ideology has always played a role in kibbutzim.

Idealism more broadly was also important. In fact, I would play devil's advocate when arguing with my uncle about this issue. Even as I articulated a cynical view of the egalitarian kibbutz, I found elements of it intuitively appealing. Few people are purely selfish; everyone cares about her family and friends. Many are driven by the wish to do good, and they devote considerable effort to behaving in a socially responsible way by being helpful and trying to improve the world. So wouldn't it be nice to live in a society where everyone put all this effort and energy toward the good of the group and, in turn, received from the group everything he needed? Wouldn't it be nice to live among people who felt mutually responsible for one another, who didn't primarily think about their own material well-being but rather cared about others?

Many people intuitively feel equality is the fair way to divide resources. The fact that so much of society's wealth is held by so few people, and that some people are starving while others have billions of dollars, is appalling to many. Indeed, societies throughout history and almost all countries today have engaged in redistribution from the rich to the poor and from the fortunate to the unfortunate members of society.

How much equality there should be, which often translates into how high the taxes that governments impose should be, is highly debated. Also debated is whether it is preferable to have equality of income or merely equality of opportunity, such as through equal access to education and health services. Equality of opportunity does not imply equality of income, because even two people with the same access to education and health services can earn very different amounts depending on their talent and effort. This is a lively and important area of research, especially because wealth inequality in Europe and the United States increased dramatically over the last two centuries, meaning that wealth is increasingly concentrated in the hands of few.[1] Generally speaking, those who believe their effort is the main driver of their income tend to favor equality of opportunity, and those who believe luck and other circumstances beyond their influence are the main determinants of their income tend to favor equality of income. But even those in favor of equality of income don't usually propose the complete income equality that was practiced in kibbutzim.

Certainly, ideology must have been important in motivating the equal sharing of resources. It enhanced the inherent loyalty of members to their kibbutz and to the egalitarian ideals. This idealistic view can explain the equal sharing in the distribution of income ("from ability to needs"). It can also explain other key features of kibbutzim: absence of private property; a non-cash economy; communal dining halls where members ate their meals together; high provision of local public goods—which are public

---

[1] For influential examples, see Piketty and Saez (2001); Atkinson, Piketty, and Saez (2011); and Piketty (2014).

goods that can only be enjoyed by kibbutz members; separate communal residences for children outside their parents' homes; collective education to instill socialist and Zionist values (Dror 2002); communal production, whereby kibbutz members worked inside their kibbutzim in agriculture or in one of the kibbutz plants; and a prohibition on outside labor, because hiring labor was considered "exploitation."

Economics and Insurance

An economic perspective suggests a different benefit of the egalitarian kibbutz. Even when abstracting from ideology and fairness, it is not surprising that the founders of kibbutzim chose equality. Equal sharing provides a safety net, valuable insurance against misfortune. As my grandmother knew all too well, a kibbutz member knew that even if she became sick, if she lost her husband, or if her occupation turned out to be unprofitable, she and her family would enjoy a decent life and get an equal share of the output despite their circumstances. People value such insurance because they dislike risk—we are all "risk averse." To illustrate that you too are risk averse, consider the following thought experiment. Would you rather get one million dollars, or flip a coin and get two million dollars if it lands on heads and zero dollars if lands on tails? Both these options would give you one million dollars on average, but I haven't yet met a person who would choose the risky bet over the certain outcome. Income equality provides great insurance. The higher the income equality, the better the insurance.

Economic theory also suggests that income equality is desirable from society's perspective. Holding everything else constant, a dollar taken from Warren Buffet and given to a homeless person increases the well-being of society as a whole, referred to as "social welfare" by economists. This social welfare is increased because taking a dollar away from the rich will hurt them little, whereas giving this dollar to the poor will benefit them much more. Note that I say "holding everything else constant," because Warren Buffet might invest his dollar and this investment might indirectly improve the welfare of the poor.

Rawls ([1971] 2009) advanced a related idea: the fair distribution of income is the one people would select from behind a "veil of ignorance," meaning that they would choose before they knew what their own situation in the society would be. This means they will want to design society so that even the worst-off people are not too miserable, because that could be them. In fact, the extreme case of income equality is generally an attractive distribution when viewed from behind a veil of ignorance. However, full equality might not be attractive even from behind a veil of ignorance if we take into account the possible distortions that equal sharing might bring. For example, it is understood that people do their best for themselves and their families given the rules. Thus people can only be taxed up to a point; beyond this point, the talented and hard-working will leave and everyone will stop working hard. The incentive to leave or work little if redistribution is too high limits the degree of equality that is feasible in society.

Although this insurance motive for equality in kibbutzim has been largely overlooked, its importance is evident in kibbutzim's bylaws, which in earlier days were to a large extent standardized across kibbutzim. In a common phrase (and in my own translation from the Hebrew), the bylaws spelled out kibbutzim's commitment to "provide for the economic, social, cultural, educational, and personal needs of members and their dependents . . . [and] to ensure a decent standard of living for kibbutz members and their dependents."

Mutual aid was practiced not only within a kibbutz but between kibbutzim: if a kibbutz found itself in trouble, it would receive support from other kibbutzim. The early bylaws stated that the kibbutz was committed to "have mutual aid with other kibbutzim and rural villages," which provided insurance against negative shocks to the specific kibbutz.

Although this may come across as an unusual arrangement, mutual aid and mutual support are actually widespread even in capitalist societies: it is not just that nobody wants to be taken advantage of, but we also all help our families and friends and many of us are part of a community of some sort. In fact, many believe that mutual aid is a fundamental law of nature. Humans have evolved to cooperate and help each other, not just to compete and pursue our self-interest.[2] Fairness, altruism, and reciprocity lead humans (as well as animals) to support mutual aid and provide valuable insurance. Mutual aid is at the heart of many societies and organizations, ranging from various organizations (cooperatives, unions, fraternities, Japan's postwar *keiretsu*[3]) to clans and welfare states.

Insurance was much needed, and mutual aid among members within a kibbutz and across kibbutzim was a fundamental principle. Kibbutz members knew that whatever their circumstances might be, and whatever their ability and income, they (and their families) would always be provided with an average income and be taken care of when necessary. Founders of kibbutzim needed insurance against potential income shocks. In early days, the newcomers often became sick with malaria, and "as much as half of the work force could be idle because of illness on a given day" (Near 1992). Itzhak

---

[2] There is a huge literature on this topic. One classic reference on mutual aid is Kropotkin [1902] 2012, and a more recent example is Beito (2003). Ridley (1997) is a nice example of the view that cooperation may be a stronger force than our "selfish gene." Hunter-and-gatherer societies tended to be egalitarian in their social structure, and traditional bands and tribes often had egalitarian social system and communal decision-making processes (e.g., Diamond 1997). It is possible that working as a tribe and sharing together gave us an evolutionary advantage that later turned us into the dominant animal (Harari 2014). In economics, Ernst Fehr and colleagues are leading examples on the importance of cooperation, altruism, and fairness in shaping human behavior and curbing free-riding (e.g., Fehr and Schmidt 1999; Fehr and Gächter 2000a, 2000b, 2002; Fehr and Fischbacher 2003; Henrich et al. 2001).

[3] The keiretsu of postwar Japan is a set of firms (e.g., Mitsubishi) that form an informal business association. Firms in a keiretsu share a common identity, often based on historical associations, that is enhanced by periodic meetings of high officials of the various component of the companies. Mutual help is strong among such firms, and the stronger firms often help the weaker firms in a way that weakens the stronger firms. The latter nevertheless feel a moral obligation to provide this help, as it would be humiliating to allow the weaker firms in the group to fail, if they could have avoided it by helping them. Despite this leveling, the keiretsu control a substantial part of Japan's economy. It is possible however, that this arrangement is subsidized by consumers who may arguably pay higher prices to support such arrangements; indeed, similar critiques have been leveled against the kibbutzim. For a nice account, see Lincoln and Gerlach (2004). I thank Mark Granovetter for pointing out this example.

Tabenkin, an early leader in the kibbutz movement, commented that "in the conquest of work in town and country, in the conquest of the soil, the need for the kvutza always appeared; for we were alone and powerless, divorced from our parents and our environment, and face to face with the difficulty of life—the search for employment, illness, and so forth."[4]

In the very early days, when most members worked in agriculture inside their kibbutz, each kibbutz faced considerable aggregate risk. As with villages in developing countries today, a drought or crop failure could cause economic hardship for the entire kibbutz. Regional associations demanded that kibbutzim distribute their grain equally among themselves and sell it collectively (these was the beginning of the Hamashbir cooperative, see Near 1992, p. 46). Such arrangements could be regarded as means to provide insurance for the individual kibbutz.

Once kibbutzim diversified their economies, they became even better forms of insurance. Because a kibbutz consists of members with different occupations and abilities working in different industries, equal sharing provides members and their families with valuable insurance against bad luck such as illness, unemployment, and disability. In early years this was the only insurance option, but eventually the state began to offer Israelis formal unemployment insurance. This alternative source of insurance reduced the need for a kibbutz to protect against some kinds of income shocks that led to temporary unemployment. However, even after outside insurance markets developed, equal sharing provided kibbutz members with an additional level of insurance that could not be obtained elsewhere (although, at some stage, employment in the Israeli public

[4] Much has been written about Tabenkin, who together with David Ben-Gurion and Berl Katznelson was a founding father of the Labor Movement in Palestine. I particularly enjoyed the wonderful book by Zeev Tzahor (2015) , a member of Kibbutz Ramat HaKovesh who later became the last secretary of Israel's prime minister Ben-Gurion. Tzahor describes how the founding generation of kibbutzim admired Tabenkin and how Ben-Gurion was fascinated by this admiration and wanted to understand its causes. In his later years, Tabenkin was opposed to territorial concessions and was an expansionist, illustrating the possible contradiction between the Zionist and Socialist ideology that I later describe.

sector that granted tenure also provided good insurance, as well as creating the incentive problems discussed in this book). This extra insurance came in part from the fact that other sources did not provide complete insurance. For example, a person who became disabled and unable to work might receive from the government a sickness benefit that paid her only a fraction of her previous income. Even if this fraction were high, it would not compensate for possible future promotions the worker might have earned. Income equality within kibbutzim also offered insurance against shocks to the market value of one's skills (or "human capital"). Such insurance was limited outside kibbutzim, and available only in the forms of life insurance and disability insurance.[5] Just as my grandmother's skills as a seamstress became obsolete, I might be in trouble if economics becomes obsolete, and I have no way to buy insurance against this possibility. If I lived in an egalitarian kibbutz, with dozens of people of different occupations and skills, the redistribution offered by the kibbutz would effectively insure me against such decline in the demand for economics.

The importance of ideology and insurance in the early days was evident in a survey conducted in the late 1960s covering over a thousand members of the first and second generations (Rosner 1990). The most important objective listed by kibbutz members was the "establishment of a just society," which includes both ideological and insurance elements. Other factors with insurance elements also were ranked as important objectives of members; specifically, the factors guaranteeing "full social security," "freedom from economic concern and competition," and "an adequate standard of living." Some ideological objectives listed as important were: "collectivity and equality," "developing a model socialist society," and "fostering fellowship among members."

As one member of Maagan Michael, a kibbutz that remained egalitarian, said when discussing the future of his kibbutz, "The bottom line is that everyone in Maagan Michael can live from cradle to grave with honor" and "there are no poor or neglected, as

---

[5] Tzahor (2015) describes how the first thing he did when he and his family left the kibbutz was to buy life insurance.

in other places. We have to preserve that reality" (Gavron 2000, p. 206). Another member of that kibbutz, who was in favor of moving away from sharing and allowing for more individualism, nevertheless remarked that she would still like the kibbutz to help weaker members and provide members with health and education services (p. 207).

Even the language used by kibbutzim many years later, as they shifted away from equal sharing, illustrates the importance of insurance. Kibbutzim that maintained equal sharing were called *shitufim* (Hebrew for "full sharing"); even ones that had shifted away from equal sharing were called *reshet-bitachon* (Hebrew for "safety net"), emphasizing that even a widely reformed kibbutz provided substantial insurance and wouldn't let weak members starve.

WHY AN ECONOMIST MIGHT CREATE AN EGALITARIAN KIBBUTZ

> Capitalism is the exploitation of man by man; socialism is exactly the opposite!
>
> —*Old anarchist joke, cited in Gavron 2000, p. 209*

Imagine (it's hard, I know) that in 1910 the founders of kibbutzim met with a Western economist. The founders would tell the economist that they wanted to set up a society based on full income equality, and ask for her advice: How should they design their new society? What rules and norms would be particularly important for its success? Just like the economist I played in the argument with my uncle, the economist would likely have told them their idea was terrible and their egalitarian society was doomed to swift failure. But if the economist had the foresight to know everything economists and other social scientists learned over the next century, she would likely have recommended that they create a society that is fundamentally the egalitarian kibbutz they ended up building without her advice, with only minor tweaks.

The founders wished to create a society that provided members with the highest degree of income equality, both because equal sharing provides a valuable safety net (insurance) and because of ideological reasons.[6] The economic challenge facing the founders was how to create a fully egalitarian society while solving the two incentive problems inherent to equal-sharing arrangements. The first is the "adverse selection" problem, or the tendency for the least-skilled people to enter and be subsidized by more-skilled members. A closely related problem is the "brain drain" problem, or the tendency for the most-skilled members to exit and earn a wage premium for their talent outside the commune. The second is the "free-rider" problem, or the tendency of members to shirk on their jobs, rely on the efforts of other members when performing team work, and not study hard or invest in their education. Let me explain why a kibbutz was a great way to solve these.

Economic theory provides guidance about how to maintain a high degree of income equality while avoiding incentive problems.[7] One way to mitigate adverse selection is to recruit members with

[6] I note again that while the discussion below suggests functional and economic benefits of various rules and norms in kibbutzim, this does not imply that the founders of kibbutzim were primarily motivated by functional economic considerations. For example, while the lack of private property might help solve the brain drain problem, Marx clearly had other considerations in mind when he analyzed the history of property formation and private property. The point is that regardless of the original intentions, kibbutzim were structured in a way that helped them deal with the various incentive problems associated with equality.

[7] The conceptual framework, which is formally presented in Abramitzky (2008a), highlights that while insurance considerations can provide a rationale for a group of individuals to agree on equal sharing before they know their own productivities, at some point their productivities are revealed. If people are permitted to exit the equal-sharing agreement and instead receive wages outside the equal-sharing agreement (what economists call "receiving their outside options"), this insurance arrangement might fail because of the lack of incentives for high-ability people to stay in it (the brain drain problem). Using economics jargon, the problem facing a kibbutz is how to provide insurance with limited commitment, that is, how to provide a high level of insurance in a world in which members cannot commit to stay in their kibbutz and can exit at will. (For optimal contracts with limited commitment in other settings, see Coate and Ravallion 1993; Ligon, Thomas and Worrall 2002; Hendel and Lizzeri 2003; Albarran and Attanasio 2003; Crocker and Moran 2003; and Morten 2016.) In addition, if productivity is not only an in-born trait, but also depends on effort, then the insurance arrangement might fail because of the lack of incentives to work hard under equal sharing (moral hazard). Similar problems afflict many forms of insurance, such as health insurance and life insurance.

similar economic prospects and similar needs for insurance. A second way, used by many countries, including the United States, is to make insurance programs such as Social Security and Medicare mandatory.

Now imagine the founders of kibbutzim gathering together in the new land, full of uncertainty, and deciding to create a kibbutz. They needed a community that would provide them a safety net—insurance against sickness, unemployment, and loneliness. They were young, they shared the same ideals, and they had similar economic prospects.[8] According to Talmon, the "main characteristic of the kibbutzim [at the outset was] homogeneity. Kibbutzim were established by young unattached individuals who share a comparatively long period of social, ideological, and vocational training" (Talmon 1972, p. 2). To be sure, founders were not exactly the same in their work attitude and innate abilities. Gavron (2000, p. 21) quotes one of the founders of the first kibbutz: "not everyone was equally conscientious, skilled and energetic. Some were careless and even lost their tools. There were crises and arguments." However, they were roughly similar in their economic prospects. The rules were designed at a point when the founders did not fully know what their prospects in the new land would be, and this homogeneity made the creation of the kibbutz easier. Such a "veil of ignorance" regarding the design of a society before members knew their fortunes naturally reduced adverse selection. This solution might not have been a conscious, calculated factor in kibbutz formation, but it helped to sustain the kibbutz, a point that I will return to below and in chapter 6.

Not only was adverse selection mitigated, but kibbutz founders might have been favorably selected. Idealistic zeal and socialist ideology drove a small fraction of the new immigrants to establish communes. The people who first chose to make the costly and risky move to settle a foreign land were probably better than average in all sorts of ways, such as more adventurous, harder working, and, in the

---

[8] Young kibbutz-born individuals can also be regarded as homogeneous in their ability. They enter an egalitarian contract that provides them with insurance, and they might leave once they grow up and learn their abilities.

case of the young Zionists and socialists, more prosocial. Those who chose to go to the kibbutz instead of the city were likely also selected on an additional set of criteria such as their attitudes toward communal living and the commitment they felt to the kibbutz ideals.

The mirror problem of brain drain can be avoided by "posting a bond" that will make exit more costly for those members who turn out to be the most productive. In the context of the kibbutz, abolishing all private property served as such a bond. According to the kibbutz movement's bylaws, whether intentionally or not, the founders committed that each member would "bring to the possession of the kibbutz his full working power and any income and assets he owns and/or receives from any source." Furthermore, the bylaws state that "the property of the kibbutz cannot be distributed among members, both when the kibbutz persists and when it is dissolved," and that "the kibbutz does not distribute profits in any way, and every surplus goes to the kibbutz." Kibbutz members are "not allowed to sell any of the assets they use, they cannot receive gifts from outside the kibbutz, and the kibbutz can seize members' property."

The lack of private property and the communal holding of all property meant that members could not save and members who exited could not take their share of the property with them. For example, they could not take their house or their share of the kibbutz profits. This made exit very costly, thus facilitating income equality while avoiding the brain-drain problem.[9] Other identifying features

---

[9] The problem is that people learn their ability over time (à la Harris and Holmstrom 1982) and might renege the contract and leave. Before people learn their ability, they would like a high degree of equality to insure themselves against shocks to their ability. The fact that they know, at the time of contracting, that they will learn their ability in the future limits their ability to implement a high degree of equality. To implement a contract that provides a high degree of equality (i.e., a high degree of insurance) requires a commitment at the time of contracting that would effectively "lock in" those who turn out to be high-ability people in the future. Otherwise, low-ability people would stay and earn low income and high-ability people would leave and earn high incomes, making the contract useless in providing insurance. Therefore, the two ingredients required to maintain a high degree of insurance are homogeneity across individuals at the time of contracting and "lock-in" devices designed to make it costly for high-ability people to renege on their contract and leave.

of kibbutzim that locked in members and facilitated income equality while avoiding brain drain included the abolition of cash, the encouragement of education that was primarily valuable within the kibbutz (what economists would call "kibbutz-specific human capital"), and the high provision of local public goods such as swimming pools, parks, tennis courts, and cultural centers, which can only be enjoyed if one stays in the kibbutz. Chapter 6 discusses these in more detail.

Finally, the free-rider problem could be minimized by penalizing shirking with social sanctions, and rewarding hard work with social rewards. The system of social sanctions and rewards was supported by the establishment of a regular general meeting of all kibbutz members, a communal dining hall and other social gathering places, and an information transmission mechanism based on gossip.[10]

Privacy in the kibbutz was very limited, and individualism was discouraged. As already discussed, members had to give up the centrality of the family in favor of their community, and children were raised in special residences outside the home. One of the founders of Degania said in a meeting that "there must be no privacy. All privacy interferes with our communal life. All of us are obligated to participate in the expense of raising children—not just the parents." Although these requirements may have been chosen for ideological reasons, they made mutual monitoring easier and social pressure more effective, which enabled equal sharing without free riding.[11] It is interesting to note that the connection between privacy (in the broad sense) and individualism has been historically explored as having arisen in the West only in the past two centuries. While humans seem to be hardwired to appreciate privacy, societies in the distant past chose survival and convenience over privacy. It is perhaps a

---

[10] It is even argued that gossip is a mechanism that was created thousands of years ago for this exact purpose (Harari 2014).

[11] Similarly to the case of religious sects studied by Iannaccone (1992) and Berman (2000), these practices can also be interpreted as "efficient prohibitions" inducing members to better monitor each other or as costly sacrifices that induce members to signal their sincere intention to live in the kibbutz.

luxury of modern societies to place high value on privacy.[12] As I discuss in more detail in chapter 5, this lack of privacy helps explain why kibbutzim are so rare and why only a small share of Israelis live in a kibbutz.

Ideology re-enters the picture here. A member with a high level of ideology and idealism was less likely to leave or shirk than was a member with a low level of ideology. Thus, the presence of ideologically committed members is important for maintaining equal sharing while mitigating brain drain and free riding. As a result, kibbutzim had an incentive to instill ideology through education, which they attempted to do. Kibbutzim put in place a collective education system that promoted altruism and socialism, encouraged a strong work ethic and norms of working hard, cooperation, an extended-family approach, caring about the collective more than about oneself, and having meaningful service in the army. The collective, rather than parents, was responsible for raising children, who learned to live communally, take responsibility, help the weak, and value cooperation over competition. A key goal was to train children to believe in the collective way of life their parents had chosen.

Such an education system was not without cost. Some claimed that the traditional kibbutz education system educated for conformism and mediocrity, pulling up weaker students but pushing down those with high individual aspirations (Spiro 1958; Bettelheim 1969). Either way, these strategies were helpful in raising members who would value or benefit from living in a kibbutz, thus supporting equal sharing.

Governmental support to kibbutzim, discussed in chapter 8, effectively increased the kibbutz budget and allowed kibbutzim to provide higher living standards to their members. Higher living standards, in turn, reduced members' incentives to exit and thus helped solve the brain-drain problem.[13]

---

[12] A fun read on this by Greg Ferenstein can be found at https://medium.com/the-ferenstein-wire/the-birth-and-death-of-privacy-3–000-years-of-history-in-50-images-614c26059e#.q3sy2z3ae.

[13] However, it does increase the incentives for adverse selection in entry, because people from the outside would find it more attractive to enter a rich kibbutz.

THE KIBBUTZ AS A SUBSTITUTE
FOR THE NUCLEAR FAMILY

One way to think about a kibbutz is as an extended family. Like a family, the kibbutz would want its members to contribute according to their ability and receive according to their needs. The kibbutz fulfilled many of the economic functions of families, which broadly fall into four categories.[14] The first is mutual insurance. One partner can work when the other is unemployed or sick, providing unemployment and health insurance, or the two partners can work in different occupations that are subject to different shocks, providing insurance against shocks to the value of one's human capital. If markets are well developed and there are market options for unemployment and health insurance, the insurance role of the family becomes less important. The average kibbutz has four hundred members who work in different occupations and industries, yet output is distributed equally. Thus, the kibbutz provides valuable health insurance, unemployment insurance, and insurance against shocks to human capital. Inside the kibbutz, as in the case of a family, monitoring is less costly than in markets, and information is more symmetric.

The second function of the family is to provide benefits from specialization or economies of scale. One partner may work at home while the other works in the market, resulting in a higher joint production due to increasing returns. Kibbutzim have traditionally tried to exploit increasing returns in food production (communal dining hall), and in raising children (separate residences for children).

The third function of the family is to facilitate the formation of human capital by transmitting values and information from parents

---

[14] The seminal paper on this topic is Weiss (1997). The institutional literature more generally examines institutions that support markets and institutions that are substitutes for markets. Coalitions of Maghribi traders (Greif 1989, 1993), Italian city-states during the commercial revolution (Greif 1994), merchant guilds of the late medieval period (Greif, Milgrom, and Weingast 1994), and institutions designed to restrain rulers' coercive power (North and Weingast 1989) are examples of institutions that supported trade. Firms, family, communes, and cooperatives and partnerships are examples of institutions that are substitutes for markets.

to children and by helping to finance schooling for the spouse. In principle, a kibbutz can do the same and send some members to school while others work and finance the students.

The fourth function of the family, which is also fulfilled by kibbutzim, is the sharing of collective goods. Kibbutzim have high levels of local public goods, and kibbutz members share information and help each other when needed. As the following chapters suggest, these various functions of kibbutzim also interact with each other: an institution that provides insurance has to overcome the problems of free-riding and adverse selection; the extensive sharing of information and networking facilitates mutual monitoring; the mutual support and the close interaction of members make peer pressure effective; and the shared wealth, high provision of local public goods, and economies of scale lock in members and mitigate adverse selection.

In summary, kibbutzim were created for a variety of different reasons—fulfilling the dreams of building a Jewish nation, taking part in creating a socialist community based on equality and social justice, and taking advantage of the insurance that equal sharing provides and the economies of scale in production and consumption that kibbutzim offered. Whether intentional or not, kibbutzim created a society that supported equal sharing while dealing quite well with incentive problems. The kibbutz also provided the kind of camaraderie that some people value a lot, even if it comes at a heavy price of loss of privacy and strict norms of behavior.

Economic theory yields a number of predictions that the remainder of the book will test using data. For example, under equal sharing, a kibbutz is expected to experience brain drain and adverse selection. At the same time, wealthier kibbutzim, and ones with stronger socialist ideology, are expected to experience less brain drain and to be able to maintain a higher degree of income equality.

PART II

THE SURVIVAL

"An experiment that has not failed."

—*Martin Buber, 1949*

INTERLUDE: HOW THE KIBBUTZ WAS A
SAFETY NET FOR MY GRANDMOTHER,
AND WHY MY MOTHER LEFT

As a young girl, my mother, Bracha, loved many aspects of her life in the kibbutz.[1] She loved the space, the nature, and her friends. She fondly remembers spending many hours outside, playing with friends, wandering in the kibbutz paths, running and swimming,

---

[1] It is curious that my mom was named Bracha, the female version of her father's name Baruch, both meaning "blessing." The name Baruch for my grandfather is understandable, because he was born in a Polish shtetl. But it is curious that my Zionist grandparents would give this name to their daughter. First, because it was not the modern Hebrew names that Jews in Palestine often gave. Second, naming your child after a living relative is not common among Ashkenazi Jews. It is even more curious given her older sister was named Naomi, a modern and fashionable Zionist name at the time.

riding horses, milking cows, celebrating joint birthdays with her entire class, and rejoicing in the Shavout harvest festival when all bring the first fruits in a big kibbutz celebration.

As my mother grew up, however, many aspects of kibbutz life started to bother her. She especially hated the lack of privacy, and the way everyone knew and talked about your comings and go-ings. To this day, when we ask my mom "Where are you going?" her instinctive answer is, "I stopped answering this question forty years ago when I left the kibbutz." She was also bothered by how individualism was suppressed in favor of conformity to communal behavioral norms—and communal life, while helpful in terrible times, could also be suffocating. She hated that people could not choose what to study at university—that, instead, such decisions were decided in the communal meetings. My mother used to say that kibbutzim are wonderful places for kids and for old people, but they might not be as great for everyone else. And those adults who might find it great might not be the ones kibbutzim want to attract.

Like her mother forty years earlier, my mother studied outside of Negba to become a teacher/instructor during her military service. Like many other kibbutz members who interacted with nonmem-bers during and after their military service, she met my father, a Je-rusalem native who would not even consider moving to the kibbutz. His father had also come from Poland, deserted Andres's army to go to Palestine (like many of the other Jewish soldiers) after he lost his parents, siblings, wife, and son in the Holocaust. As an aside, my paternal grandfather actually first joined Kibbutz Mizra in the North of Israel, but he left after only two days. He could not toler-ate the communal living, the work in the field, and other aspects of kibbutz life. Like many other enterprising men and women, he preferred the excitement of "making it" in the city. My father, who at the time studied mechanical engineering at the Technion, the Israeli Institute for Technology, was the same way.

The truth was that my mother didn't want to stay in the kibbutz either. She felt that while older Negba members, like kibbutzniks everywhere, were proud of being both farmers and intellectuals with high culture, individual creativity and talent were discouraged and frowned upon.[2] In 1970, when she decided to leave Negba and move in with my father in Jerusalem, she had no idea how her mother would react to such news. She worried her mother might be very disappointed in her. Her older sister had married someone on a different kibbutz—so my mother might have also felt guilty about leaving her mother without any family in Negba.

During this period, increasingly more kibbutz-born children left their kibbutz in search for a new life that was more individualistic and free of the various restrictions imposed by the kibbutz. Leaving the kibbutz was viewed in kibbutzim as a failure, almost a betrayal of kibbutz values. But members nevertheless often left either because life was hard, because they were fed up with kibbutz life, or because they stopped believing in kibbutz values. Yaakov (Yankale) Rotblit, an Israeli songwriter and composer who helped form Kibbutz Metzer, wrote his now classic ballad about a member who left his kibbutz (*balada leozev kibbutz*). The ballad tells the story of a young kibbutz member who leaves with all his belongings in one suitcase, and how all the other kibbutz members consider him a "deserter." Lines such as "we'll see how he gets along outside," "you will see that he will come back crawling to the dairy barn," and the verse "he will come back" convey how members were sure he would not make it outside and would return after his failed attempt to abandon the kibbutz and its values.

My grandmother's reaction was thus a pleasant surprise, and my mother admires her for this until this day. Breindel said: "We made our own choices, and you should make your own. I am happy whenever you are. You have my blessing." My grandmother recognized that my mother's generation wasn't as idealistic as hers and she respected my mother's right to make her own decisions. After all, she herself had made a more radical one years earlier, with much bigger consequences for herself and her family.

Our family stayed very close to both my grandmother and Negba. We would visit every Saturday, coming in the morning always to find my grandmother waiting for us at the door. She would bake cookies and prepare iced coffee for us. These Saturdays were

[2] Golan (2012, chap. 7) describes a similar experience in her kibbutz.

so special for her that she would sometimes ride her three-wheeled bike to the dining hall beforehand and carry back food for us in her *menaska* (a multilayered container for food used in kibbutzim) so we could enjoy our meal together in the privacy of her room rather than with the entire kibbutz in the dining hall. My brother and I loved those visits, especially swimming and playing basketball and table tennis.

My grandmother's health declined sharply in the last few years of her life. By the time she was seventy-eight, she had developed severe Alzheimer's, which gradually prevented her from going to work, singing in the choir, and doing the things she loved. Soon she could not live by herself, and eventually barely recognized us. But the kibbutz made her last years more livable: like a large surrogate family, the commune continued to buffer her from misfortune in her final years, just as it had when she had been a young widow. Though she'd worked all her life as a simple seamstress, my grandmother died with round-the-clock nursing care delivered with the kind of compassion money can't buy.

CHAPTER 4

On the creation versus survival of societies

IDEALISM AND PRACTICAL CONSIDERATIONS

Three dimensions were important in the creation of kibbutzim: ideology, economics, and historical contingencies. Over time, ideology and the favorable historical conditions have declined, and economic forces have become more important. In particular, for the kibbutz founders, living in a kibbutz was an active choice. For later generations who were born in a kibbutz, it was the default option. Therefore, practical considerations became more important in later generations. The decision of whether or not to stay in the kibbutz was less idealistic and more often involved cost-benefit analysis, for example: Would I earn more outside? Is the safety net provided by the kibbutz worth it (more on this later)? Will my life be as comfortable outside the kibbutz? And is there a better place to raise my children? Such attitudes made equal sharing more difficult to sustain. Kibbutz-born people were more likely than founders to free-ride and to consider leaving their kibbutz in expectation of higher wages outside. Amir Helman, a kibbutz member who taught at Ruppin College, was quoted by Daniel Gavron (2000, p. 280) saying, "My father was prepared to work without personal incentives. I needed the motivation of interesting work. My children quite simply don't see why they should support others."

Such an erosion of idealism is not unique to kibbutzim; a similar process may have taken place in Israel as a whole.[1] Many societies and institutions start out as idealistic but lose their idealistic zeal over time.

In this sense, the reasons for the creation of an institution can be very different from the reasons for its continuing success. This does not mean that societies and institutions necessarily become weaker over time. It does suggest that societies and institutions are often able to survive in the long term because they set rules and norms that create good incentives even after idealism is gone. This certainly happened in kibbutzim.

While the pioneers emphasized idealism in their attraction to the kibbutz, later generations gave more practical reasons. The reflections of one of the pioneers of Kibbutz Givat Brenner on his past reveal the mindset of the kibbutz founders (quoted in Gavron 2001, p. 45):

> All of us who lived on that peak can never forget the wonderful experience, which is forever engraved on our hearts. Those were days filled with beauty, the innocence of youth and the magic of friendship, the search for truth and for a new way of life.

In contrast, here is what Omri Lulav, a second-generation kibbutz-born member, wrote in an article in 1965 (quoted in Near 1997, p. 271):

> True, we are not imbued with the same spirit of mission which accompanied your deeds in the early days. True, our days are made up of small deeds, and the evenings do not raise us to

---

[1] In early generations, the attachment of Israeli Jews to Israel was strong, and many chose to stay even if they could find higher-paying jobs abroad. The attachment to Israel, while it still exists, has fallen substantially and a process of brain drain from Israel has begun (see, e.g., Gould and Moav 2007). As with the kibbutz, the stigma against Israeli emigrants declined. Emigrating from Israel is called "descending," and descenders were looked down upon. Israel's prime minister Itzhak Rabin in a 1976 interview referred to Israeli emigrants as "fall-outs of weaklings," a term that has been used ever since to criticize emigrants. But while this negative sentiment about emigrants is still sometimes present, it is much less pronounced today. Another parallel between Israel as a whole and kibbutzim is that the increase in outside opportunities for Israelis might have been a contributing factor in the brain drain from Israel.

peaks of enthusiasm, as yours did in the past. True, we do not appreciate equality and community in the way you did, just as we do not know how to appreciate satiety—for we have never been hungry. We simply love our way of life.

Gavron (2000, p. 35–36) describes how one leader of Degania, decided to survey members' motivations to stay in Degania when he became the kibbutz secretary in the 1960s:

> He was appalled to discover that the reason they remained was because it was a pleasant way of life, or because their parents lived there, or because their friends were there, or simply because it was convenient. Not one of them gave him an ideological reason or even said that they believed in the communal way of life."

A young member of Hatzor told Mort and Brenner (2003, p. 110) that "[he had] no sentiments to the communal way of life, only to the grass on which [he] ran as a child." A member of Kibbutz Maagan Michael explained his practical motives for staying in the kibbutz (Gavron 2000, p. 205): "I can become a schoolteacher, for example, without it affecting my standard of living in the tiniest respect. Where else in the world can you find a way of life that gives you that?"

In his wonderful novel—which is unique because it is also a documentary piece—Inbari (2009) describes how even among the pioneers there was a tension between idealism and practice. This tension was reflected in passionate discussions about topics such as whether kibbutzniks are communists or socialists, how socialism squares with Zionism, and the difference between needs and luxuries.

HISTORICAL CONTINGENCIES

Historical contingencies also played a role in the origin of kibbutzim. First, the Jewish agencies in Palestine viewed the newly established communes as an efficient way of protecting the Jewish residents of Palestine (the Jewish Yishuv) and as a legitimate way of implementing the Zionist idea. Second, it is largely because of unique historical circumstances that the founders of kibbutzim left Europe and came to Palestine. The kibbutzim strove for full equality at least in part because the founders were influenced by socialist movements in their country of origin and by the Soviet revolution, and were committed to equality and communal living. Before migrating, they were trained in youth movements such as He'chaluz ("the pioneer") and Ha'shomer Ha'tzair for hard physical work and communal life. They were joined by Palestine-born Jews who rejected their parents' way of life and sought to experience a better way. Free-riding and adverse selection were mitigated at least in part because founders cared deeply about the collective and because the Zionists' organizations supported and encouraged the kibbutz movement. Many other types of communes did not enjoy such support from the societies in which they existed and in fact were often persecuted (more on this in chapter 11).

THE KIBBUTZ AND THE MOSHAV

The combination of socialist ideology and the support of the Zionist entities were pivotal factors in the creation of the kibbutz movement; in Palestine, at the beginning of the twentieth century, a different ideology and set of historical circumstances led to the creation of moshavim. A comparison between kibbutzim and moshavim has the potential to illuminate the roles of ideology and history in institutional choice. A moshav is an agricultural cooperative, a village whose members are independent individual farmers. Members work by themselves and hold private means of production and property, but they maintain cooperation in supply and marketing. Like the early kibbutz, the moshav was originally based on agriculture and bought its inputs and marketed its products collectively. Moreover, one ingredient of the moshav, at least in theory, was mutual assistance among members. Unlike the kibbutz movement, however, each individual or family worked its own land and earned its own profits. The family, rather than the collective, was the basic entity that made consumption decisions.

People who joined a moshav could (in theory) have instead joined or established a kibbutz, but did not, potentially for cultural and ideological reasons. The fiercely collectivist kibbutz was better suited to those who placed little value on privacy or the institution of the family. The moshav was founded to answer "a distinct need for farmers who believed in cooperation but rejected the intense communal way of life of the Kvutza" (Gavron 2000, p. 29). Later, when many Sephardic Jews from Middle Eastern countries poured into the new state of Israel, rather than joining a kibbutz, they opted for a more individualistic moshav or settled in a city. This is hardly surprising: they were more individualist and cared more about their privacy. The family was very important to them, and they rejected the kibbutz concept of placing the commune ahead of it.[2] The moshav allowed the individual and the family to remain at the center, while still providing partial insurance through mutual assistance. Ashkenazic Eastern European Jews, in contrast, joined kibbutzim and enjoyed full insurance. It's likely many of the Sephardic Jews would never have been accepted into kibbutzim, as entry was selective and kibbutzniks at the time tended to consider the new immigrants unsuited to living in a kibbutz. However, Sephardic Jews could have created their own kibbutzim. Since free-riding is potentially more severe in a kibbutz (full insurance) than in a moshav (partial insurance), organizations supporting peer pressure developed in the kibbutz movement more than in the moshav movement. Since adverse selection is similarly potentially more severe in a kibbutz, kibbutzim developed more lock-in devices and a heavy reliance on local public goods (as described earlier), which served as a "bond" that made it costly for members to leave.

In fact, there are several variants of moshavim, some of which are more similar to kibbutzim. The worker's moshav (*moshav ovdim*) is a workers' cooperative settlement. This is the more common type and relies on cooperative purchasing of supplies and marketing of produce; the family or household is, however, the basic unit of production and consumption. The collective moshav (*moshav shitufi*) is a collective smallholder's settlement that combines the economic features of a kibbutz with the social features of a moshav. Farming is done collectively and profits are shared equally. This form is closer to the collectivity of the kibbutz: although consumption is family-based, production and marketing are collective. Unlike the

---

[2] Such differences in cultural beliefs can have substantial effects on subsequent institutional development (see, e.g., North 1990; Greif 1994; Temin 1997b; Mokyr 2002; and Botticini and Eckstein 2005, 2012).

worker's moshav, land is not allotted to families or individuals but is collectively cultivated.

The original *Manual for Establishing a Moshav Ovdim* (Jaffe 1919) lists five principles: land is government owned and can only be leased; members will cultivate their own land, and no employment relationships will occur; each moshav will produce several different crops to reduce risk and seasonality; members will support and assist each other; the moshav will buy and sell in bulk to get better terms and prices. The theory was not always implemented in practice. A common complaint was that mutual assistance was implemented inefficiently. Many members felt the cost of the safety net was too high, and most members saw little benefit from it (Yannay, 1940). One member of Moshav Yamit said:

> I have no problems with mutual assistance, but it became immediately obvious that not all of us are set for that. . . . members connect to the water hose but not to the monitoring clock, some fuel their tractors but forget to record it in the notebook . . . some market their produce to private contractors and not via the central system. I understood I was signed up for mutual assistance in a Moshav where members steal from their own pockets (Visler, 2001).[3]

MEANS TO AN END

In any event, the unique historical circumstances surrounding the creation of kibbutzim help explain why they are so rare and can be found only in Israel. However, ideology and favorable conditions only took kibbutzim so far. After the ideological zeal and outside support that had created them were gone, they needed to work harder to remain attractive.

Ideology and the principle of equality in kibbutzim both had intrinsic value and were means to an end. Along these lines, political philosophers distinguish between noninstrumental egalitarianism, which values equality as an end in itself, and instrumental egalitarianism, which values equality only because it helps achieve

[3] My translation from Hebrew.

something else.[4] In the context of kibbutzim, equality was both a sacred principle—the key to a just society—and a means of achieving objectives such as insurance.

In the creation of kibbutzim, both instrumental and noninstrumental egalitarianism played roles.[5] Equality was an inherently desirable ideal, but it also had practical benefits: insurance against illness, unemployment, and advancements that made an individual's skills obsolete; and access to social capital in the form of companionship and networks.

Similarly, many other identifying features of kibbutzim—such as separate residences for kids, the communal dining hall, requiring members to work within the kibbutz, prohibiting external labor, the large agricultural base, and the high provision of local public goods—have economic rationales in addition to their intrinsic value in kibbutz ideology.[6] Many seemingly ideological features of kibbutzim are even more consistent with an economic interpretation of kibbutzim, even if they were not created for an explicit economic purpose.

For example, a pure taste for equality does not in itself justify not allowing members to use cash. The use of cash would allow members

[4] In a more general context, an instrumental ideology is one that rationalizes a certain behavior, like cooperation or honesty. Douglass North (1981) defines ideology as a social force designed to overcome the free-rider problem. Avner Greif (1994) thinks about cultural beliefs as ones that support the equilibrium strategies. Both North's and Greif's definition would fall into the instrumental-ideology category, since the ideology is not desired for its own sake, but is adopted to support an independent goal. Instrumental and noninstrumental ideology do not have to be mutually exclusive. The Maghribi traders in Greif's papers (1989, 1993) could be trustworthy either because they had a taste for honesty—perhaps since they feared god—or since being honest was their best response in equilibrium. The first reason illustrates a noninstrumental ideology and the second illustrates an instrumental one; Maghribi traders might have been honest for a combination of both reasons.

[5] Like many other institutions that persisted over long periods of time (e.g., Greif 1989, 1993, 1994; North and Weingast 1989; Greif, Milgrom, and Weingast 1994), kibbutzim were a solution to a problem—they were a substitute for insurance markets that could not provide full insurance against income shocks.

[6] Scholars of kibbutzim (e.g., Don 1995; Leviatan and Rosner 2000) adopted the view of Abell (1983), a researcher of cooperatives, who argues that cooperatives can only succeed when forces such as ideology and solidarity are more important than economic incentives. Unique features of kibbutzim discussed in chapters 1 and 2 are regarded as evidence that kibbutzim are ideological institutions.

to purchase according to their needs, rather than imposing a consumption bundle on them. However, not using cash actually has an important economic benefit: it prevents members from saving money, thus making it more costly for them to leave the kibbutz. A similar logic applies to other unique features of kibbutzim, such as the policy of making members acquire kibbutz-specific human capital. A taste for equality does not justify training members to be agronomists rather than engineers, but the desire to lock in members does.

Moreover, at the outset, people were required to give up their private property when they joined a kibbutz. Kibbutzim would rather that people not join than that they not share their personal possessions with other members. It was considered better to refuse a gift from the outside than to not share it. This included sizable reparations for holocaust survivors. Inbari (2009) tells stories of how all personal clothes became communal property and how clothes were sorted into categories in the communal laundry for members to take whatever socks, underwear, and pants were available. There are stories of someone arriving with clothes in a trunk and these being given to another member of a different size. This goes beyond a taste for redistribution, since it destroys value without making anyone better off. Inbari (2009) describes how some members secretly kept in their possession a piece of clothing that had sentimental value. It is difficult to know exactly why such policies were practiced. It is possible that they simply reflect strict ideology. But such policies can also be interpreted as costly sacrifices demanded at entry, exactly what one would expect from an insurance organization worried about free-riding and exiting.[7]

I next discuss in detail the roles of local public goods, the communal dining hall, and the sharing of information in preventing free-riding and adverse selection. Such economic mechanisms help explain how kibbutzim were able to survive long after their ideology had faded and external support was gone. I discuss these instrumental and noninstrumental concepts in more detail in chapter 11, on the stability of communes.

---

[7] See Berman (2000) for a discussion of sacrifices in ultra-orthodox communities.

CHAPTER 5

The free-rider problem

I worked in the banana groves. . . . I couldn't take it any longer! It was hard work; you guys work hard in Israel. I didn't like the kibbutz. Nice Jewish boys from Long Island don't like to get up at six in the morning to pick bananas. At six in the morning you should be sleeping! And bananas? All summer long I found ways to get out of work.

—*Jerry Seinfeld, 1998*[1]

WHY ECONOMISTS EXPECT FREE RIDING UNDER EQUAL SHARING: THE EQUITY-EFFICIENCY TRADE-OFF

The first threat to income equality is the free-rider problem—also known as the shirking problem or the moral hazard problem, terms that I will use interchangeably, depending on the aspect of the problem I want to emphasize. When kibbutz members stand to get an equal share of the whole kibbutz pie regardless of how hard they work, that is, when the material reward is independent of effort, they have no incentive to work hard.[2] This shirking problem in the

---

[1] From the article "Seinfeld's Kibbutz Days" by Ellis Shuman, Israeli Culture Daily, April 20, 1998, https://archive.li/qBusi.

[2] In many kibbutzim the problem was even worse, because the spending on consumption was standardized by a "norm" shared by all kibbutzim in a kibbutz movement, regardless of the income in the specific kibbutz.

kibbutz is often a manifestation of the so-called free-rider problem, the incentive to undercontribute when everyone benefits from the contributions of anyone, even though each contributor pays the full cost of his own contribution. In the egalitarian kibbutz, a member benefited from other members' hard work because the incomes they generated were shared with him. At the same time, he gained a lot and lost little by not working hard, since he saved on effort yet still received an equal share of the kibbutz's total income. If all members (mis)behaved in this way, little work would get done, the kibbutz would not produce much, and all members would be poor.

"Moral hazard" is a term that originates in the study of insurance markets.[3] Moral hazard occurs when a person has an incentive to behave inappropriately because he does not bear the full consequences of his actions, and the one who does bear the rest of the consequences cannot fully monitor his actions.[4] Why would a team member work hard if nobody could see how much effort he put in? Why would a worker work hard if he only got a fixed wage regardless of his contribution to the firm? Why would a manager take bold moves and do his best to maximize the firm's profits if his earnings were unrelated to the performance of the firm?

Moral hazard is viewed as a threat to insurance markets and for societies that share output equally. The "moral" part originally implied that the insured was acting immorally by abusing the insurance contract. Economists today don't consider such behavior either "moral" or "immoral" but instead focus on the inefficiencies

---

[3] Think of the market for car insurance, for example. Imagine an insurance company offers comprehensive insurance that will cover any damage to the car at no additional cost to the driver. Such insurance doesn't give the owner much incentive to take good care of the car. For example, why lock the car, park it safely, or get it serviced regularly if the insurance company will cover the full monetary cost if it is damaged, stolen, or breaks down? In other words, the driver might behave inappropriately because he doesn't bear the full consequences of damaging the car.

[4] Beyond a large body of theory, there is an empirical literature on asymmetric information and moral hazard (e.g., the survey by Chiappori and Salanie, 2000). The focus of the empirical literature on free-riding is profit sharing in firms and its association with performance. See Prendergast (1999, 2002) for a survey on the literature of the provision of incentives in firms, and Knez and Simester (2001) for a contribution on firm-wide incentives and monitoring.

that arise in such situations. But when studying a society that strove to be virtuous, such as the kibbutz, it is tempting to think in terms of moral judgments as well.

Most relevant to the kibbutz is the problem of "moral hazard in teams,"[5] which is a free-rider problem: a team member contributes little to a group task when others can't tell the extent of his effort and only the team's overall output is observed. For example, a member doesn't pull his weight in the cotton fields because his effort is not monitored, and instead he relies on the hard work of others.

Besides shirking, moral hazard problems resulting from the communal ownership of property also threatened the kibbutz. Just like no one washes a rental car before he returns it (to use a famous example), moral hazard happened in the egalitarian kibbutz every time a member took too much food in the dining hall or left the air conditioning on all day because he did not pay the full price of his meals and electricity; it happened every time he walked dirt into the swimming pool or carelessly scuffed the ping-pong table surface just because they weren't his own. In fact, many of the moral hazard and free-rider problems in kibbutzim stem from the lack of private property rights in the presence of incomplete monitoring.

Equal sharing might also discourage entrepreneurship and innovation. Entrepreneurs often take big risks because the rewards could be very high if their innovations are successful. In an egalitarian kibbutz, an entrepreneur will never receive the bulk of the rewards—any successful innovation will be shared with the entire kibbutz membership. On the other hand, two by-products of income equality might actually encourage entrepreneurship. The first is that equal sharing encourages taking risks, because the risk is borne by the entire membership rather than solely by the worker or manager herself. This shared responsibility means that being entrepreneurial and trying to innovate did not entail much risk under the equal-sharing system. The second is that equal sharing encourages

---

[5] Classic references on this are Alchian and Demsetz (1972) and Holmstrom (1982). See also Corgnet et al. (2015) for a survey and experimental evidence on peer pressure and moral hazard in teams.

consultation and collaboration. Outside the kibbutz, people might worry about others stealing their ideas or have career concerns and want to appear as the main contributors to the project. Equal sharing in kibbutzim meant that members had incentives to ask for advice from the best experts in the kibbutz on any matter, because they would benefit from any project succeeding whether or not they were responsible for it. Perhaps partially as a consequence of this, kibbutzim have been responsible for many major innovations in agriculture. Take Kibbutz Hatzerim, for example. Their factory, Netafim, is a highly successful, high-tech company that is among the world leaders in micro-irrigation products such as drippers and driplines.

Nevertheless, free-rider problems, and the inefficiency that goes along with them, are inherent in any society that strives for equality. In fact, the equity-efficiency trade-off is an important concept in modern economics.[6] Efficiency requires that society produces at full capacity, employing workers, as well as other factors of production such as capital and land, effectively. But a genuinely equal society has little leeway to reward people for their efforts and thus incentivize them to act in ways that benefit the society. The more equal the society, the less incentive its members have to work hard, study hard, create new businesses, or innovate. Hence, the equity-efficiency trade-off: the greater the income equality, the better the safety net, but the lower the incentives. The higher the rewards for effort, the greater the incentives, but the lower the safety net.

This equity-efficiency trade-off is a central point in the debates between capitalism and socialism, between US Republicans and Democrats, on the benefits of long-term unemployment insurance, and on how generous welfare programs should be.

The equity-efficiency trade-off is often invoked to explain why Europeans work fewer hours than Americans. In European welfare states, tax rates are often very high. A Swedish citizen knows that for any dollar she earns above 1.5 times the Swedish average

---

[6] As illustrated by the most recent 2016 Nobel Prize winners, Oliver Hart and Bengt Holmstrom, who made important contributions in contract theory and the insurance-incentives tradeoff.

income, she will only get to keep 43 cents out of every additional dollar she earns, while the rest will be taken as tax. When a similar American earns 1.5 times the US average, she gets to keep about 75 cents out of every dollar she earns. Even when she earns 8.5 times the US average, she gets to keep 53 cents out of each additional dollar she earns. When faced with the choice of working more hours or spending more time with the family, the Swedish citizen would be more likely to choose the family, whereas a similar American is more likely to choose the work.[7]

Economic theory suggests that very high tax rates may be causing a free rider problem: everyone is content to work less hard himself and rely on others to work hard and pay the taxes that fund the redistribution. But when everyone in the country thinks like this, everyone works less hard, the country produces less, and average income is lower. Sweden, however, is a rich country full of hard workers, suggesting the story is more complex, and high tax rates don't necessarily lead to free-riding.[8] Cross-country comparisons, and even comparisons within countries over time, are imperfect because many other things are different across countries and over time—some high-tax countries are richer than the United States,

[7] One paper that makes this point is Prescott (2004), and Davis and Henrekson (2004) provides some supporting evidence. There are, of course, other reasons besides taxes that might explain differences in working hours between Europeans and Americans. For example, Europeans may have different preferences. Blanchard (2004, p. 4) argued that "Europe has used some of the increase in productivity to increase leisure rather than income, while the United States has done the opposite." Another reason is differences in labor market regulations. Alesina, Glaeser, and Sacerdote (2006, paper's abstract) suggest that "European labor market regulations, advocated by unions in declining European industries who argued 'work less, work all,' explain the bulk of the difference between U.S. and Europe."

[8] Economic theory suggests that taxes affect the trade-off between leisure and labor. Higher marginal taxes reduce labor supply through the substitution effect, by making the cost of leisure lower relative to the cost of goods. At the same time, they increase the labor supply through the income effect, or the decrease in total income that makes each marginal dollar earned more valuable. In general, whether labor increases or decreases depends on the balance between the two income and substitution effects; in the case of traditional kibbutzim with 100% tax rates and high lump-sum transfers, economic theory clearly predicts labor supply will decrease.

and it is not at all clear that in the 1950s, when the United States had very high marginal taxes, people worked any less than they do today. Still, some argue that high European tax rates may help explain why average incomes in Europe are below typical US levels.

In the extreme case of a 100 percent tax rate, the free-rider problem is expected to be devastating. Indeed, many believe that the free-rider problem was a major reason for the failure of socialism in general and the former Soviet Union in particular. In kibbutzim, a member's earnings were also effectively 100 percent taxed. There was no link between effort and reward, meaning there was no financial incentive for members to work hard and pull their weight. Yet, kibbutzim have often been invoked as the social experiment that demonstrated that socialism could indeed be successful and that the free-rider problem could be overcome without the use of financial incentives. Here I discuss how.

Most disagreements between the Democrat and Republican political parties in the United States on economic issues are exactly over the equality-incentives trade-off, manifesting itself in all kinds of issues including education, taxation, and welfare. Democrats seem to worry more about equality, while Republicans seem more worried about incentives; both parties want equality and incentives, but since there is a trade-off, each must choose a position on this continuum. This trade-off also helps explain why CEOs and other managers rarely receive wages that are entirely unrelated to the firm's performance, and instead receive large parts of their wages as stocks and options,[9] and why the market does not provide full insurance contracts.

Did kibbutz members indeed work hard, or did they shirk on their jobs and free-ride on others? This question bothered kibbutz members for many years. Nobody likes free riders—in the kibbutz or anywhere else. In the egalitarian kibbutz, free-riding could cause the whole system to collapse. By chance or intentional design, mechanisms to deal with free-riding were developed in the kibbutz,

---

[9] Such stocks create a link between a manager's performance (which is often difficult to observe) and the firm's success, thereby better aligning the manager's incentives with those of the firm.

in part because of a universal dislike of free-riding, and in part because of the long-term view that the free-rider problem should be solved to improve the well-being of the group.

WAS THERE FREE-RIDING IN
THE EGALITARIAN KIBBUTZ?

Measuring free-riding and shirking are inherently difficult, so we don't have much evidence about the extent of the free-rider problem in the kibbutz. There is plenty of anecdotal evidence suggesting that members were concerned about this problem from the outset, and that members always needed to demonstrate to the others that they worked hard and did their best to contribute.[10] Free-riding naturally became more severe in later generations once idealism declined. One later-generation member claimed, "people like me who started as socialists concluded that you can work hard and get nothing while others don't work hard. It is so unfair." Another member said that his kibbutz was a "paradise for parasites."[11] Another member who left his kibbutz when he was eighteen is quoted in a 2007 *New York Times* article as saying, "My parents worked all their lives, carrying at least 10 parasites on their backs. If they'd worked that hard in the city for as many years, I'd have had quite an inheritance coming to me by now."[12]

While the potential problem of free-riders and "parasites" has bothered kibbutz members for many years, researchers of the kibbutz movement have found little evidence of free-riding as reflected in a lack of motivation in the workplace.[13] Quoting Helman, a kibbutz member and an economist who taught in Ruppin College, Gavron summarized (Gavron 2000, pp. 154–155):

---

[10] See, e.g., a discussion in Lieblich, Tuval-Mashiach, and Zilber (1998), and Inbari (2009, pp. 118–119, 143).

[11] Quoted in Muravchik 2003, p. 333.

[12] Isabel Kershner, "The Kibbutz Sheds Socialism and Gains Popularity," *New York Times*, August 27, 2007, http://www.nytimes.com/2007/08/27/world /middleeast/27kibbutz.html?_r=0.

[13] See, e.g., Tannenbaum et al. (1974), Palgi (1984), Rosner and Tannenbaum (1987b), and Shimony et al. (1994).

[I]n the 1920s, the professional economists were sure that, without the usual material incentives, kibbutz members would produce less and consume more than those in private concerns. They were wrong: the kibbutz members were diligent, and they volunteered for—and even competed for—the most difficult jobs, without material rewards.

One way to measure free-riding would be to compare electricity use, air conditioning use, water and food consumption, and the frequency of washing laundry in egalitarian kibbutzim and in similar households living outside kibbutzim. I don't know of any systematic quantitative research on this topic, although this route could be a promising direction for research. Anecdotally, kibbutzim often urged members to cut back on food, water, and electricity consumption. One kibbutz reported saving a substantial amount of money by urging members to reduce consumption (Gavron 2000, p. 85).

Another way to capture some aspect of free-riding by shirking on the job is to test whether kibbutz members were more likely to be unemployed or whether they worked shorter hours than similar people did outside the kibbutz. The hypothesis here is that kibbutz members could expect to earn the same regardless of whether and how much they worked, so they might be less likely to work or at least more likely to choose not to work as many hours.

To study this, I looked at the employment status and hours worked of kibbutz members relative to Jewish people living in cities and relative to those living in non-kibbutzim rural areas such as moshavim. My information comes from the Israeli population censuses conducted between 1961 and 1995, a period in which all kibbutzim were still based on full equal sharing and so members had incentives to free-ride by shirking on their jobs.

I compared the self-reported weekly hours worked by kibbutz members aged twenty-five to sixty-four with those worked by the rest of the Ashkenazi Jewish population, acknowledging that this is an imperfect measure because misreporting may be different between kibbutz members and city people. Figure 5.1 shows that in all years, kibbutz members worked *longer* hours than the population averages for both urban and rural Ashkenazi Jews. Figure 5.2 shows that

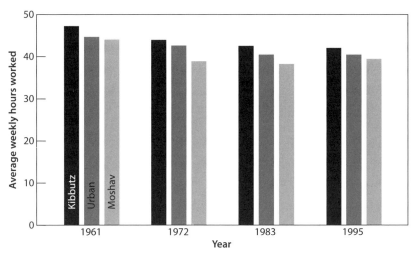

FIGURE 5.1: Kibbutz members worked longer hours than nonmembers: This figure shows the average weekly hours worked by kibbutz members ("kibbutz"), the Ashkenazi Jewish city population ("urban"), and the Ashkenazi Jewish population in other non-kibbutz rural areas ("moshav"). The sample is individuals aged 25 to 64 who worked non-zero hours (because employment is near universal in kibbutzim). Numbers are averages of categorical data, not of continuous numbers. Data source: Israel population censuses of 1961, 1972, 1983, and 1995.

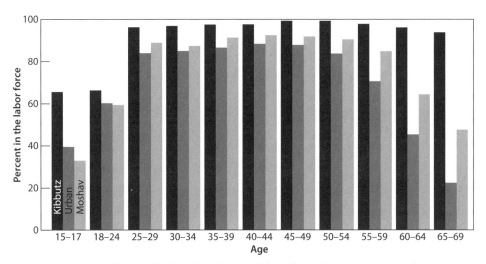

FIGURE 5.2: Share of individuals in the labor force by age group and settlement type in 1995. Settlement types are kibbutz, urban, and moshav. Data source: Israel population census of 1995.

kibbutz members were almost all in the labor force, and they were more likely to be employed than the Ashkenazi Jewish average. These figures suggest that, at least as measured by self-reported employment and the quantity of hours devoted to work, kibbutz members did not free-ride relative to a similar population outside the kibbutz.

One potential issue with the statistics that indicate that kibbutz members worked more hours and had higher labor force participation rates is that they might report home production as work, while nonmembers don't. This is because unlike a non-kibbutz member, who provides labor for income and in addition is engaged in "home production" (taking care of the garden, shopping, preparing food, child care, laundry, cleaning the house, taking the car to be repaired, and many other tasks), a kibbutznik who works in typical home-production activities such as in the laundry room or the dining hall would report these as work. Nevertheless, one clear takeaway is that kibbutzniks did not just play video games or sit on the beach all day—whether their jobs were productive or not, they all went to work and they worked long hours.

Employment status and the number of hours worked do not capture all types of potential free-riding. For example, a member might shirk on the job, playing on his computer all day while appearing to work long hours, but getting little real work done. Unfortunately, I could not find systematic data on productivity per worker. Still, it appears that the egalitarian kibbutz was able to solve at least part of the free-riding problem, as reflected in the facts that kibbutz members were more likely to work and worked longer hours than other Israeli Jews.

HOW DID KIBBUTZIM DEAL WITH THE FREE-RIDER PROBLEM?

There's no way to know exactly how much shirking went on in kibbutzim, but the evidence presented above suggests the level of shirking was lower than we might expect, given the incentives faced by kibbutz members. So how did kibbutzim limit shirking?

Culture has always been an important glue that kept the kibbutz together. Members of the kibbutz were proud to be called kibbutzniks. They were proud of their overrepresentation in the Israeli Defense Force as officers and in elite units, as well as in the Knesset and in academia. The tightness of the social network ensured that such a culture of pride in the community and hard work was widespread within a kibbutz and across kibbutzim.

Overall, the story of kibbutzim supports the economic sociologists' view originated by Polanyi (1968) and Granovetter (1985) that economic exchanges take place within the social context, and that social structures and social networks affect economic outcomes (Granovetter 2005). Economic exchanges often take place between people who are involved in long-term relationships and repeating interactions. The economy and economic transactions do not occur in a vacuum, and they are embedded in social institutions. Consistent with this idea, a field experiment conducted by Ruffle and Sosis (2006) found that kibbutz members were more cooperative toward (anonymous) kibbutz members than they were toward (anonymous) city residents. When paired with city residents, kibbutz members cooperated just as much as city residents. Kibbutzniks were thus not more cooperative than non-kibbutzniks, but they were more cooperative with others from their group. In this sense, kibbutzniks confirmed the psychological foundation of in-group–out-group bias (see Hewston et al. 2002 for a recent survey).

Beyond culture, a set of rules, rewards, and sanctions helped kibbutzim deal with incentive problems. For starters, in a traditional kibbutz, the last thing you wanted to do was to appear as if you were not putting enough effort into your job. If other members noticed you were slacking, they could make your life miserable. As in the army, social sanctions could be made highly effective in the small and cohesive kibbutz.[14] A veteran of Degania describes how social sanctions were implemented when a member shirked: "[N]obody said a word to him. But in the evening, in the dining hall, the atmosphere around him was such that the following morning he got up and left the kvutza" (Near 1992, p. 38). The way a kibbutz

---

[14] Social sanctions may be effective in inducing members to work hard, but they are likely to be less effective at preventing brain drain, because once a member exits he forms a new social group outside the kibbutz.

community was organized put it in a particularly good position for members to monitor each other and apply social sanctions. This could be one reason why kibbutzim survived as equal-sharing communities for so long.

In the traditional kibbutz, working was mandatory. If you didn't find a job, the work organizer (*sadran haavoda*), an official who was elected by the kibbutz general assembly to assign members to tasks, would simply assign you to the kitchen to peel potatoes and serve meals to members. Therefore, few members were unemployed. In later years, especially since the 1990s, finding a job became the responsibility of the members. All members were expected to find a job that fit their skills and contributed to the kibbutz, with help from the kibbutz if necessary. Unemployment in kibbutzim remained low.

This strategy of making sure no one was without a job made sense for an egalitarian community, because such a society had to worry about free-riders. In contrast, free-riding is less of a problem in a capitalist society. Take an extreme example of a purely capitalist society without any redistribution (of which there are actually very few). In such a society, people who don't work would simply starve to death. Such a purely capitalist society wouldn't have to find a job for you because you would have strong incentives to find a job for yourself.

While social sanctions were used as the stick to convince members to work, social esteem was used as the carrot. In particular, members who were appreciated by their peers and considered to be the highest contributors were promoted to prestigious leadership positions such as the kibbutz secretary, treasurer, or farm manager. The chance to be a big fish in a small pond could increase motivation and provide incentives to work hard even in the absence of monetary rewards. Such motivation might have been less effective if the kibbutz already had a capable and entrenched leadership team; to alleviate this possibility, leadership positions were rotated every few years, so members always knew they had a chance to win the roles.[15] More broadly, positive reinforcement has always been

---

[15] Many authors have highlighted the importance of both social sanctions and social esteem in kibbutzim. See, e.g., Lieblich (1981); Barkai (1986); Keren et al. (2006); Keren, Levhari, and Byalsky (2006); and Shenker (2011).

important. In every kibbutz, there are stories of key figures who were devoted to their work and the community, and they served as role models for the rest.

In theory, a focus on social sanctions and rewards is just one way to avoid the shirking problem in egalitarian communities. There are alternatives. For example, another solution to the shirking problem could have been to cast out commune members who put in low effort. Alternatively, shirkers could have been penalized monetarily. In practice, in traditional kibbutzim, not only did wages not reward effort, but firing was not a realistic threat and members were rarely expelled (e.g., Shenker 2011). One reason why members were rarely expelled could be that, unlike in the case of a firm, a kibbutz contained whole families, and expelling a shirking member would mean expelling an entire family even if other family members had not shirked.[16] More generally, each kibbutz was to a large extent an extended family, and just like in an extended family—where there is always the cousin who annoys everyone but is still invited to the holiday dinner—kibbutzim did not expel members. Instead, they used other ways to ensure cooperation.

The option of casting out members or punishing them monetarily was not used because it might have risked opening the door to decisions to expel members for arbitrary reasons, even on grounds of low contribution due to disability or lack of talent. This would have reduced the insurance value of the kibbutz. Expelling members and fining shirkers might also have been considered undesirable on ideological grounds.

Outside the world of the kibbutz, a similar logic applies to co-operatives, professional partnerships and to tenured professors in academia. For example, members in German cooperatives used monitoring and social sanctions to enforce the return of loans by fellow members, and this made them better than banks at supporting loans to risky individuals (Guinnane 2001). Tenured professors

---

[16] More generally, the institution of the family within the larger institution of the kibbutz affected people's economic behavior; I will return to this in chapter 7. Here, it suffices to say that kibbutz members were not unconnected economic actors—most were members of families, of circles of friends, and of other tight-knit social networks that exerted even more influence over them than the kibbutz did as a whole.

are rarely dismissed but (often) continue to publish, mostly because they are committed to scholarship but perhaps partly because their peers can observe how hard they work and apply peer pressure. Similarly, partners frequently work hard despite the gains from their effort being split with their partners in part because of mutual monitoring.[17] Kendel and Lazear (1992, p. 816) predicted that "partnerships tend to be formed among individuals who perform similar tasks because mutual monitoring is more effective." However, at least in later years, the kibbutz consisted of people with different occupations working in different industries and who performed different tasks. Mutual monitoring was able to remain effective in the kibbutz because the interaction among members and the information transmission mechanisms were more intensive than in professional partnerships.

These mechanisms could explain, for example, why members worked longer hours—to show other members that they were hardworking. Whether you did your best quality work during those long hours could be more difficult to observe. In this sense, monitoring and social sanctions might be more effective in improving work quantity than in improving work quality. Some tasks are easier to monitor than others; the importance of observing effort could help explain why kibbutz members tended to work in easier-to-observe occupations and industries. For example, how much effort you put in while picking oranges was straightforward to observe: just count how many bags you picked. Other jobs like designing gadgets or writing novels might be harder to observe; the kibbutz tended to shy away from such jobs. Moreover, various mechanisms used in kibbutzim and discussed next made them especially effective in observing effort.

The kibbutz improved the effectiveness of its social monitoring system in several ways: by making effort more observable (so that a kibbutz member can see if another shirks); by improving information flows among members (so everyone else finds out if someone shirks); and by maximizing interactions between members (so

---

[17] See, e.g., Kandel and Lazear (1992), Lang and Gordon (1995), and Gaynor and Gertler (1995).

informal social sanctions were more unpleasant for the shirker). On the flip side, the kibbutz rewarded good workers in ways other than financial incentives. I will discuss these aspects in turn.

First, kibbutzim instituted various mechanisms to facilitate monitoring by making effort observable. Typical tasks in kibbutzim were activities that produced easily quantifiable or measurable results, such as working in the kitchen (Are the meals prepared? Is the kitchen clean?) and milking cows (How much milk was collected?). Relatedly, members were expected to live and work inside the kibbutz, where they were surrounded by other members and there were plenty of eyes to notice any lack of output.

Second, various mechanisms were used to facilitate monitoring by improving information flows among members. Privacy was severely limited, as a member's colleagues were also neighbors, their children attended the same schools, and they all ate in a communal dining hall. The close proximity of members and their repeated interaction—coupled with the fact that gossip was rampant—facilitated information transmission and increased the effectiveness of social sanctions. Similar to an extended family, there was not much privacy. As Inbari (2009, p. 27; my translation) puts it, "in a family, there are no secrets." The truth is that just like in a family, there are secrets in the kibbutz, but those are hard to keep and typically frowned upon when discovered.

Indeed, while gossip is often associated with negative connotations, social psychologists have argued that gossip may help bonding in social groups that are growing (Dunbar 1998, 2004). Gossip can promote prosocial behavior in the sense that sharing negative information about the behavior of one person alerts others so they can avoid being exploited by him.[18] Kniffin and Wilson (2010), for example, drew on case studies involving cattle ranchers, members of a competitive rowing team, and airline company employees to

[18] See, e.g., Kniffin and Wilson (2010); Feinberg et al. (2012); Feinberg, Willer, and Schultz (2014). However, while sanctioning is often meant to increase trust and cooperation, it may also generate a backlash and actually end up reducing cooperation (Tenbrunsel and Messick 1999). It might give people the idea that others act in their own self-interest rather than being internally motivated (Mulder et al. 2006).

argue that gossip may serve a socially useful function to promote prosocial behavior.

Similarly, sociologists often talk about normative control, by which they mean the internalization of norms and the effective policing of them through peer enforcement. Especially relevant here is the concept of network closure, or social capital more generally—in a nutshell, the argument is that normative enforcement is more effective in tight-knit communities where everyone knows everyone. Let's say I am friends with you and Nick, and you and Nick are also friends. If I misbehave toward you, I also jeopardize my relationship with Nick. In this way, network closure facilitates trust and effective sanctioning. A classic reference here is Coleman (1988, 1994). More recently, Burt (2005) introduced the idea of the "structural hole": people who bridge parts of the network that are disconnected are at an advantage, and are less subject to normative control.

Third, the small population size of kibbutzim increased interactions between members and made social sanctions more effective. In the early days of kibbutzim, there was an ideological debate over whether the goal of kibbutzim should be to create one big kibbutz. This was never attempted and was unlikely to have been successful. Social sanctions are more effective in small communities, where people know each other well, where there is plenty of social interaction, and where reputation matters.

All kibbutzim are small and consist of approximately one hundred to one thousand members, with an average of 440 members. Even the largest kibbutz is sufficiently small for social sanctions to be effective. As Mancur Olson noted in his 1965 seminal book, people in groups have incentives to free-ride on the efforts of others if the group is working to provide public goods, and the free-rider problem is expected to be stronger as the group becomes larger. It is possible that the relatively small size of kibbutzim made it easier for them to sustain equality.[19] I show in chapter 9 that even when

[19] Some anthropologists seem to think that a community can remain equal and without hierarchy more easily when it is smaller than about 1,000 people: people can organize themselves without permanent institutions above small families until communities reach about 100–150 people. They can then do fine up to 300–350 people if they add a few kinship structures such as simple clans,

kibbutzim shifted away from full equality, the size of a kibbutz did not affect its degree of equality. This is surprising because we expect smaller kibbutzim to solve the free-rider problem better and thus to be able to support greater equality. My results suggest all kibbutzim were of a size at which free-riding could be mitigated, at least to a certain extent.

Kibbutz members who truly believed in cooperation and mutual aid were inherently motivated to help others and contribute to the kibbutz. The intrinsic rewards of pleasure or satisfaction that they gained from engaging in cooperative behavior were sufficient to motivate such behavior.[20]

Finally, kibbutzim share many characteristics of other sects and communes (see Iannaccone 1992; Berman 2000): prohibitions, sacrifices, and screening were used to deal with free-riding (and also helped with the problem of adverse selection, as we will see later). Prohibitions included occupational and educational restrictions, restrictions on outside work, and dress codes. Such prohibitions increased interactions within the kibbutz, made effort partially observable, and increased the cost of exit.

As well as being an attempt to avoid the entry of less productive workers, screening reflected an attempt to deal with free-riding by selecting people who were mentally suited to communal living and would not free-ride upon entry. This could explain why many entrants were people who signaled their serious intentions by belonging to a socialist youth movement in Israel or abroad, or who joined

---

but by the time they reach 500 people, they normally have to have some kind of leaders with coercive powers. By the time settlements get to over 1,000 people, we typically start to see institutionalized politics and economic inequality. See, e.g., G. Foster (1960), Carneiro (1967), Johnson and Earle (2000), and Bandy (2004). Dunbar suggests that people can maintain only about 150 stable relationships. However, these numbers should be taken with a grain of salt. Classic anthropological studies, like Evans-Pritchard's *The Nuer* (1940) describe tribal groups numbering in the thousands that do not have a central authority. See also essays in Middleton and Tait's *Tribes without Rulers* (2013) and in Neville Dyson-Hudson's *Karimojong Politics* (1966).

[20] Less intrinsically motivated individuals may also have been encouraged to work through precommitments to match the contributions of other members, as suggested by Guttman (1978) and Guttman and Schnytzer (1989).

through military service as part of a coherent unit that trained people to live in a kibbutz.

Another way the free-rider problem manifested itself was through members' decisions of how much to study and what skills to acquire. From the individual member's perspective, excelling in school and acquiring a high level of education provide no financial benefit. Thus, members have limited incentives to excel in school and acquire education. From the perspective of the kibbutzim, all members benefited when any one member increased his education or skills. At the same time, there was a downside to encouraging too much education among members: those whose education and skills were more valuable outside the kibbutz were more likely to exit. For this reason, kibbutzim faced conflicting incentives about how much to encourage education and skill. In chapter 8, I discuss this issue in more detail. In chapter 11, I test whether the shift away from equal sharing, which increased members' returns to education, led members to acquire more and better education.

Another manifestation of the free-rider problem in the kibbutz could be in members' decisions of how many children to have. The financial and time costs of raising and educating children in the traditional kibbutz were divided among all members, which may have encouraged members to have more children than they would have chosen if they had borne these costs in their entirety. This shared responsibility was especially true in the period when children all lived together outside their parents' homes. As a balancing factor, the benefit of having children in a traditional kibbutz might have been lower, given that the child "belonged" to all in the kibbutz and parents only saw their children for a few hours a day. Regardless, having many children might have been desirable to the kibbutz, as it increased the potential pool of future members and helped ensure the future of the kibbutz. I discuss members' decisions of how many children to have in more detail in chapter 11.

CHAPTER 6

The adverse selection and brain drain problems

THE ECONOMICS OF ADVERSE SELECTION AND BRAIN DRAIN

The other problem with income equality is adverse selection, which is the tendency of bad workers to try to enter equal-sharing arrangements, and its mirror image, brain drain, which is the tendency of the best workers to leave such arrangements. In the context of kibbutzim, adverse selection refers to the strong incentives for people who are unemployed, earn low wages, or are just lazy to apply to a kibbutz and share incomes equally with better workers. The related problem of brain drain refers to the strong incentives for the best and most talented workers to leave the kibbutz in favor of a city, where they can earn higher wages.

Why might an egalitarian society end up with the worst workers? Imagine a kibbutz member who chooses whether to migrate to an Israeli city or stay in her egalitarian kibbutz. In the kibbutz, the member will receive a fixed wage, say 8,000 New Israeli Shekels (NIS) per month. In the city labor market, education and skill are rewarded. An average person with an elementary school education might receive only 6,000 NIS in the city, an average person with high school education might receive 7,500 NIS, someone with a BA degree might receive 8,500 NIS, and someone with higher level of schooling might earn 10,000 NIS. It is easy to see that members with higher levels of education expect to earn more outside the kibbutz and thus have stronger economic incentive to exit.

In this example, if moving were costless, we would expect members with BA degrees or higher to exit, and ones with a high school education or below to stay. That is, we would expect kibbutz-to-city migrants to be positively selected in their education and skill from the kibbutz population. The city-to-kibbutz migration can be described similarly. Because the kibbutz offers lower returns to education and skill, we expect city-to-kibbutz migrants to be negatively selected in their education and skill from the city population.[1] Figure 6.1 illustrates this point.

Outside the kibbutz, wages increase as skills increase, so that higher-skilled people earn more. In contrast, in the kibbutz, equal sharing implies that wages are independent of skills; everyone earns a fixed amount (8,000 NIS in the example above) regardless of skill level. The point of intersection of these two lines represents a skill level such that the individual is equally motivated to stay or leave. At this skill level, wages are the same in the kibbutz and in the city. If wages were the only consideration, people with skill levels above the point of intersection would leave, and those below it would stay. The vertical distance between the two lines is a measure of the loss or gain that the individual would experience by moving to the city. The intuition behind this relationship is simple: because skills are more rewarded in the city than in the kibbutz, the higher a member's skill, the more incentive he or she has to exit. If this process of brain drain takes place over time, the kibbutz may unravel as the higher-skilled people leave and wages in the kibbutz declines.

In reality, exit is economically costly, not just in terms of direct costs such as those involved with renting or buying an apartment,

---

[1] It is worth noting that this insight is used in the context of understanding whether migrants to and from origins with different returns to skills are positively or negatively selected (e.g., Roy 1951, Borjas 1987, Chiquiar and Hanson 2005, Abramitzky 2009). Migrants from origins with low returns to skill are expected to be positively selected, i.e., have higher-than-average skill; migrants from origins with high returns to skill are expected to be negatively selected, i.e., have lower-than-average skill. A kibbutz with equal sharing is a limit case where returns to skills are zero.

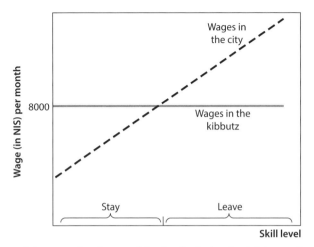

FIGURE 6.1: Adverse selection and brain drain in the kibbutz. In this hypothetical example, the dashed line depicts the relationship between wages and skills outside the kibbutz and the solid line shows this same relationship in the kibbutz.

buying new appliances, and wages lost during the move, but also in terms of indirect costs to members, who cannot take their physical assets (e.g., their house and their share of the public goods) with them when they exit. I discuss such costs in the next section. To the extent exit is costly, it is as if the wage in the city is lowered by the cost of exit, so that the dashed line in figure 6.1 (above) is shifted downwards, as illustrated in figure 6.2 (below). In this case, more members stay in their kibbutz and exit rates from the kibbutz are lower. Even some of the more-educated and -skilled members, who would leave if exit were costless, end up staying if exit is costly. With costly exit, those who leave are even more positively selected (more educated and skilled) than when exit is costless. In other words, when exiting is costly or otherwise difficult, only those with very high skill levels find it worth incurring the cost of leaving the kibbutz. Similarly, when entry is costly, the solid line would be shifted downwards. Fewer city residents enter a kibbutz in this case, and those who do enter are even more negatively selected in terms of their skills.

These comparisons so far have focused on the relative financial costs and benefits of living in a kibbutz, but kibbutz life is more

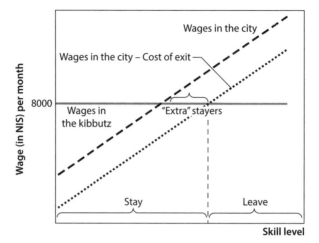

FIGURE 6.2: The effect of exit costs on the decision to stay in the kibbutz instead of moving to the city. The dashed line depicts the relationship between wages and skills outside the kibbutz, the dotted line exhibits the real wage (the wage after subtracting the exit cost) and the solid line shows the relationship between wages and skills in the case of the kibbutz.

attractive for idealistic people. For a more realistic story, let's add idealism to the calculation. Members differ both in their skill level and in their level of commitment to the kibbutz (idealism). Figure 6.3 illustrates the selection process from kibbutzim in this case. For a given skill level, those with lower idealism tend to leave the kibbutz. The higher the member's skill level, the higher the level of idealism that is required for her to wish to stay. Among those with high skill levels, only those with high idealism stay. Those with very low skill levels always stay in their kibbutz, even if they have low idealism. High-skilled members with low idealism leave, and higher-skilled members with high idealism stay. Those who leave have higher average skills than stayers, and those who stay have higher average idealism than movers. In contrast, entrants to kibbutzim will have lower average skills than non-entrants, and higher average idealism.

Adverse selection also arises in a number of other situations. It is a potential threat to insurance markets, just as much as it is a threat

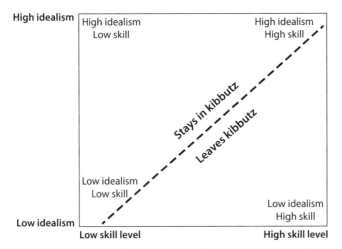

FIGURE 6.3: Movers have higher average skills than stayers, and stayers have higher average idealism than movers. The figure shows who is expected to stay and who is expected to leave the kibbutz when individuals differ in both their skill level and their idealism.

to societies and organizations that share incomes equally. Consider car insurance, for example. Insurance companies that offer full insurance against any damage to the car might attract the worst drivers in the same way that all-you-can-eat buffets attract big eaters. Insurance companies that don't want to suffer large losses will thus not offer full insurance, even though all drivers would enjoy it.[2] Another classic example of how adverse selection might destroy the

---

[2] Drivers want to insure themselves and their cars against accidents. Ideally, they would like to get full insurance (full coverage of all repairs and damage caused by any accident). Anticipating bad drivers will be disproportionally more attracted to full insurance contracts, the insurance company that doesn't want to go bankrupt would have to charge very high premiums, which good drivers will find too expensive to buy. The insurance company realizes that this adverse selection process attracts only bad drivers, and therefore the company will not offer full insurance (or will offer full insurance at very high prices that will attract only the worst drivers). Note that if the insurance company could know who is a good driver and who is a bad driver, it could charge different premiums for different types of drivers. But because it can't, the process of adverse selection would lead to a market failure, whereby full insurance contracts are not offered even though such contracts are desirable to drivers.

market is the used-car market, in which the fact that sellers know more about the condition of their car might lead buyers to avoid buying a used car because they believe the seller will only sell his car if it has unseen problems.[3]

Insurance and adverse selection also play a role in labor markets. Fixed monthly wages provide insurance in the sense that, unless you actually lose your job, you get the same wage regardless of your performance and in both good and bad times. In a labor market where some jobs offer fixed wages and others offer wages that vary based on performance, the fixed-wage jobs are likely to attract less-productive workers. In contrast, more-productive workers might tend to opt for jobs that offer per-task wage or performance-based bonuses.[4]

---

[3] In an article titled "The Market for Lemons," George Akerlof, who later won the Nobel Prize for his insight, analyzed how information asymmetries between buyer and sellers affect the market for used cars. Some used cars are good quality and some are bad quality, and while the seller of a car is likely to know which type he has, in many cases the buyer will not. A buyer who can't be sure he's buying a good car won't be willing to pay as much as a good car is worth. But this means owners of good cars won't be able to get high prices for them, and many will decide not to sell them at all. The more potential sellers of good cars drop out of the market, the more likely a car any buyer considers will be a bad car, and the less he'll be willing to pay for it. This unraveling process may in theory continue until no good used cars are offered for sale at all. This is what economists call "market failure": no market for high-quality used cars exists even though many buyers would be happy to buy high-quality cars at prices that sellers would be willing to sell them.

[4] Consider two firms that offer on average the same compensation for workers, but one offers a fixed hourly wage and the other offers workers a per-task wage or stocks of the firm. Which would a worker prefer? On one hand, a fixed wage is good because it offers insurance against undesirable fluctuations in earnings. On the other hand, per-task wages or stocks in the firm tie the worker's wage to his performance, meaning a good worker is likely to be able to earn more under such a wage scheme. Now think about two workers, who seem to the firm equally qualified in terms of their education and skills, but the workers know themselves better than the firms knows them. One is motivated and ambitious and expects to excel on the job; the other tends to get bored quickly and expects to have trouble motivating himself to work hard. In such case, the firm that offers fixed wages could expect adverse selection, whereby the less motivated worker will choose to join and the more motivated and ambitious worker will instead choose the competitor firm that offers a per-task wage or stocks in the firm. Notice that even the worker who ended up choosing the per-task wage would have preferred a fixed

Adverse selection is also a risk for social insurance programs such as Social Security. If participation in such an insurance policy were voluntary, so that citizens could opt in or out as they wished, adverse selection might destroy the policy. Only sick and unskilled people would join, whereas the healthy and skilled would opt out.[5] Insurance payouts could end up being unsustainably high and leading to the collapse of the policy. Such adverse selection concerns help explain why social insurance programs such as Social Security, Medicare, and Medicaid are mandatory: when everyone must join, adverse selection is not a problem.

The flip side of adverse selection is brain drain: the tendency of desirable, skilled kibbutz members to exit. A kibbutz member whose above-average skills would enable him to earn more outside the kibbutz has an incentive to exit the kibbutz for the sake of this wage premium, as illustrated in figure 6.1. A society based on equality that loses all its most productive members will be doomed to a low level of income. It is thus no accident that Communist countries have traditionally been run as totalitarian regimes that made it difficult, if not impossible, for their citizens to leave.[6]

Unlike citizens of Communist nations, kibbutz members have always been able to exit at will. Kibbutz founders valued freedom and democracy as much as they valued equality. But this right to

---

wage because fixed wage offers better insurance—that is, he might have chosen a fixed wage even if it paid less than the per-task wage. However, the fixed wage that will make the firm not lose money would be much lower, because fixed wages attract all the less-motivated workers who will be less productive. A classic paper on how performance pay improves productivity is Lazear (2000a).

[5] The reason is *not* that healthy and skilled people do not want insurance—in fact, they would like insurance very much. But for the government to break even and not lose tons of money, the premiums it charges would have to be high enough to cover the expected medical expenses of both the sick and the healthy, or the cost of unemployment by the unskilled and by the skilled. This makes such an insurance policy a great deal for the sick and unskilled but a terrible deal for the healthy and skilled.

[6] In totalitarian socialist countries such as North Korea and the former Soviet Union, citizens were often not allowed to leave, or even move internally. In China, the Hokku system didn't allow people to move to cities and forced them to stay where they were born. In the former Soviet Union, people born in rural areas could not move to the cities. If you lived in a Russian kolkhoz, the collective farm that emerged under Stalin, exit was not an option.

exit makes it challenging for kibbutzim to maintain equal sharing because of the brain drain problem. In fact, brain drain is a potential challenge for all societies with greater redistribution, kibbutzim being an extreme example.[7] Similarly, in worker-managed firms, which have a more compressed compensation structure than conventional firms, high-ability members were shown to be more likely than other members to exit (Burdin 2016).

Was there brain drain from kibbutzim? That is, did the most educated and skilled members exit? Why did many members, including educated ones, choose to stay in the kibbutz over the years? How did kibbutzim deal with the problem of brain drain?

As figure 6.1 illustrated, when a member considered whether or not to stay in a kibbutz, he or she thought about the value of staying ("inside option"), the value of living outside the kibbutz ("outside option"), and the cost of moving. Members' inside and outside options changed over the years. In the early days, kibbutzim were relatively poor and living standards were low. One main value of living in a kibbutz was idealism. The other was the safety net. At that time, members' outside options were also not very attractive, both because life outside was risky and because standards of living in Palestine in general were low. The idealism and safety net involved in living in a kibbutz, combined with the low outside option and the difficulty of leaving the kibbutz and starting fresh outside, meant that brain drain was limited.

In later generations, idealism declined, but material living standards in kibbutzim increased. As long as the living standards inside

[7] The insight that brain drain is more likely to occur when people move from origins with high taxes (and thus high redistribution) to destinations with low taxes and vice versa is based on the classical Roy (1951) self-selection model, and was used to test the selection of immigrants in Borjas (1987) and Abramitzky (2009). The Roy self-selection model has also served as a framework for studying other labor market choices (see Heckman and Honore, 1990). Examples include women's labor force participation (Gronau 1973, 1974; Heckman 1974), self-selection of workers into unions (Lee 1978), selection of schooling levels (Willis and Rosen 1979), and self-selection across industries and occupations (Heckman and Sedlacek 1990). Other migration studies that use the Roy framework include Robinson and Tomes (1982); Ferrie (1999a, 1999b); Chiquiar and Hanson (2005); Borjas, Bronars, and Trejo (1992); Ramos (1992); and Abramitzky and Braggion (2006).

kibbutzim were sufficiently high relative to members' outside options, brain drain remained low, though some productive members who expected to earn high wages outside the kibbutz still left. In addition, the rules and norms kibbutzim put in place in the earlier days made it difficult for members to leave the kibbutz and start a fresh life outside. These lock-in devices reduced the incentive of even productive members to leave, reducing brain drain.

However, as I discuss later in detail, everything changed with the high-tech boom in Israel in the mid-1990s. The boom substantially increased the earnings that productive members could expect to earn outside and triggered a process of brain drain. Although the number of highly skilled members who exited kibbutzim was high, it would have been even greater without the lock-in devices kibbutzim put in place.

WAS THERE ADVERSE SELECTION AMONG ENTRANTS TO THE EGALITARIAN KIBBUTZ?

Less-educated and less-skilled people expect to gain more from entering a kibbutz, as figure 6.1 above shows. Does this prediction play out in real life? Were the Israeli Jews who entered kibbutzim less educated and less skilled than those who did not? And how did kibbutzim deal with adverse selection?

Kibbutzim were well aware of the potential for adverse selection and expressed concern about people who might try to enter for the "wrong reasons." The concern was that people who didn't have any interest otherwise in living in a commune and didn't share the kibbutz principles might seek to enter simply because they couldn't find a job or make a living outside the kibbutz. One character in Inbari's novel was a painter who entered a kibbutz in the early days. "Had he told them he was a painter, he would not have been accepted, so he invented a curriculum vitae of a serious candidate. The members saw in front of them a blond young man who was short but strong, capable of any job" (Inbari 2009, p. 79; my translation).

In the early 1980s, in an attempt to be more inclusive and to attract more people to communal life in the kibbutz, kibbutzim experimented with a relatively open-door policy. According to anecdotal accounts, entrants were not the kind that kibbutzim were hoping for: most were not skilled or hard workers, and shared little of kibbutz ideology. Once kibbutzim realized they were disproportionately attracting the wrong people, they started to screen applicants more carefully. They began to admit mostly applicants who had at least a high school diploma, held a desirable profession, and were still young enough to work. They even set up a joint central body, the kibbutz's Department of Absorption and Demographic Growth, which is in charge of the screening process for individual applicants to the kibbutz and imposes strict rules on entry. It is legitimate to ask whether being selective and not admitting weak members of society is consistent with the ideals of equality and mutual aid. There is no easy answer, but in practical terms, the alternative seems to have proved infeasible.

In my conversations with them in 2002, officials at the Department of Absorption had many good stories about applicants: one wanted to enter a kibbutz because he figured it would be a cheaper place to raise his five kids; another had lost his job and wanted to enter a kibbutz just until he found a new one; and an eighty-year old applicant said after all her experience living in a capitalist world she would now like to try equal sharing.

The officials pointed out that kibbutzim preferred applicants who were between twenty and fifty years old, had finished high school, had served in the military, and had an occupation that would allow them to "find a job within the kibbutz or its surroundings immediately." The current online application form (last accessed on March 25 2015) also leaves little doubt that kibbutzim care about high education level, desirable occupation, and employment status. Applicants are asked for their date of birth, number of children, level of education, field of study, profession, and current job. Such questions are easier to understand when viewed from the perspective of a community that tries to avoid adverse selection than when viewed from the perspective of a socialist commune that seeks to attract ideologically committed people regardless of their education and skill.

Applicants also had to go through a lengthy interview, fill out forms about their own and their children's physical and mental health, and submit a curriculum vitae. The committee even sent a sample of applicants' handwriting to be analyzed by a graphologist, with the hope of gaining more insight into applicants' character and intentions. Finally, applicants had to answer a long questionnaire meant to assess whether they were suited to living in a kibbutz.

Note that this description of joining a kibbutz relates to the 2000s and may not accurately represent the situation in earlier years. Only about one-third of the kibbutzim absorbed new members from the outside. These kibbutzim are typically of medium wealth, and are more likely to be located in Israel's far south or far north. Poor kibbutzim often cannot absorb outsiders because they lack the resources to build new apartments for children who decide to stay, who are still the main source of population growth. Poor kibbutzim also face unemployment, which makes it difficult to use new labor profitably. At the other end of the spectrum, rich kibbutzim also often do not accept outsiders, as they face high demand for apartments by their own children. Kibbutzim in the center of Israel and those close to the sea are crowded with members and often do not have room for new housing. Some kibbutzim require an entry fee, but this may be recoverable in part upon leaving. Applicants cannot fully choose the kibbutz they join: they list their preferences to join particular kibbutzim, but the final decision takes into account both applicants' preferences and kibbutzim's needs.

I tested for adverse selection of entrants to kibbutzim between 1983 and 1995, a period when kibbutzim were all based on income equality and mostly had a screening process in place. The people considered were Israeli Jews who in 1983 lived outside a kibbutz in Israel.[8] I looked at where they were living twelve years later in 1995, and asked whether those who in 1983 earned less and had lower wealth were more likely to have entered a kibbutz by 1995.

In the representative sample I analyzed, using census data, about one out of every two hundred of the country's non-kibbutz population entered a kibbutz. The admission process, which screened out many people and favored skilled people who could contribute

---

[8] For more details about the data construction and econometrics analysis, see Abramitzky (2009).

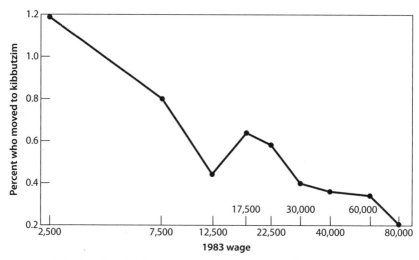

FIGURE 6.4: People with lower wages were more likely to enter kibbutzim. The figure shows the proportion of people living in cities in 1983 who entered kibbutzim between 1983 and 1995, broken down by wage categories in 1983. Only 90 out of the 16,789 Jewish Israelis in the sample who lived outside of kibbutzim in 1983 (with non-missing earnings) entered a kibbutz between 1983 and 1995, about 0.5%. Data source: Linked censuses of 1983 and 1995.

economically to the kibbutz helps explain why individual entry to kibbutzim from the outside was so low.

Moreover, figure 6.4, which again uses the merged 1983 and 1995 population censuses and examines Jewish Israelis between the ages of twenty-one and fifty-four who lived outside a kibbutz in 1983, shows that despite the strict screening, people with lower earnings were more likely to enter a kibbutz in this period, which suggests a process of negative selection.[9]

There is a subtle but important difference between negative selection and adverse selection. Negative selection of entrants means those who enter have lower potential earnings on average than those who do not, which may result from lower skills, lower education, lower motivation, or any number of other factors. Adverse

[9] It is, of course, possible that kibbutzim were ineffective in screening.

selection, in contrast, means those who enter are poorer in terms of qualities that are unobservable to the kibbutz, such as ambition and motivation, though they may be similar to non-entrants in observable qualities. Adverse selection is therefore a specific type of negative selection, and results from an asymmetry of information between kibbutzim and potential entrants. The kibbutz, of course, is concerned about negative selection even if it has nothing to do with asymmetric information. For example, the kibbutz might not like to accept people with lower levels of education and ones without a profession, but education and profession are typically easy to observe, so the kibbutz should be able to successfully screen out such applicants. Adverse selection is by definition harder for the kibbutz to deal with, because it is difficult for the kibbutz to find out factors such as applicants' ambition and motivation.

This tendency of people who earned less to enter a kibbutz likely understates the negative selection of applicants because the least promising applicants were eliminated by the screening process.[10] Indeed, I show in table 6.1 below that less educated and less skilled people, who are typically screened out, were not more likely to enter a kibbutz despite their stronger incentive to do so.

Even if kibbutz officials were well aware of the tendency of people with low levels of education and skills to enter, they couldn't avoid adverse selection because potential entrants have private information regarding their skills and about how much they can contribute to the kibbutz. The census data contain information on people's wages before they entered the kibbutz. However, wage was not used as a criterion in the application process, for two reasons. First, wages might be difficult to verify. Second, kibbutzim may care more about entrants' skills and education than about the wages they had prior to entry. Note that the determination of whether or not the

---

[10] Note that I only observe individuals who actually entered, rather than all applicants. However, this should make it harder to document negative selection, because it includes only applicants who were accepted by the kibbutz. Hence, my results are likely to provide a lower bound on the negative selection of people who wish to enter kibbutzim. Although I find significant evidence of negative selection in entry, it should be noted that the size of the sample of entrants is very small.

negative selection documented here can be interpreted literally as adverse selection due to asymmetric information depends on which is the true reason.[11]

Moreover, to test whether entrants to kibbutzim were negatively selected because of the equal sharing the kibbutz offers rather than because city-to-rural immigrants in general tend to be negatively selected, it is important not only to compare kibbutz entrants with non-entrants, but also to compare migrants from the city to a kibbutz with those from the city to other rural locations.

Table 6.1 presents the average characteristics of people who lived in the city in both 1983 and 1995, city-to-kibbutz movers, and city-to-other rural location movers, respectively. The average person who entered a kibbutz earned a wage that is about 20 percent lower than that of non-entrants (25,877 vs. 32,120 shekels). In contrast, the table shows that city-to-other rural migrants earned a wage similar to city natives who did not move (31,211 vs. 32,120 shekels). The average person who entered a kibbutz was also younger than the average Israeli who did not move (26.5 vs. 33.3 years old) and was more likely to have at least a high school diploma than nonmovers (64% vs. 51%). An entrant was less likely to work in a high-skill occupation than the average city worker (6.6% vs. 14.1%), and was somewhat less likely to work in a low-skill occupation (7.3% vs. 8.4%).

Then I tested more formally the hypothesis that entrants to the kibbutz were negatively selected in the sense that they earned less before they entered a kibbutz. Next, I conducted an econometric analysis of entry to the kibbutz in the period 1983–1995, in which I evaluated whether people who earned lower wages were more likely to enter, controlling for their various characteristics that I could observe, namely their age, gender, family size, education, occupation, marital status, and previous residence in Israel's South or North Region.

The econometric analysis, presented in the appendix to this chapter, confirms the findings that higher-educated people were in fact

---

[11] This approach of relying on observable characteristics that were not used by the kibbutz in the application process follow the approach developed in Finkelstein and McGarry (2003, 2006), and Finkelstein and Poterba (2006).

TABLE 6.1: The Selection in Entry to the Kibbutz, 1983–1995

Variable	(1)	(2)	(3)
	City natives	City-to-kibbutz migrants	City-to-other rural migrants
1983 monthly earnings	32,130	25,877	31,211
At least high school diploma	50.70%	64.20%	69.20%
High skill	14.10%	6.60%	14.90%
Low skill	8.40%	7.30%	6.10%
Age	33.327	26.57	28.434
Male	57.60%	55.60%	53.30%
Married	74.30%	34.40%	64.10%
Family size	4.068	3.311	3.687
Born in Israel	53.80%	77.50%	73.10%
Israel's north region	7.20%	6.60%	10.50%
Israel's south region	11.80%	13.90%	10.50%
Observations	20,617	151	610

Note: This table presents the means of the explanatory variables for different groups of individuals. All variables are measured in 1983, i.e., prior to exit/entry. "High skill" signifies individuals working in either academic or managerial occupations. "Low skill" signifies individuals working either in unskilled occupations in industry or as service workers. A third omitted group contains all other occupants. "Israel's north region" includes the following districts: Sefad, Kinneret, Yizrael, Akko, and Golan. "Israel's south region" includes Ashkelon and Beer-Sheva districts. A third omitted group contains all other regions. The numbers of observations for 1983 monthly earnings are fewer than for the other variables: 15,456 observations in column 1; 77 in column 2; and 415 in column 3.

more likely to enter kibbutzim, but people with lower wages were also more likely to enter. The formal econometric analysis also suggested that even among people of the same ages and same marital status who had the same level of education and held a similar occupation, those with lower wages were more likely to enter a kibbutz, suggesting adverse selection in entering kibbutzim.

To summarize, we have seen that entrants to kibbutzim between 1983 and 1985 were negatively selected in their wages, in the sense that people who earned less were more likely to enter a kibbutz. This is despite the fact that kibbutzim engaged in screening and wouldn't let in people with low education and skills. Entrants thus had at least high school degrees and worked in skilled occupations, but they were the ones among the educated and skilled who didn't manage to earn high wages in the outside world, possibly reflecting information asymmetries between the entrant and the kibbutz.

HOW DID KIBBUTZIM DEAL WITH ADVERSE SELECTION?

While adverse selection took place as economic theory predicted, the screening process kept entry low and ensured negative selection was minimal in the sense that entrants had high enough levels of education and skill. It is likely that many unskilled people with limited job prospects would have entered kibbutzim if prospective entrants hadn't been screened. Such unskilled entrants would have contributed on average less to kibbutz production and would have reduced average income and thus the standard of living in the kibbutz. This rationale helps explain why the admission process in kibbutzim focused on screening out people who were unlikely to contribute their fair share to the kibbutz economy.

Another layer of screening took place once people entered the kibbutz. Applicants didn't automatically become members but instead had to live in the kibbutz for a trial period of one or two years, at the end of which existing members would vote on whether to accept the applicants as members. The trial period was designed to allow members to learn whether applicants were a good fit for the kibbutz, whether they contributed their share, whether they were cooperative and friendly, and any other dimension members cared about.

The unavoidable problem of adverse selection of entrants helps explain why entry to kibbutzim is highly restricted, and why in the last half-century, kibbutz population growth mostly came from kibbutz-born members deciding to stay, rather than entry from the outside. In earlier days, when entry from the outside was the main source of population growth in kibbutzim, entrants were more often young idealists committed to communal life and more similar in their economic prospects. They took a number of actions to try to signal their serious intentions. Before the 1970s, most were young people who belonged to socialist youth movements in Israel and abroad, or young Israelis who formed kibbutz-inspired units called Nahal during their mandatory military service and asked to join a kibbutz when they finished their service.[12] Such people were less likely to be adversely selected: they were idealists, they demonstrated commitment to socialism and communal life before they joined, and they were young enough to avoid the suspicion that they entered simply because they wanted to take advantage of income equality in the kibbutz.

My grandparents fit this story: Breindel and Buzik both belonged to the Ha'shomer Ha'tzair youth movement in their shtetl in Poland from the time they were young teenagers. I imagine my young grandparents having tea with their friends in the cold winters of Poryck, passionately discussing the ideas of Ben Borochov, Martin Buber, and other Zionist-socialist leaders. I imagine my grandmother becoming increasingly worried as she watched her sweetheart and friends shifting from thinking about making aliyah and joining a kibbutz as abstract ideas to making concrete plans to move to Palestine. Even if my grandmother was not as idealistic and passionate about moving to the Levant and joining a kibbutz as my grandfather, she joined at a point in her life when she was still young and had all her life ahead of her. I wonder if Kibbutz Negba would have accepted my grandmother ten years later as a forty-year-old seamstress, a widow with two young daughters.

Concerns about adverse selection also rationalize various seemingly irrational sacrifices required by kibbutzim of entrants, norms that stigmatized certain behaviors, and costly signals of commitment in the kibbutz. Larry Iannaccone, a pioneer in the study of the economics of religion, suggested that seemingly puzzling human behaviors such as sacrifices, stigmatizing actions, and costly signals can be rationalized as practices that help strengthen sects and religious groups. Otherwise, why would Krishnas shave their heads? Why would Mormons abstain from caffeine? Why would Orthodox Jews wear side curls and yarmulkes? And why would monks take vows for celibacy and silence? Such seemingly irrational behaviors and sacrifice might actually build group strength and help avoid adverse selection and free-riding. Note, however, that

---

[12] Military service is mandatory in Israel for three years for men (typically ages 18–21) and two years for women (typically ages 18–20).

this "economic" approach does not deny the importance of faith, ideology and idealism but rather offers a complementary rationale.

Such sacrifices and stigmatizing behaviors are prevalent in sects and religious groups. Costly sacrifices mitigate the problem of adverse selection by a self-selection process (unlike the screening done through membership applications) that helps exclude those members who want the benefit of the group without contributing to the group's success. In other words, only people who are most committed to the cause find it worthwhile to enter given the sacrifices and costly signals of commitment. As a result, free-riders tend to stay out. Members who do enter or remain in the group are those for whom the benefits are higher than the costs of the sacrifice or stigma.

Even kibbutzim, most of which are secular, used stigma and sacrifice to ensure that people didn't just seek to enter to take advantage of the abundant food, spacious recreational facilities, and valuable safety net rather than because they actually wanted to live in a kibbutz. By demanding members to sacrifice and by stigmatizing unwanted behavior, kibbutzim ensured that only people who were committed to the kibbutz ideals would enter.

One such sacrifice that must have discouraged some people from entering was the separation of parents from their children by creating separate children's residences outside parents' homes. Children slept together in these residences, and parents and children could only see each other in a designated period each day. While not the official intention of this policy, such separation was a big sacrifice for most parents. Eventually, in the late 1970s and 1980s, all kibbutzim decided to move children back into their parents' homes.

Other norms included strict mutual monitoring to ensure that members would not free-ride. Kibbutzniks were expected to give up a lot of their privacy and their individualism in almost every aspect of life; they were expected to socialize with one another, including eating all their meals in the communal dining hall rather than with their own families. The cost of not abiding by norms is higher in small groups where everyone knows everyone; this explains why all kibbutzim are relatively small. Another norm that was stigmatized had to do with a "meaningful" service in the military. Everyone in Israel has to serve in the military, but military service can involve different degrees of personal sacrifice and difficulty. Serving in an elite combat unit in the military was highly valued in the kibbutz; the share of kibbutz members in such units was much higher than their share in the general population. Kibbutz members knew that they and their children were expected to serve in combat units unless they had a health problem, and they were frowned upon if they didn't.

WAS THERE BRAIN DRAIN FROM THE EGALITARIAN KIBBUTZ?

It is difficult to test systematically for brain drain from kibbutzim for most periods in their existence because of a lack of consistent data. Over thirty years ago, Bruno Bettelheim (1969) conjectured that the kibbutz educates to mediocrity and that the best and worst members would tend to leave. In fact, kibbutz scholars have always suspected that the "best" members might be the first to leave. They found little evidence for this hypothesis for the decade of the 1970s (e.g., Leviatan 1975, 1996; Helman 1982; Nathan, Shenbal, and Paskin 1982), but some suggestive evidence for brain drain for the period starting the late 1980s.[13]

---

[13] Natan, Shenbal-Brandes, and Paskin (1982) followed an entire high school class for seven years. Before graduating, the minors were asked to fill in a CPI questionnaire (personality questionnaire) combined with a "talent test." Seven years later, the researchers found no differences between movers and stayers in either the "talent test" or in their education and their job positions. Similarly, Helman (1982) found no such evidence in movers' and stayers' "talent levels" as evaluated by their former high-school teachers. Leviatan and Orchan (1982) based their research on members under thirty-five years old from ten kibbutzim and found no difference in a self-assigned "talent level" between movers and stayers. On the flip side, Leviatan (1993) considers the increase in the percentage of movers who are older than thirty as evidence for the exodus of "good" members, as these people are generally more experienced and more educated due to their age. He also found a 4% exit rate of members who held major positions in their kibbutz over a period of five years and viewed this as evidence that the best members tend to leave.

For the period between 1983 and 1995, however, it is possible to test for brain drain from kibbutzim using linked population censuses. I followed kibbutz members who left their kibbutz during this period and those who stayed, and compared movers with stayers. I also examined how kibbutz members who moved performed in the outside labor market. I started by constructing an individual-level dataset based on the population censuses conducted in Israel in 1983 and 1995, a period when kibbutzim were still based on income equality.

I focused on kibbutz members who lived in a kibbutz when the census was taken in 1983, and then located them in the census of 1995 when some still lived in a kibbutz but others had left. This allowed me to test whether the most educated and skilled members left in higher numbers. Because kibbutzim are rural and most people who leave them move to cities, it is informative to compare the selection of people who leave kibbutzim to that of people who leave other rural areas for cities. If brain drain were equal from kibbutzim and other rural areas, this would suggest it was the rural nature of kibbutzim, not their equal sharing, that caused the higher-skilled and more-educated members to leave. I thus constructed a similar sample that follows other rural-to-urban Jewish migrants and rural stayers over the same time period. Comparing the two samples lets me test whether brain drain was greater from kibbutzim than from other rural areas. This matched sample accounts for a representative 4 percent of kibbutz members and of Israeli Jews outside the kibbutz.[14]

---

[14] The 1983 and 1995 census data include all Israeli citizens who answered the "extensive questionnaire" in both years. At each census, this questionnaire was given to 20% of households in a way that adequately represented the entire population. To follow the same kibbutz members over time, I needed to observe the same kibbutz members in both 1983 and 1995, so I used a representative sample of 4% (20% of 20% is 4%) of kibbutz members constructed by the Israeli Central Bureau of Statistics. I similarly used a 4% representative sample of other rural-to-urban Jewish migrants and rural nonmigrants over the same time period.

Because kibbutz members are always Jewish, I compare kibbutz members to non-kibbutz Jewish people. I focus on adults who are at least 21 in 1983 (the age by which men complete their mandatory military service) and thus old enough to make their own migration decision, but younger than 54 in 1983 (66 in 1995) so they are likely still in the labor force. A total of 343 out of the 1,577 individuals

An important shortcoming of the data is that, because of confidentiality concerns of the Israeli Central Bureau of Statistics, I cannot identify in which kibbutz a person lived (though I do know in which region of Israel the kibbutz was located). This means the data do not allow me to identify which kibbutz members moved to another kibbutz. A second shortcoming is that incomes inside the kibbutz are not recorded in the census, and these incomes anyway did not reflect rewards to skill. Thus, when examining kibbutz-to-city migrants, I compared movers to stayers in their education and occupation rather than in their wages.

As figures 6.5a and 6.5b show, I found that more-educated and higher-skilled kibbutz members left in higher numbers, indicating brain drain from the kibbutz. To test whether the primary driver of brain drain was the rural nature of kibbutzim or their equal sharing, I compared kibbutz-to-city migrants with other rural-to-urban migrants. Figures 6.5a and 6.5b show that the positive selection of kibbutz movers was more pronounced than that of other rural-to-urban migrants, suggesting stronger brain drain from the egalitarian kibbutz than from other rural locations.

To better characterize those who left the kibbutz, table 6.2 shows the average demographics of members who stayed in their kibbutz, left their kibbutz for a city, left their kibbutz for another rural location, and stayed in a city, respectively. The table shows that kibbutz members who moved to a city were more educated (over 61.5% of kibbutz movers had at least a high school diploma vs. 50% of stayers), more likely to work in a high-skill occupation (9.9% vs. 8.4%), and less likely to work in a low-skill occupation (14.9% vs. 22.6%). Also, the average kibbutz mover in 1983 (before migration) was younger (less than thirty years old) than the average stayer (thirty-six years old). This evidence suggests brain drain from the kibbutz, whereby more-educated and higher-skilled kibbutz members were more likely to leave their kibbutz.

The appendix to this chapter shows these basic patterns hold in a formal econometric regression analysis. This analysis is important

---

in the sample who lived in a kibbutz in 1983 left the kibbutz (262 to the city and 81 to non-kibbutz rural areas) between 1983 and 1995, over 20% of the sample.

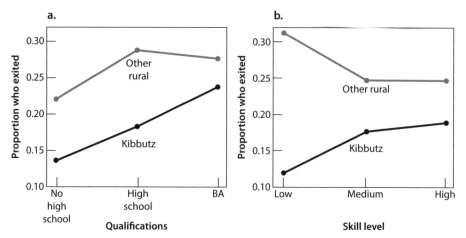

FIGURE 6.5A and B: More-educated and higher-skilled kibbutz members were more likely to exit to the city. The left-hand panel (a) shows the proportion of kibbutz members (black line) and individuals from other rural areas (gray line) who moved to the city between 1983 and 1995 by level of qualifications in 1983. The right-hand panel (b) shows the same, but broken down by the skill level of the member's occupation in 1983. To make these comparisons meaningful, I concentrate on Jewish individuals who were between the ages of 21 and 54 in 1983 (and thus between the ages of 33 and 66 in 1995). A total of 343 out of the 1,577 individuals in the sample who lived in a kibbutz in 1983 left the kibbutz between 1983 and 1995, over 20%. "High-skill" individuals are those working in either academic or managerial occupations. "Low-skill" individuals are those working either in unskilled occupations in industry or as service workers. A third omitted group contains all other occupations. Source: Linked censuses of 1983 and 1995.

because it allowed me to test whether the more-educated and higher-skilled were more likely to exit even when accounting for different tendencies to exit of members of different age, gender, marital status, and country of birth. I showed that brain drain occurred even among members with similar such personal characteristics.

Anecdotal evidence supports the statistics. Ariel Halperin, who between the years 1992 and 2000 led the Kibbutz Arrangement Board as a trustee of the government, kibbutzim, and the banks, was quoted in Mort and Brenner (2003, p. 43) saying in 1997: "[I]n many kibbutzim we are witnessing a mass desertion by kibbutz

TABLE 6.2: The Selection in Exit from the Kibbutz, 1983–1995

Variable	(1) Stayed in kibbutz	(2) Kibbutz-to-city migrants	(3) Kibbutz-to-other rural migrants	(4) City natives
At least high school diploma	50.00%	61.50%	63.00%	50.70%
High skill	8.40%	9.90%	9.90%	14.10%
Low skill	22.60%	14.90%	8.60%	8.40%
Age	36.295	29.5	29.963	33.327
Male	49.40%	55.00%	54.30%	57.60%
Married	79.60%	52.30%	70.40%	74.30%
Family size	3.57	2.576	3.136	4.068
Born in Israel	66.90%	75.20%	65.40%	53.80%
Israel's north region	52.40%	50.80%	56.80%	7.20%
Israel's south region	19.90%	25.60%	25.90%	11.80%
Observations	1,234	262	81	20,617

Note: This table presents the means of the explanatory variables for different groups of individuals. All variables are measured in 1983, i.e., prior to exit/entry. "High skill" signifies individuals working in either academic or managerial occupations. "Low skill" signifies individuals working either in unskilled occupations in industry or as service workers. A third omitted group contains all other occupants. "Israel's north region" includes the following districts: Sefad, Kinneret, Yizrael, Akko, and Golan. "Israel's south region" includes Ashkelon and Beer-Sheva districts. A third omitted group contains all other regions.

members of the workplace and the hiring of outside labor to fill the gap." And those who left were typically the more educated and higher skilled. A member of Degania told Gavron (2000, p. 34) that her son studied law in the university, and "he saw that he was bringing in a lot of money . . . and that some members were not working all that hard. He left." Similarly, the secretary of kibbutz Givat Brenner in 2001 summarized the process that had taken place in his kibbutz during the previous two decades: "I don't want to shout it out loud, but there is a negative selection process [from the kibbutz perspective] at work here. We have lost some of the best and brightest of our young adults. . . . We do not have enough members in the twenty-five to forty age group, and frankly, those who have stayed are not the best."[15]

[15] Quoted in Gavron (2000, p. 68).

The statistical analysis (see appendix, table 6.A6) revealed other factors that predicted the decision to stay in the kibbutz. Young members were more likely to leave. Members with bigger families might prefer to stay in the kibbutz and let other members subsidize them, rather than leave and finance their big family outside the kibbutz. An additional family member decreased the exit probability by two percentage points (from 20%, on average, to 18%). Overseas immigrants are four percentage points more likely to leave the kibbutz than Israeli-born Jews, although this parameter is not measured precisely. Members from kibbutzim in the far north and south of Israel were five percentage points more likely to leave their kibbutz.[16]

The next step of the research was to test whether kibbutz-to-city migrants were positively selected in their characteristics that are not observable to the researcher, such as ambition, motivation, work attitudes and abilities. The challenge was to test selection over characteristics I couldn't observe in the census. In a nutshell, I inferred this indirectly by asking whether kibbutz members who left earned more than similarly skilled workers in the city. That is, I compared the earnings of kibbutz movers in the city with the earnings of both the city labor force and other rural-to-city migrants.[17] If members who left their kibbutz earned in the city more than city natives and other rural migrants with similar observable characteristics, then we would conclude that kibbutz members were positively selected in their unobservable characteristics.

[16] It is also interesting to note differences by gender in the migration decision. Summary statistics and the reduced form equation did not reveal big differences in behavior between men and women and, if anything, suggest that more men than women had left the kibbutz in the late 1980s and early 1990s. On the other hand, the structural wage regressions suggest that men tended to earn more than women outside the kibbutz, which is why we see more men leaving. When controlling for this income effect, it turns out that men are 20% less likely to leave the kibbutz than are women. This statistic may be a result of more women marrying out of the kibbutz than men, but this issue requires further investigation.

[17] Specifically, I evaluate how former kibbutz members who left their kibbutz between 1983 and 1995 performed, in terms of their earnings, in the city in 1995 relative to similar people already in the city and relative to other rural-to-city migrants. A similar regression model was analyzed in the work of Chiswick (1978) and Carliner (1980).

The main findings were that the average kibbutz mover earned higher wages than both city natives and other rural-to-city migrants.

I also found that, once in the city, less-educated kibbutz-to-city movers earned higher wages than less-educated city natives. This finding is consistent with the idea that only the most productive less-educated members decided to leave their kibbutz. In contrast, all educated members had an increased incentive to exit, and indeed I found that more-educated workers who left the kibbutz did not earn higher wages than similar city natives. I present these findings in table 6.A7 and figure 6.A2. The appendix to this chapter presents the more formal econometric analysis of these patterns.

HOW DID KIBBUTZIM DEAL WITH BRAIN DRAIN?

Figures 6.5a and 6.5b illustrated that brain drain from kibbutzim was stronger than from other rural places. Nevertheless, this figure also shows that the overall exit rate from kibbutzim was lower than that from other rural areas, suggesting kibbutzim were successful in retaining members. In fact, even the educated and skilled people living in kibbutzim were less likely to leave than were similar people living in other rural areas. That is, while some members left and the most-educated and higher-skilled left in higher numbers, many members stayed in their kibbutz, including many of the higher-skilled and most-educated members.

This last finding might seem puzzling because kibbutzim's equal sharing is particularly unattractive for those with high earning potential in the city. It suggests kibbutzim had mechanisms in place that successfully reduced the brain drain problem. Whether intentional or not, various rules and norms in the kibbutz made exit more costly and reduced members' incentive to leave; brain drain would have been much more severe had such rules and norms not been in place.

One such mechanism was the communal ownership of all property. Upon arrival, members had to give their private property to the kibbutz, including their personal belongings, clothing, and jewelry, and they could not acquire private property while they lived in the kibbutz.[18] Kibbutz members did not own their houses, and could enjoy their share of the community assets only as long as they stayed in the commune. The kibbutz bylaws state that "each kibbutz member must live inside the kibbutz, bring to the possession of the kibbutz his full working power and any income and assets he owns and/or receives from any source"; "the property of the kibbutz cannot be distributed among members, both when the kibbutz persists and when it is dissolved"; "the kibbutz does not distribute profits in any way, and every surplus goes to the kibbutz."[19]

Importantly in the context of brain drain, a kibbutz member who left could not take her house or her share of the kibbutz property (e.g., of the swimming pool or of the kibbutz factory) with her. The communal property thus served as a bond that increased the cost of exit. A higher cost of exit facilitated equal sharing in the kibbutz, because many educated and skilled members stayed in order to avoid that cost.

Similarly, a kibbutz member did not inherit anything from her parents, had no savings, and was not allowed to receive gifts from the outside (although this rule was hard to enforce and many flouted it), which increased the cost of exit. When someone received a gift from the outside—for example, if a family member from Tel Aviv gave a radio to his cousin in a kibbutz—the kibbutz member was required to give the radio to the kibbutz so that all members could enjoy it. In some cases, such a gift triggered the kibbutz to buy radios for all members.

Kibbutz-born children didn't technically join, so they never had property to forfeit to the kibbutz. Nevertheless, they could not receive bequests or other financial support from their parents, who owned no private property. This meant that they could not save much money to leave, and could not easily rent or buy an apartment if they left. In effect, their entire family savings belonged to the kibbutz, making it difficult to start a new life outside.

---

[18] Anecdotes tell of a bride who had to give away her wedding dress, and the next morning someone wore it to work in the field, while others who got married were given workers' clothing for their weddings.

[19] My translation from the Hebrew.

One episode in particular challenged the rule of no private property, and tested members' commitment to ideals of equality. In the 1950s, Germany decided to pay reparations for Holocaust survivors, many of whom lived in kibbutzim. According to an agreement between the Federal Republic of Germany and the Israeli government signed in Luxembourg in September 1952, West Germany would pay the Israeli government 3,450 million German marks (about 800 million US dollars), in the form of goods and monetary transfers. Much of this sum was used to buy products such as metal and raw material for industrial and agricultural production, but a nontrivial sum was allocated to compensate individual Holocaust survivors.

The sizable German reparations were paid to the survivors personally rather than to their kibbutzim, but kibbutz members were expected to turn in their new fortunes to their kibbutzim. Members who received reparations faced the tough decision of whether to take the money and leave, or comply with the rules and surrender the money to the kibbutz. According to one calculation (Tzur 1984), about 85 percent of kibbutz members who received compensation stayed in their kibbutz, and only 15 percent left. Some members were able to reach various agreements with their kibbutz, for example, that they would be able use part of the money for a one-time expense of their choice that was subject to the approval of the kibbutz (Inbari 2009, p. 178), or that their child would be able to recover some of the reparations if they decided to leave. One possible interpretation (Yariv 2004) is that "giving up the payments to the collective use of the kibbutz was a signal for the strong ideological holding the kibbutz had for a substantial subgroup of members."[20]

---

[20] The compensations likely improved the kibbutz finances quite a bit. Even beyond the direct monetary compensations for kibbutz members who survived the Holocaust, the compensations benefited kibbutzim indirectly by reducing the cost of equipment kibbutzim used in industry and agriculture, allocating large sums to Tnuva, the main dairy company that got its milk supplies primarily from the kibbutzim, among other things. Yariv (2004) even raised the possibility that the compensations were in part responsible for the industrialization progress in kibbutzim over the following decade: "[K]ibbutzim had both the motive and the means to industrialize in the mid 1950's, and they did."

Beyond the lack of private property, other rules and norms served as lock-in devices that increased the cost of exit and allowed kibbutzim to reduce brain drain. Local public goods such as swimming pools, basketball and tennis courts, cultural centers, and parks could only be enjoyed by current kibbutz members. To be sure, the fact that member incomes all belonged to the kibbutz meant that kibbutzim could afford more local public goods, in the same way that welfare states with high tax rates can afford more public goods. Whether this was intentional or not, local public goods raised the cost of exit because only members could enjoy them, and those who left could not.

As already discussed, not allowing cash to be used was another lock-in device. A member had no savings, even if she was the kibbutz manager and contributed to the kibbutz greatly. The income she generated for the kibbutz translated into things like local public goods, food, and investment in kibbutz industry and agriculture.

In early days, instead of cash income, goods were distributed in kind. Needs were divided into different categories, such as food, clothing, travel, and so on, and members were provided with what they required. Members ate their meals in the communal dining hall—buffet style—and they could take as much food as they wanted. Members who served the kibbutz in official positions and had to travel were given higher travel expenses and were sometimes provided one of the kibbutz-owned cars for trips. The kibbutz also provided them some money for expenses, and they returned the change to the kibbutz upon their return. For day-to-day use, however, members did not have their own money and did not own private bank accounts. So members who wanted to leave their kibbutz could not rely on their savings and had to make it from scratch outside the kibbutz. This lack of financial backup also meant parents could not leave a bequest to their children, which made kibbutz-born children more dependent on their kibbutz and made exit more difficult for them.

Even after money became more widely used, members did not get their full salaries. Rather, they received relatively small monthly allowances and could buy whatever they wanted with this money. When kibbutzim privatized in the late 1990s, many kibbutz members were forced to deal with money for the first time, which often caused considerable distress. Note that salaries in and of themselves are not incompatible with equality, because the kibbutz can still divide all incomes equally. On the contrary, salaries might be more consistent with the Marxist idea of "from each according to ability, to each according to needs," because a member knows her needs and preferences better than the kibbutz, meaning she can spend her equal salary in a way that best matches her needs. So the fact that kibbutzim did not just collect all member incomes and distribute the funds equally, but rather kept most of them and paid only small allowances, was not necessary to maintain equality; what it did was make exit costly.

Another norm that locked in members was that they were expected to work inside their kibbutz. This rule of working inside the kibbutz, strictly enforced in early days, made it difficult for a kibbutz member to know what the outside world had to offer her, what economists call a member's "outside option." A member who lived and worked in her kibbutz would not know if she could find a good job outside the kibbutz, how valuable her skills would be, and how much she could earn, and so she would be less likely to leave. Over time, as more members began working outside their kibbutzim and interacting with nonmembers, this mechanism became weaker. Moreover, kibbutz members' jobs were often specific to the kibbutz—members worked in kibbutz agriculture, in the kibbutz industrial factory, or in the kibbutz shops or services—so a member who left could not expect to find a similar job outside. As economists would say, members' human capital (profession, skill) was kibbutz-specific and was less useful outside their kibbutz, making leaving less appealing.[21]

To be clear, lock-in of personal assets was not complete. Members who left did often receive modest amounts that increased with the number of years they had spent in the kibbutz. More importantly, members who left took their human capital with

---

[21] A nice paper that also makes this point is Gould and Moav (2016). In their model, people stay in a country if their country-specific skills are high in comparison with their general skills—the skills they take with them.

them, which had been paid for by their kibbutz, and of course they could not be deprived of their future earnings after they left. Moreover, in many kibbutzim today, people who are born and raised in the kibbutz do not have to decide whether they wish to become members until they are in their late 20s or 30s. The next chapter discusses kibbutzim's human capital investment problem in more detail.

In summary, brain drain was certainly a problem in kibbutzim, but the problem was not as severe as simple economic theory would predict. Many educated and skilled members ended up staying in their kibbutz rather than leaving and earning higher wages outside. The kibbutz used a number of mechanisms, which increased members cost of leaving their kibbutz. Members had no private property and could not take their share of the kibbutz and its factories and local public goods upon leaving. Members had no savings and no bequests they could use to make the move, they were not always aware of the possibilities for them outside their kibbutz, and they often had human capital that was kibbutz-specific and not very valuable outside. These made it harder for members to leave, even for members who brought in large incomes to the kibbutz and could potentially make a good living outside. Thus the kibbutz could maintain full equal sharing of all incomes without losing all the brightest and most talented members.

Of course, ideology played a role too. A member brimming with idealism and socialist ideology would not leave even if she could earn more outside the kibbutz. A member filled with guilt about questioning kibbutz values would also not leave. As we will see, this also helps explain why kibbutzim have always tried to instill idealism and ideology in their children, trying to convince them that living in a kibbutz was the best choice, and using guilt (an important driving force in extended families) to prevent members from leaving.

APPENDIX: ADVERSE SELECTION

I add below the econometric analysis of the adverse selection. The econometric method involves running a regression analysis on the data. The most commonly used regression is the linear regression, which I will use, along with different regression methods.[22]

The logit regression results of entering a kibbutz are presented in columns 1 and 2 of table 6.A1. The regressions provide little evidence of negative selection over characteristics that were observable to the kibbutz. While high-skill workers were less likely to enter and low-skill workers were more likely to enter (both coefficients are not significant), workers with at least a high school diploma were actually significantly more likely to enter kibbutzim than were less-educated individuals.

At the same time, the regressions provide evidence of adverse selection, that is, negative selection on characteristics not observed by the kibbutz. Specifically, people with lower wages were more likely to enter. The negative coefficient on wage declines somewhat in magnitude but remains significant when controls are added for individual characteristics that were observable to the kibbutz, such as education and age.[23]

I tested whether this negative selection on wage held for migrants from the city to other rural locations that do not engage in redistribution. Formally, I ran a multinomial logit that modeled the decision of people who lived in the city in 1983 to stay in the city, move to a kibbutz, or move to another rural location. The results are presented in column 3 (without controls) and column 4 (with controls) of table 6.A1. The regressions suggest that although people who earned lower wages were more likely to enter a kibbutz, similar people were not more likely to move to non-kibbutz rural localities, although the multinomial results with controls are not measured precisely.

[22] For the sake of fluent reading, I will assume minimal knowledge of these methods, though further information is available in *Introductory Econometrics: A Modern Approach* (Wooldridge 2015).

[23] The table in the appendix of Abramitzky (2009) shows how the magnitude of the wage coefficient changes with different subsets of the control variables. The magnitude of the wage coefficient does not decrease when controlling for the level of education, but is halved when age and marital status are added. The reason for this is that younger and single individuals are more likely to enter, but also more likely to earn lower wages. This is natural and does not imply adverse selection, which is small but significant after adding such observable controls.

TABLE 6.A1: Entry to Kibbutz vs. Moving from City to Other Rural Areas (Logit and Multinomial Logit Regressions), 1983–1995

Variable	(1)	(2)	(3)		(4)	
	Logit of moving to kibbutz from either city or other rural area		Multinomial logit of moving from city to			
			Kibbutz	Other rural area	Kibbutz	Other rural area
Pre-entry (1983)	-4.285***	-2.678*	-4.240***	-0.941	-2.073	0.215
	[1.241]	[1.381]	[1.335]	[0.649]	[1.506]	[0.769]
log wage (/10)					0.692***	0.785***
					[0.265]	[0.118]
At least high school diploma		0.842***				
		[0.246]				
High skill		-0.556			-0.396	0.151
		[0.373]			[0.379]	[0.140]
Low skill		0.164			0.181	0.002
		[0.362]			[0.386]	[0.198]
Age (/10)		2.406*			2.614	-0.584
		[1.436]			[1.626]	[0.605]
Age squared (/100)		-0.410*			-0.466*	-0.027
		[0.221]			[0.253]	[0.089]
Male		0.363			0.209	0.173
		[0.225]			[0.241]	[0.110]
Married		-0.891			-0.855***	0.214*
		[0.244]			[0.264]	[0.128]
Family size		-0.205***			-0.245***	-0.107***
		[0.074]			[0.083]	[0.038]

Born in Israel		1.010***		0.866***	0.377***
		[0.288]		[0.300]	[0.116]
Region dummies	no	yes	no	yes	yes
Predicted probability	0.005	0.003	0.026	0.002	0.019
Observations	16,789	16,789	15,948	15,948	
Chi-squared for same effect of wage			5.00**	1.87	

Note: Columns 1 and 2 present logit regressions on the sample of people living outside kibbutzim in 1983, where the dependent variable is equal to 1 if the individual moved to a kibbutz between 1983 and 1995. Columns 3 and 4 present multinomial logit regressions on the sample of people living in the city in 1983, where the base category is remained in the city, and the other options are moved to a kibbutz or moved to another rural area. All explanatory variables are measured in 1983, i.e., prior to exit. "High skill" signifies individuals working in either academic or managerial occupations. "Low skill" signifies individuals working either in unskilled occupations in industry or as service workers. A third omitted group contains all other occupations. "Israel's north region" includes the following districts: Sefad, Kinneret, Yizrael, Akko, and Golan. "Israel's south region" includes Ashkelon and Beer-Sheva districts. A third omitted group contains all other regions. Standard errors are given in brackets. The row "Chi-squared for same effect of wage" reports the chi-squared from the test that the coefficient on wage in the equation predicting moving to a kibbutz is the same as in the equation predicting moving to another rural area. Asterisks indicate significance at ***1% **5% *10%.

As an alternative test for negative selection in entry, I tested whether city-to-kibbutz migrants were more negatively selected on pre-entry unobservable abilities than both city stayers and city-to-other-rural migrants (see table 6.A2). Entrants to a kibbutz, ceteris paribus, were expected to earn lower pre-entry wages than both non-entrants and entrants to other rural areas. Formally, I ran the following OLS regressions (with and without the interactions of moving with education):

$$\ln wage_i^{83} = \alpha + x_i^{83} \cdot \beta + \delta_1 \cdot KibbutzEntrant_i$$
$$+ \delta_2 \cdot EducatedKibbutzEntrant_i + \varepsilon_i \qquad (1)$$

$$\ln wage_i^{83} = \alpha + x_i^{83} \cdot \beta + \delta_1 \cdot KibbutzEntrant_i$$
$$+ \delta_2 \cdot EducatedKibbutzEntrant_i + \delta_3 \cdot AnyRuralEntrant_i$$
$$+ \delta_4 \cdot EducatedAnyRuralEntrant_i + \varepsilon_i \qquad (2)$$

Where $\ln wage_i^{83}$ is the natural log of individual i's wage earned outside the kibbutz in 1983; x_i^{83} is a vector of characteristics of individual i believed to affect wages (including age, age squared, gender, a dummy for Israeli born, region dummies, education, and occupation); $KibbutzEntrant_i$ is a dummy indicating whether the individual entered a kibbutz between 1983 and 1995; $Educated$-$KibbutzEntrant_i$ is a dummy that equals 1 if individual i entered a kibbutz between 1983 and 1995 with at least a high school diploma (in 1983); $AnyRuralEntrant_i$ is a dummy that equals 1 if individual i entered either a kibbutz or another rural location; $Educated$-$AnyRuralEntrant_i$ is a dummy that equals 1 if individual i entered either a kibbutz or another rural location and had at least a high school diploma in 1983.

In regression equation (1), the earnings of city-to-kibbutz entrants were compared with the earnings of city stayers, and in regression equation (2) the earnings of kibbutz entrants were compared with the earnings of city-to-other rural migrants. If redistribution (income equality) in kibbutzim encouraged low earners to enter, then we should expect kibbutz entrants to earn less than both city stayers and city-to-other rural migrants, that is, I expect δ_1 to be negative in both regressions. The coefficient δ_2 in both regressions tests whether more educated people who entered a kibbutz earned especially lower wages, before they entered, relative to the average income of the educated person. More-educated people earn on average more than less-educated people. We may thus expect all uneducated people to seek to enter a kibbutz, where their earnings would be shared with more educated people. In contrast, we expect more educated people to only enter if they earn particularly low earnings relative to the kibbutz average (which means lower earnings than their more-educated peers); otherwise they would have no reason to enter a community that would have them share their earnings with less educated people.

Table 6.A2 presents the main results of selection in entry to the kibbutz. The regression results suggest that city-to-kibbutz migrants were negatively selected. Columns 1–3 present the results of the regression corresponding to equation 1 with and without controls. The coefficient on "entered kibbutz" (δ_1) is negative, large, and significant, suggesting that entrants to the kibbutz earned lower wages prior to entry than non-entrants. Column 3 reveals that the negative selection is coming from the more-educated entrants (δ_1 is close to zero and δ_2 is negative and large). In particular, people who entered a kibbutz with at least a high school diploma earned lower wages prior to entering a kibbutz than similarly educated city stayers.

The results from the regressions corresponding to equation 2, presented in columns 4–6, suggest that city-to-kibbutz migrants were more negatively selected than city-to-other rural migrants (i.e., δ_1 is negative). However, column 6 suggests that this negative selection was not more pronounced for more-educated kibbutz entrants.

As with exit, another way of illustrating that educated entrants to kibbutzim were negatively selected in their pre-entry wages is to compare the part of their wage that cannot be explained by the attributes I observed with that of non-entrants. Formally, I compared the density of kibbutz entrants' earnings residuals from an OLS regression of earnings on education, skill level, and controls with the density for non-entrants. Figure 6.A1 shows that the kernel density of the residuals for highly educated entrants to kibbutzim is shifted to the left of the density of others, whereas the residuals of less-educated entrants to kibbutzim lie to the right of the density

TABLE 6.A2: Pre-entry Earnings of City-to-Kibbutz Migrants, City-to-Other Rural Migrants, and Nonmigrants (OLS Regressions), 1983

Variable	(1)	(2)	(3)	(4)	(5)	(6)
			Comparing kibbutz entrants with:			
		Non-entrants			*City-to-other rural migrants*	
Entered kibbutz	-0.027***	-0.016**	0.003	-0.022**	-0.016**	-0.016
	(0.009)	(0.007)	(0.013)	(0.009)	(0.008)	(0.014)
Entered kibbutz * At least school diploma			-0.028*			-0.000
			(0.016)			(0.017)
Any migrant				-0.005	-0.000	0.019***
				(0.004)	(0.003)	(0.006)
Any migrant * At least high school diploma						-0.028***
						(0.007)
At least high school diploma		0.0206***	0.0208***		0.0206***	0.0214***
		(0.0011)	(0.0011)		(0.0011)	(0.0011)
High skill		0.0277***	0.0277***		0.0277***	0.0277***
		(0.0015)	(0.0015)		(0.0015)	(0.0015)
Low skill		-0.0266***	-0.0266***		-0.0266***	-0.0265***
		(0.0018)	(0.0018)		(0.0018)	(0.0018)
Age		0.1120***	0.1121***		0.1120***	0.1122***
		(0.0049)	(0.0049)		(0.0049)	(0.0049)
Age squared		-0.0128***	-0.0128***		-0.0128***	-0.0128***
		(0.0007)	(0.0007)		(0.0007)	(0.0007)

	(1)	(2)	(3)	(4)	(5)	(6)
Male		0.0538***	0.0538***		0.0538***	0.0539***
		(0.0010)	(0.0010)		(0.0010)	(0.0010)
Born in Israel		0.0068***	0.0068***		0.0068***	0.0069***
		(0.0011)	(0.0011)		(0.0011)	(0.0011)
Region dummies	no	yes	yes	no	yes	yes
R^2	0.001	0.279	0.279	0.001	0.279	0.280
Observations	15,948	15,948	15,948	15,948	15,948	15,948

Note: Each column in this table presents an OLS regression of the log of earnings in 1983 (scaled by 1/10) for individuals living in a specified type of area outside kibbutzim at the time. "Entered kibbutz" is a dummy variable that equals 1 if the individual moved to a kibbutz between 1983 and 1995. "Entered kibbutz . At least high school diploma" is the interaction of "Entered kibbutz" with a dummy variable that equals 1 if the individual had at least a high school diploma in 1983. "Any migrant" is a dummy variable that equals 1 if the individual moved from a city to either a kibbutz or a non-kibbutz rural location between 1983 and 1995. "Any migrant . At least high school diploma" is the interaction of "Any migrant" and a dummy variable that equals 1 if the individual had at least a high school diploma in 1983. All other explanatory variables are measured in 1983 (before exit). "High skill" signifies individuals who worked in either academic or managerial occupations. "Low skill" signifies individuals who worked either in unskilled occupations in industry or as service workers. A third omitted group contains all other occupations. "Israel's north region" includes the following districts: Sefad, Kinneret, Yizrael, Akko, and Golan. "Israel's south region" includes Ashkelon and Beer-Sheva districts. A third omitted group contains all other regions. Standard errors are given in parentheses.

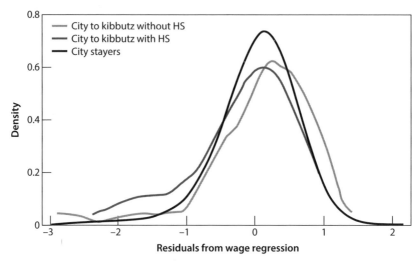

FIGURE 6.A1: Highly educated entrants earned less than highly educated non-entrants; less educated entrants did not earn less than less educated non-entrants. This figure plots kernel densities of residuals from an OLS regression of log earnings in 1983 on a dummy variable for having at least a high school diploma, dummies for having a high-skill or low-skill occupation, age and age squared, dummies for being male and for being born in Israel, and region dummies. The sample is Jewish individuals living in cities in 1983. All explanatory variables are measured in 1983. "City to kibbutz without HS" denotes people without high school diplomas who moved to a kibbutz between 1983 and 1995. "City to kibbutz with HS" denotes people with at least high school diplomas who moved to a kibbutz between 1983 and 1995. "City stayers" denotes people who were still living in a city in 1995.

for others. Consistent with economic theory, this figure suggests that highly educated people who entered a kibbutz were adversely selected—they earned lower wages than similarly highly educated people who didn't enter. In contrast, less-educated people who entered a kibbutz did not earn less than similarly less educated people who did not enter.

APPENDIX: BRAIN DRAIN

This appendix subjects the data to a more formal econometric regression analysis. I will use the familiar linear regression (OLS) along with different regression methods. This analysis is important because it allowed me to test whether the more-educated and higher-skilled members were more likely to exit even when accounting for the different tendency to exit of members with different age, gender, marital status, and country of birth. I can thus test whether brain drain occurred even among members with similar personal characteristics. The regression analysis also allowed me to test directly how much more pronounced the brain drain was from kibbutzim relative to other rural places.

To do so, I used the individual-level data to test the prediction that more-productive individuals are more likely to exit under equal sharing. To test for selection in exit, I ran a so-called probit regression analysis, which is an econometric procedure that examines whether members with higher education and more-skilled occupation, who otherwise were of the same age, marital status, family size, and country of birth, were more likely to exit. For those familiar with regression analysis, I ran a probit regression where the dependent variable takes the value 1 if the individual left the kibbutz (between 1983 and 1995). This regression is a reduced-form specification of individuals' decisions on whether to stay or leave. Intuitively, the probit regression analysis assumes that an individual chooses whether to exit based on her demographic characteristics and how much she values living in a kibbutz, in a city and in a moshav or other rural place.

Table 6.A3 suggests that kibbutz-to-city migrants are more educated and more skilled than stayers. Column 1 shows the average demographics of individuals who stayed in their kibbutz between 1983 and 1995; column 2 shows the average characteristics of people who left their kibbutz for a city during this period; and column 3 shows the marginal increase in the chance of leaving the kibbutz.

The regression analysis suggests that having at least a high school education increases the probability of exit by 9.8 percentage points as compared with members having less than a high school education. Members with high-skill occupations are over 8 percentage points more likely to leave the kibbutz, and members with low-skill occupation are over 9 percentage points less likely to exit as compared with those having medium-skill occupations.

TABLE 6.A3: Who Chose to Exit the Kibbutz, 1983–1995

	Stayed in kibbutz	Left the kibbutz	Increase chance of leaving by
	(1)	(2)	(3)
At least high school diploma	50%	61.9%	9.8%*** [0.021]
High skill	8.4%	9.9%	8.4%** [0.043]
Low skill	22.6%	13.4%	−9.2%** [0.023]
Age	36.295	29.609	−3.8%*** [0.011]
Born in Israel	66.9%	72.9%	−4.5%* [0.025]
Married	79.6%	56.6%	−6.4%* [0.038]
Family size	3.57	2.708	−0. 06% [0.01]
Israel's north region	52.4%	52.2%	5.0%** [0.024]
Israel's south region	19.9%	25.7%	−5.5%* [0.033]
Observations	1,234	343	1,577
Predicted exit probability			18.2%
LR²			237.7

Note: The dependent variable in column 3 equals 1 if the individual exited from the kibbutz and 0 otherwise. The coefficients reported are marginal probabilities of exit. Entries in column 1 represent the mean characteristics of individuals who stayed in their kibbutz between 1983 and 1995. Entries in column 2 represent the mean characteristics of individuals who left their kibbutz between 1983 and 1995. "High skill" signifies individuals working in either academic or managerial occupations. "Low skill" signifies individuals working either in unskilled occupations in industry or as service workers. A third omitted group contains all other occupations. "Israel's north region" includes the following districts: Sefad, Kinneret, Yizrael, Akko, and Golan. "Israel's south region" includes Ashkelon and Beer-Sheva districts. A third omitted group contains all other regions. Standard errors in brackets. "Predicted exit probability" is the predicted probability of the average kibbutz member to exit. All explanatory variables are measured in 1983 (before exit), t-test significant at ***1%, **5%, *10%.

One potential issue with the interpretation of this regression analysis as brain drain from kibbutzim, is that the skill bias in exit could be attributed to "selective" investment in human capital. That is, members who intended to leave invested more in their skills because they would get greater returns to these skills outside the kibbutz. Under this alternative story, two members of equal talent would acquire different levels of education and skills depending on whether they planned to exit. Members who planned to leave would acquire more education and skill, and this departure would generate a positive correlation between education and the propensity to exit that has nothing to do with brain drain.

Note that the period of study is one of increased migration (over 20% of members in the sample exit between 1983 and 1995) following the financial crisis. Under these circumstances, the finding that educated and skilled members were more likely to move probably reflects brain drain and unlikely reflects the alternative story of differential investment in human capital depending on intention to exit.

To disentangle brain drain more formally, I conducted the same analysis on subsamples of members who were over 30, 35, and 40 years of age in 1983. The older members had already invested in their human capital years before the period studied here (probably with the intention of staying; otherwise they would have left much earlier) and their decisions were less likely to represent selective investment in human capital. In the context of the kibbutz, it was even more costly for members to exit at an older age, because they couldn't save money for the move and couldn't take their share upon leaving.

The results of the probit regression for subsamples of individuals at different ages are reported in table 6.A4. The first column considers all individuals over age 21 in 1983. The second column considers only members who were at least 30 in 1983. The third column considers members over 35 and the fourth column considers individuals over 40. The regression results suggest that, in all age groups, the more-educated and higher-skilled workers were more likely to exit, and the lower-skilled workers were less likely to exit. That is, the effects of education and skill on the probability of migrating were large and statistically significant, even when focusing on older members whose education was completed years before they migrated.

One issue with the interpretation of the finding that educated and skilled members were more likely to exit is that this finding has nothing to do with brain drain as a result of equal sharing in kibbutzim, but rather represents a general pattern of rural-to-urban migration. To overcome this issue, I compared kibbutz members

TABLE 6.A4: Probit Analysis of Exit from the Kibbutz
between 1983 and 1995, by Age

Variable	Marginal exit probabilities for individuals of age			
	≥ 21	≥ 30	≥ 35	≥ 40
	(1)	(2)	(3)	(4)
At least high school diploma	9.8%***	5.9%***	7.1%***	5.5%**
	[0.021]	[0.019]	[0.022]	[0.024]
High skill	8.4%**	8.0%**	8.8%**	12.8%***
	[0.043]	[0.037]	[0.043]	[0.053]
Low skill	−9.2%**	−7.2%***	−6.1%**	−2.5%
	[0.023]	[0.021]	[0.024]	[0.029]
Age	−3.8%***	3.4%	−5.1%	−16%
	[0.011]	[0.023]	[0.044]	[0.093]
Age squared	0. 03%**	−00.05%*	0.05%	0. 2%
	[0.0002]	[0.0003]	[0.0005]	[0.001]
Male	2.2%	2.2%	1.1%	2.2%
	[0.022]	[0.020]	[0.022]	[0.024]
Born in Israel	−4.5%*	−5.6%***	−4.0%*	−0. 9%
	[0.025]	[0.021]	[0.022]	[0.023]
Married	−6.4%*	−0.5%	−2.6%	−0. 2%
	[0.038]	[0.040]	[0.050]	[0.045]
Family size	−0. 06%	−0. 6%	−0. 4%	−1.4%
	[0.01]	[0.009]	[0.010]	[0.011]
Israel's north region	5.0%**	3.4%	2.6%	−0. 2%
	[0.024]	[0.023]	[0.025]	[0.026]
Israel's south region	−5.5%*	2.1%	−1.7%	−0. 7%
	[0.033]	[0.032]	[0.031]	[0.032]
Observations	1,577	1,085	773	457
Predicted probability	18.2%	10.9%	9.8%	6.1%
LR²	237.7	61.63	53.57	33.63

Note: The dependent variable equals 1 if the individual exited from the kibbutz and 0 otherwise. Each of columns 1–4 reports regression results for subsamples of individuals at different ages. The coefficients reported are marginal probabilities. "High skill" signifies individuals working in either academic or managerial occupations. "Low skill" signifies individuals working either in unskilled occupations in industry or as service workers. A third omitted group contains all other occupations. "Israel's north region" includes the following districts: Sefad, Kinneret, Yizrael, Akko, and Golan. "Israel's south region" includes Ashkelon and Beer-Sheva districts. A third omitted group contains all other regions. Standard errors in brackets. All explanatory variables are measured in 1983 (before exit). t-test significant at ***1%, **5%, *10%.

who stayed with those who moved to other rural locations. Table 6.A5 shows that the finding that more-educated and higher-skilled members left their kibbutz was true not only among members who left to a city but also among members who left for other rural locations, suggesting brain drain away from equal sharing among rural-to-rural migrants.

Another approach was to try to predict the earnings of kibbutz members upon moving, and test whether members who expected higher earnings were more likely to exit. Econometrically, the idea is to predict the (natural log of) earnings upon moving, which is the 1995 city log of earnings expected by a mover with certain observable characteristics from 1983 (obtained from an OLS regression of 1995 city log of earnings on education, high- and low-skill occupations, and controls).[24] I ran logit regressions, which are similar in spirit to the probit regressions discussed above, that take the value 1 if the individual left the kibbutz between 1983 and 1995, and I tested whether higher-skilled members were more likely to leave their kibbutz, and whether they were more likely to move than higher-skilled individuals in other rural areas.

Table 6.A6 suggests that kibbutz members who left were more educated, were higher skilled, and could expect higher earnings upon exit than stayers. The first two columns present the results from alternative specifications of the logit regression. In column 1, the coefficient on having at least a high school diploma is 0.656, suggesting that having at least a high school education increases the probability of exit by 9.4 percentage points,[25] which is more than 50 percent of the average probability of exit, 17.5 percent. Members

---

[24] The coefficients of interest from this regression are: 0.352 on education, 0.360 on high skill, and 0.216 on low skill. This suggests that having at least a high school diploma increases predicted outside-of-kibbutz earnings by 35.2%, having a high-skill occupation increases expected earnings by 36.0%, and having a low-skill occupation decreases expected earnings by 21.6%. The controls are the same as those I later use in the logit regression.

[25] A probit regression model outputs coefficients that are harder to interpret. Thus the 0.656 magnitude is not a percentage increase. In order to get the percentage increase, one needs to do a short calculation, resulting in the 9.4%. For further information, see Wooldridge (2015).

TABLE 6.A5: Summary Statistics, Probit and Multinomial Logit of Exit from Kibbutzim, 1983–1995

	(1)	(2)	(3)	(4)	(5)	
	Stayed in kibbutz	Moved to city	Moved to other rural	Probit of exit	Multinomial logit of exit	
				Marginal effects	Coefficients	
Variable	Mean	Mean	Mean		Moved to city	Moved to other rural
At least high school diploma	0.500	0.615	0.630	0.098***	0.677***	0.580**
	(0.500)	(0.488)	(0.486)	(0.021)	(0.159)	(0.258)
High skill	0.084	0.099	0.099	0.084**	0.550**	0.348
	(0.278)	(0.300)	(0.300)	(0.043)	(0.257)	(0.417)
Low skill	0.226	0.149	0.086	-0.092***	-0.527**	-1.292***
	(0.418)	(0.357)	(0.283)	(0.023)	(0.213)	(0.427)
Age	36.295	29.500	29.963	-0.038***	-0.236***	-0.279*
	(8.719)	(7.900)	(7.279)	(0.011)	(0.080)	(0.147)
Age squared	1393	932	950	0.0003**	0.002*	0.002
	(649)	(532)	(478)	(0.0002)	(0.001)	(0.002)
Male	0.494	0.550	0.543	0.022	0.150	0.099
	(0.500)	(0.498)	(0.501)	(0.022)	(0.160)	(0.254)
Married	0.796	0.523	0.704	-0.064*	-0.527**	0.159
	(0.403)	(0.500)	(0.459)	(0.038)	(0.252)	(0.407)
Family size	3.570	2.576	3.136	-0.001	-0.031	0.099
	(1.627)	(1.663)	(1.730)	(0.011)	(0.079)	(0.124)

Born in Israel	0.669	0.752	0.654	−0.045*	−0.186	−0.620**
	(0.471)	(0.433)	(0.479)	(0.025)	(0.176)	(0.264)
Israel's north region	0.524	0.508	0.568	0.050**	0.250	0.639**
	(0.500)	(0.501)	(0.498)	(0.024)	(0.180)	(0.321)
Israel's south region	0.199	0.256	0.259	0.055*	0.318	0.536
	(0.400)	(0.437)	(0.441)	(0.033)	(0.176)	(0.367)
Observations	1234	262	81	1,577		1,577

Note: Dependent variable in probit regressions is equal to 1 if the person left a kibbutz. Dependent variable in multinomial logit regressions is equal to 0 if the person stayed in a kibbutz, 1 if the person moved to a city, and 2 if the person moved to another rural location. All explanatory variables are measured in 1983, i.e., prior to exit. "High skill" signifies individuals working in either academic or managerial occupations. "Low skill" signifies individuals working either in unskilled occupations in industry or as service workers. A third omitted group contains all other occupations. "Israel's north region" includes the following districts: Sefad, Kinneret, Yizrael, Akko, and Golan. "Israel's south region" includes Ashkelon and Beer-Sheva districts. A third omitted group contains all other regions. Standard errors in parentheses. t-test difference in means significant at ***1% **5% *10%.

TABLE 6.A6: Exit from Kibbutzim and Other Rural Areas (Logit and Multinomial Logit Regressions), 1983–1995

Variable	(1)	(2)	(3)	(4)	(5)	(6)	(7)
	Logit of exit from kibbutz	Multinomial logit of exit from kibbutz to		Logit of exit to city of kibbutz members relative to residents of			
		City	Other rural	Other rural areas		Other non-metropolitan rural	
Kibbutz* Predicted 1995 log earnings				0.777**	0.413*	0.965***	0.461**
				[0.326]	[0.223]	[0.334]	[0.229]
Kibbutz				-6.863**	-3.602*	-8.396***	-3.920**
				[2.772]	[1.900]	[2.838]	[1.954]
Predicted 1995 log earnings	1.922***	1.900***	1.986***	0.177	1.306**	-0.01	1.238***
	[0.284]	[0.314]	[0.500]	[0.225]	[0.222]	[0.237]	[0.232]
At least high school diploma	0.656***						
	[0.144]						
High skill	0.502**						
	[0.233]						
Low skill	-0.682***						
	[0.197]						
Age (/10)	-2.416***	-3.843***	-4.224***		-3.095***		-3.035***
	[0.744]	[0.865]	[1.550]		[0.517]		[0.536]
Age squared (/100)	0.201*	0.413***	0.414*		0.329***		0.311***
	[0.103]	[0.120]	[0.218]		[0.073]		[0.076]
Male	0.137	-0.982***	-0.958**		-0.894***		-0.854***
	[0.144]	[0.247]	[0.399]		[0.146]		[0.149]

Married	−0.391*	−0.478**	−0.608**	0.035	−0.753***	−0.760***
	[0.228]	[0.229]	[0.253]	[0.410]	[0.124]	[0.126]
Family size	−0.002	0.027	−0.002	0.119	0.041	0.051*
	[0.071]	[0.071]	[0.079]	[0.124]	[0.027]	[0.027]
Born in Israel	−0.297*	−0.492***	−0.382**	−0.798***	−0.506***	−0.494***
	[0.157]	[0.160]	[0.180]	[0.268]	[0.112]	[0.116]
Region dummies	Yes	Yes	Yes	Yes	Yes	Yes
Predicted probability	0.175	0.176	0.134	0.039	0.212	0.202
Observations	1,577	1,577	1,577	3,091	3,091	3,044

Note: Columns 1 and 2 present logit regressions on the sample of kibbutz members where the dependent variable is equal to 1 if the individual left his kibbutz between 1983 and 1995. Column 3 presents a multinomial logit regression on the sample of kibbutz members, where the base category is remained in the kibbutz, and the other options are moved to a city or moved to another rural area. Columns 4–7 present logits of moving to the city using the sample of individuals living in either a kibbutz or other rural area in 1983. All explanatory variables are measured in 1983, i.e., prior to exit. "High skill" signifies individuals working in either academic or managerial occupations. "Low skill" signifies individuals working either in unskilled occupations in industry or as service workers. A third omitted group contains all other occupations. "Israel's north region" includes the following districts: Sefad, Kinneret, Yizrael, Akko, and Golan. "Israel's south region" includes Ashkelon and Beer-Sheva districts. A third omitted group contains all other regions. Standard errors are given in brackets. Asterisks indicate the coefficient is significant at ***1% **5% *10%.

with high-skill occupations are over 8.2 percentage points more likely to exit than members with medium-skill occupations (the omitted skill category against which the effects of high and low skills are shown), and low-skill members are 8.7 percentage points less likely to exit.[26] The second column shows that the coefficient on predicted log of earnings is 1.92, suggesting that kibbutz members with a standard deviation higher log of expected earnings (which, at the mean, corresponds to 2,400 shekels) were 12 percentage points more likely to exit.[27]

Since kibbutzim are located in rural areas, a possible concern is that kibbutz movers were positively selected because rural-to-urban migrants tend to be positively selected rather than because of the intensive redistribution in kibbutzim. To account for this possibility, I tested whether kibbutz members who moved to other rural locations that did not engage in intensive redistribution are also positively selected on observable characteristics. Specifically, I ran a multinomial logit regression analysis that explicitly models the possibility that members will stay in their kibbutz, move to a city, or move to another rural location. Column 3 of table 6.2 suggests that kibbutz members with higher skills were more likely to exit, both to cities and to rural locations where earnings were not based on equal sharing.

As a robustness check, to account for the possibility that non-kibbutz rural areas also included rural communities that might be more similar to suburbs of major cities than to rural areas, I also categorized such rural communities as cities rather than as rural areas. The results (not presented) remained the same under this

[26] When the regression uses either education or high/low-skill occupations (but not both), the coefficients on education and skill are even larger in magnitude. When the regression uses the eight occupation categories provided by the census instead of dummies for high-, low-, and medium-skill occupations, the regression shows that kibbutz members with academic occupations are the most likely to exit and that unskilled industrial workers are the least likely to exit. Finally, results are similar when using a BA degree instead of a high school diploma as the measure of education.

[27] A coefficient of 1.92 corresponds to a marginal probability of 0.279. An increase in a standard deviation in predicted log of earnings (which is 0.425) thus corresponds to 0.279*0.425, which is 0.12.

specification.[28] These findings support the idea that equal sharing, rather than the preference of productive individuals for living in the city, drove out educated and skilled kibbutz members.

A related possible issue with the interpretation of the findings as brain drain is that it is possible, and plausible, that more-educated and higher-skilled people are more likely to move simply because they are more mobile in the sense that they have fewer structural barriers to moving. To address this concern, I tested whether kibbutz members with higher observable skills were more likely to move than high-skill individuals from other rural locations that did not engage in intensive redistribution. Specifically, I examined people who lived in either a kibbutz or other rural area in 1983 and either stayed or left by 1995. The idea was to test whether educated and skilled kibbutz members were more likely to move, compared with educated and skilled people who lived in other rural localities. Formally, I ran a logit regression where the dependent variable takes the value 1 if the individual moved to a city between 1983 and 1995, and the main explanatory variable of interest is an interaction term of whether the individual lived in a kibbutz in 1983 and had high skills.

Columns 4 and 5 of table 6.A6 above present the regression results. The regressions suggest that kibbutz members with higher skills were more likely to move than were high-skill people living in other rural areas. The coefficient on the interaction term in the logit regression is 0.413 (0.777 in the regression without controls), suggesting that a one standard deviation increase in expected log earnings increased the probability of moving by 3 percentage points more for kibbutz members than for other rural people.[29] Specifically, kibbutz members whose expected log earnings upon moving are a standard deviation higher are 12 percentage points more likely to exit than their lower-earning counterparts; this difference is only

[28] The coefficients on "Predicted 1995 log of earnings" in a regression similar to column 3 are 1.945 (city) and 1.826 (rural), and they have the same significance level as those in column 3.

[29] A coefficient of 0.413 corresponds to a marginal probability of 0.069. A one standard deviation (which is 0.425) increase in predicted log of earnings thus correponds to 0.069*0.425, which is 0.03.

9 percentage points for similar non-kibbutz individuals. This difference between the effect of expected earnings on the exit probabilities of kibbutz members and of non-kibbutz individuals, which is statistically significant at the 10 percent level (5% in the regression without controls), amounts to 15 percent of the average 21 percent predicted probability of moving. As a robustness check, I restricted the sample of rural areas to only include individuals who in 1983 lived in rural areas outside of metropolitan areas. Columns 3 and 4 of table 6.2 suggest that results were similar when looking at this comparison group.

Do Kibbutz-Members Who Exit Earn More than Similarly Skilled Workers in the City?

Formally, to test how kibbutz-to-city migrants perform in the city labor market, I ran the following OLS regressions of 1995 city earnings on characteristics in 1983 and dummy variables for whether the individual exited from a kibbutz, and whether he exited with a high level of education (I run these regressions with and without the interaction of exit with education):

$$\ln wage_i^{95} = \alpha + x_i^{83} \cdot \beta + \delta_1 \cdot KibbutzMigrant_i$$
$$+ \delta_2 \cdot EducatedKibbutzMigrant_i + \varepsilon_i \qquad (3)$$

Where $\ln wage_i^{95}$ is the natural log of 1995 wage of individual i in the city; x_i^{83} is individual i's 1983 characteristics expected to affect her wage; $KibbutzMigrant_i$ is a dummy variable that equals 1 if individual i left her kibbutz between 1983 and 1995; $EducatedKibbutzMigrant_i$ is a dummy variable that equals 1 if individual i left her kibbutz between 1983 and 1995, and had at least a high school diploma in 1983. In the absence of the interaction with education, the coefficient δ_1 tests whether kibbutz-to-city migrants had pre-move unobservable characteristics that were associated with higher post-move wages than city natives. When the interaction with education is added, the coefficient δ_1 tests whether less-educated kibbutz-to-city migrants earned higher wages than less-educated city natives, and δ_2 tests the hypothesis that this effect is smaller for more-educated migrants.

The first two columns of table 6.A7 present the results of OLS regressions of 1995 city earnings on 1983 (pre-moving) characteristics. The regressions suggest that the average kibbutz mover earned higher wages than the average city native, indicating that kibbutz movers had unobservable characteristics that were associated with higher wages in the outside labor market. Kibbutz members without high school diplomas who moved to cities earned 18 percent more than others with their education level living in the city, but educated kibbutz movers did not earn higher wages than similar city natives (i.e., δ_2 is negative and similar in magnitude to δ_1).[30] It is very natural for less-educated people to stay in the kibbutz and be subsidized by other more-educated members. It is thus not surprising that those less-educated members who nevertheless chose to leave were positively selected on unobservable abilities such as motivation and ambition. In contrast, it is more natural for high school graduates to leave the kibbutz, and perhaps they did not do as well in the city because their high schools were not as good or because they did not put much effort into their schooling, thinking they would stay in their kibbutz.

Another way of illustrating that kibbutz members who left, especially the less-educated, were positively selected on unobservable abilities such as motivation and ambition is to graph the part of the post-exit wages of members who left their kibbutz that cannot be explained in the statistical analysis by any of the observed variables (such as age, gender, marital status, and place of birth), called the kernel density of the residuals. Formally, the idea is to compare the density of the OLS residuals from the regression of 1995 earnings on skill level of occupation, education, and other controls for kibbutz-leavers with the density for the rest of the population (along the lines of Dinardo, Fortin, and Lemieux 1996). Figure 6.A2 shows that the kernel density of the residuals for more-educated kibbutz members who left largely overlaps with the density for others, while

---

[30] A similar regression of 1995 rural earnings shows that kibbutz-to-rural migrants earn higher wages than rural natives, and that this premium is also mainly driven by less-educated kibbutz leavers, who earned 37% more than similar rural natives.

TABLE 6.A7: Earnings in 1995 of Kibbutz-to-City Migrants vs. Other Rural-to-City Migrants (OLS Regressions)

Variable	(1)	(2)	(3)	(4)	(5)	(6)
			Comparing kibbutz migrants with			
	City natives		*Other rural migrants*		*Other rural migrants from outside metropolitan areas*	
Kibbutz migrant	0.068	0.181***	0.098*	0.170**	0.110**	0.169*
	[0.043]	[0.068]	[0.054]	[0.086]	[0.055]	[0.087]
Kibbutz migrant × At least high school diploma		-0.184**		-0.113		-0.088
		[0.086]		[0.111]		[0.112]
Any migrant			-0.032	0.011	-0.044	0.012
			[0.035]	[0.054]	[0.037]	[0.055]
Any migrant × At least high school diploma				-0.073		-0.099
				[0.071]		[0.073]
At least high school diploma	0.357***	0.359***	0.357***	0.361***	0.358***	0.362***
	[0.010]	[0.010]	[0.010]	[0.010]	[0.010]	[0.010]
High skill	0.363***	0.362***	0.363***	0.362***	0.363***	0.362***
	[0.015]	[0.015]	[0.015]	[0.015]	[0.015]	[0.015]
Low skill	-0.226***	-0.226***	-0.226***	-0.226***	-0.226***	-0.226***
	[0.017]	[0.017]	[0.017]	[0.017]	[0.017]	[0.017]
Age (/10)	0.870***	0.871***	0.869***	0.871***	0.869***	0.871***
	[0.042]	[0.042]	[0.042]	[0.042]	[0.042]	[0.042]
Age squared (/100)	-0.121***	-0.121***	-0.121***	-0.121***	-0.121***	-0.121***
	[0.006]	[0.006]	[0.006]	[0.006]	[0.006]	[0.006]

Male	0.600***	0.600***	0.601***	0.601***	0.601***	0.601***
	[0.010]	[0.010]	[0.010]	[0.010]	[0.010]	[0.010]
Born in Israel	0.113***	0.113***	0.113***	0.113***	0.113***	0.113***
	[0.010]	[0.010]	[0.010]	[0.010]	[0.010]	[0.010]
Region dummies	Yes	Yes	Yes	Yes	Yes	Yes
R²	0.264	0.264	0.265	0.265	0.265	0.265
Observations	21,150	21,150	21,132	21,132	21,132	21,132

Note: Each column in this table presents an OLS regression of log earnings in 1995 for individuals living in the city in 1995. "Kibbutz migrant" is a dummy variable for individuals who lived in a kibbutz in 1983. "Kibbutz migrant × At least high school diploma" is a dummy variable for people who lived in a kibbutz and had at least a high school diploma in 1983. "Any migrant" is a dummy variable for people who lived in either a kibbutz or a non-kibbutz rural area in 1983 and lived in a city in 1995. "Any migrant" is a dummy variable for people who lived in either a kibbutz or a non-kibbutz rural area in 1983 and lived in a city in 1995. "Any migrant × At least high school diploma" is the interaction of the previous variable with a dummy for having at least a high school diploma in 1983. All the other explanatory variables are measured in 1983 (before exit). "High skill" signifies individuals who worked in either academic or managerial occupations. "Low skill" signifies individuals who worked either in unskilled occupations in industry or as service workers. A third omitted group contains all other occupations. "Region dummies" include dummy variables for Israel's north region and Israel's south region, and a third omitted group that contains all other regions. Standard errors are given in brackets.

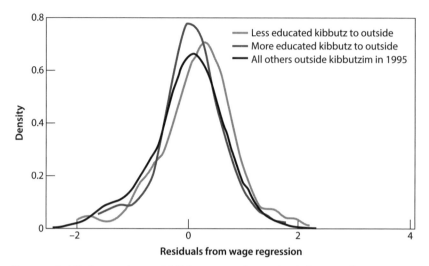

FIGURE 6.A2: Less-educated kibbutz members who left earned more than similarly educated nonmembers. This figure plots kernel densities of residuals from an OLS regression of log earnings in 1995 on a dummy variable for having at least a high school diploma, dummies for having a high-skill or low-skill occupation, age and age squared, dummies for being male and for being born in Israel, and region dummies. The sample is Jewish people living outside kibbutzim in 1995. All explanatory variables are measured in 1983. "Uneducated kibbutz to outside" denotes people without high school diplomas who exited a kibbutz between 1983 and 1995. "Educated kibbutz to outside" denotes people with at least high school diplomas who exited a kibbutz between 1983 and 1995. "All others outside kibbutzim in 1995" denotes Jewish individuals who lived outside kibbutzim in both 1983 and 1995.

the density for less-educated kibbutz members who left is shifted to the right of the density of others. These graphs support the hypothesis that less-educated kibbutz members who left ended up earning more than their observable characteristics would suggest, meaning they had characteristics unobservable to the researcher (but observable to the employer)—for example, high motivation—that were associated with higher wages. Beyond motivation, ambition, and charm, military service was another unobservable characteristic that would be observable to the employer but not the researcher. Employers might be rewarding service in elite units in the military, and kibbutz members disproportionately served in such units. Unfortunately, I could not find data connecting military service to kibbutz members.

Next, I tested whether kibbutz-to-city migrants were more positively selected on unobservable abilities than other rural-to-urban migrants. Specifically, I tested whether the wages of kibbutz-to-city migrants were higher than the wages of other rural-to-city migrants, and whether this wage premium was higher for less-educated kibbutz members. I ran the following OLS regressions (with and without the interactions of moving with education):

$$\ln wage_i^{95} = \alpha + x_i^{83} \cdot \beta + \delta_1 \cdot KibbutzMigrant_i$$
$$+ \delta_2 \cdot EducatedKibbutzMigrant_i + \delta_3 \cdot AnyRuralMigrant_i$$
$$+ \delta_4 \cdot EducatedAnyRuralMigrant_i + \varepsilon_i \qquad (4)$$

Where $\ln wage_i^{95}$ is the natural log of 1995 wage of individual i in the city; x_i^{83} is individual i's 1983 characteristics expected to affect her wage; $KibbutzMigrant_i$ is a dummy variable that equals 1 if individual i left her kibbutz between 1983 and 1995; $EducatedKibbutzMigrant_i$ is a dummy variable that equals 1 if individual i left her kibbutz between 1983 and 1995, and had at least a high school diploma in 1983; $AnyRuralMigrant_i$ is a dummy variable that equals 1 if individual i left either a kibbutz or any other rural location between 1983 and 1995; and $EducatedAnyRuralMigrant_i$ is a dummy variable that equals 1 if individual i left either a kibbutz or any other rural location in the same period and had at least a high school diploma in 1983. In the absence of interactions with education, the coefficient δ_1 tests whether kibbutz-to-city migrants earned higher wages than other rural-to-city migrants. When interactions with education are added, the coefficient δ_1 tests whether less-educated kibbutz-to-city migrants earned higher wages than less-educated other rural-to-city migrants, and δ_2 tests whether this effect is smaller for more-educated migrants.

The OLS regression results are shown in columns 3 and 4 of table 6.A7. Column 3 shows that kibbutz-to-city migrants earn higher wages than other rural-to-city migrants. Column 4 shows that this result is mainly driven by the less-educated kibbutz-to-city migrants, who earn higher wages than other less-educated rural-to-city migrants. This earnings premium is smaller for more-educated kibbutz-to-city migrants, though the coefficient on the interaction of a kibbutz migrant with at least a high school education (δ_2) is not statistically significant.[31] Columns 5 and 6 show that these results are robust when comparing kibbutz-to-city movers to individuals who moved to a city from other rural areas located outside of metropolitan areas.

Wages of former kibbutz members outside depended on a number of factors (column 4). As expected, more-educated individuals fared better and so did members with academic and managerial occupations. Unskilled workers in industry and service workers who left the kibbutz could expect to earn less outside the kibbutz than did other industry and service workers. Income was larger for older individuals, but its rate of increase decreases with age. Men earned higher incomes than women outside the kibbutz.

---

[31] I note that while I can reject the hypothesis that less-educated kibbutz-to-city migrants earn the same as less-educated other rural migrants (i.e. δ_1 is positive and significant), I cannot reject the hypothesis that more-educated kibbutz-to-city migrants earn the same as other more-educated rural-to-city migrants (i.e. that $\delta_1 + \delta_2 = 0$).

CHAPTER 7

The problem of human capital investment

Amos Oz, one of Israel's most celebrated authors, recalled: "I was a disaster as a laborer. I became the joke of the kibbutz." When his book *My Michael* turned out to be a bestseller, Oz "became a branch of the farm, yet they still said I could have just three days a week to write," he recalled. "It was only in the eighties when I got four days for my writing, two days for teaching, and Saturday turns as a waiter in the dining hall."[1]

Why would a kibbutz member study hard if a high school dropout working in the kibbutz kitchen and a computer scientist running the most profitable business in the kibbutz enjoyed the same living standards? Did kibbutz members put less effort into gaining an education and developing skills than did those outside of kibbutzim? How did the kibbutz decide on the appropriate level and type of education for its members and encourage them to attain it?

INVESTMENT IN EDUCATION— THE KIBBUTZ POINT OF VIEW

From kibbutzim's perspective, solving the human capital problem was always challenging. Kibbutzim had conflicting incentives to invest in members' human capital, many of which stemmed from

---

[1] From David Remnick, "The Spirit Level," *New Yorker*, November 8, 2004, http://www.newyorker.com/magazine/2004/11/08/the-spirit-level.

the tension between desiring their members to be skilled and thus productive, and not wanting them to be lured away by the rewards for their skill in the outside world. As employers, kibbutzim had incentives to make it difficult for productive members to leave. To this end, they preferred members to acquire kibbutz-specific, rather than general, human capital. They also encouraged occupations that facilitated mutual monitoring and peer pressure to minimize shirking. Sending members to university did not just cost the kibbutz money, but also lost the kibbutz the member's labor while she studied. Finally, as communities that provided insurance, kibbutzim benefited from having members working in diverse industries and in different occupations. In these ways, kibbutzim as employers have much in common with professional partnerships.

Kibbutz members, like lawyers, base their partnership on revenue sharing and enjoy valuable insurance against shocks to their income and human capital. Both kibbutzim and law firms try to make it costly for partners to leave by forcing them to lose some of their investment upon leaving (e.g., local public goods in the kibbutz, customers in law firms). In both kibbutzim and law firms, the best partners tend to leave, and both entities rely on mutual monitoring and peer pressure to alleviate shirking. However, partnerships tend to be more prevalent among professionals (lawyers, medical groups) and less prevalent in industry (plywood cooperatives are an exception). One reason advanced in the literature for this fact is that professionals have invested heavily in their human capital and would like insurance for shocks to the value of their specific skills. Partnerships tend to be homogenous in their occupations (i.e., only lawyers, not lawyers and doctors together), which enables better mutual monitoring. Kibbutzim, in contrast, have members with various occupations and tend to be concentrated in agriculture and industry, rather than in professional occupations. The greater diversity in occupations allows the kibbutzim to provide potentially better insurance than professional partnerships but makes monitoring more difficult.[2]

---

[2] For a relevant literature on partnerships, see, e.g., Ward (1958); Farrell and Scotchmer (1988); Kandel and Lazear (1992); Lang and Gordon (1995); Gaynor and Gertler (1995); Craig and Pencavel (1992); Levin and Tadelis (2005);

As an extended family, a kibbutz would like its children to be educated, even if members might subsequently leave. This is true especially since many of the founders of kibbutzim were intellectuals who valued education highly. Even from an employer's perspective, kibbutzim have an incentive to encourage members to acquire education and skill for a number of reasons.

The first reason is that members surrender their entire incomes to the kibbutz even if they are very high. In economic terminology, the kibbutz receives the full returns to the human capital of its members.

The second reason is that if all members are equally highly educated and skilled, equal sharing of member incomes will be easier to maintain. Large differences in human capital levels among members threaten the stability of kibbutzim, because members with human capital levels above that of the average member face financial incentives to exit. As a result, kibbutzim should be concerned not only about the average level of education of their members, but also about educational disparities among them. Note that we expect equality to be easier to maintain if only basic education is encouraged: most members would benefit from basic education, whereas higher education is expected to disproportionately benefit the most productive members, thus exacerbating initial differences in earnings potential.

The last reason is that a member who is not permitted to study the subject she is passionate about, or who is prohibited from pursuing her dream career, might leave the kibbutz in order to pursue her interests. The kibbutz would lose the contributions of talented members who would have stayed if only they were allowed to pursue their desired field of study and career choice. On the other hand, providing members with too much, or too general, human capital would increase members' incentives to leave the kibbutz by increasing what they could earn in the outside world. Such was the core individual-versus-collective balancing act.

Garicano and Hubbard (2009); Kremer (1997) is an insightful paper about why cooperatives are so rare.

INVESTMENT IN EDUCATION—A
KIBBUTZ MEMBER'S POINT OF VIEW

From the perspective of individual kibbutz members, economic incentives to acquire education and skill are low: returns to education are expected to be limited. Economists distinguish between private and social returns to education: private returns are benefits reaped by the individual herself, whereas social returns are those reaped by society as a whole. In the kibbutz context, the social returns to education are the returns to the kibbutz as a whole from members' education. When people think about whether to study hard during high school or whether to go to college, they don't always consider how their education contributes to society. This is despite the fact that our education might increase other people's productivity and output, not just our own. Just as one person smoking reduces the well-being of anyone around him, creating what economists call a negative externality, education might create a positive externality on others. Educated kibbutz members might benefit the larger community in many ways, such as by being better citizens, by sharing their knowledge with workmates and so increasing their productivity, or by coming up with better ways to do things in the workplace. Indeed, this is one reason why kibbutzim preferred their members to be educated.

However, people often think about the private returns to their education; a kibbutz member is likely to think about how much she expects her education to increase her wages. Generally speaking, economists believe that education helps us in the job market via two main channels.[3] First, education is an investment. Education improves our knowledge, creativity, and critical thinking (our human capital, in economics lingo), which make us more productive on the job and enable us to earn higher wages.[4] Second, education signals high future productivity. Attributes like creativity and perseverance are difficult to convey through a resume or interview, but education

---

[3] See Oreopoulos and Kjell (2011) for a survey of the literature on the non-monetary returns to education.

[4] Becker (1962) is a classic reference here.

signals a job applicant has desirable attributes.[5] The higher the return to education, the more incentive people have to keep studying. In the kibbutz context, members had little incentive to go to college and acquire education beyond the potential enjoyment of the learning process because equal sharing of incomes meant the financial returns to education were low.

At the same time, higher education provided kibbutzniks with better employment options within the kibbutz, opened a better outside option, and had a low personal cost. Members could study instead of working, with no financial consequences. Furthermore, because their education had no bearing on their earnings as long as they remained in the kibbutz, kibbutz members tended to prefer to study subjects they found interesting, whereas the kibbutz wanted them to study something useful. As we'll see next, kibbutz members have always demanded education; there was often a queue for studying at university.

EDUCATION OF KIBBUTZ
MEMBERS SINCE THE 1960S

The education of kibbutz members over the years reflected these conflicting goals. Figure 7.1 shows that kibbutz members have always been quite highly educated, more so than the Jewish population on average (even more than the Ashkenazi Jewish population, which typically had a high education level). Basic education was always encouraged in kibbutzim, and illiteracy was eliminated. The prevalence of basic education among kibbutz members could reflect both the high social returns of this type of education and the kibbutz's desire to increase homogeneity among its members. As can be seen from figure 7.2, the share of kibbutz members with less than five years of schooling has always been negligible, and considerably lower than the share in the general Israeli Jewish population. At the same time, the share of kibbutz members with very high

---

[5] Note that under this channel, education might help you in the job market even if the content of your education itself does not apply directly. Spence (1973) is a classic reference.

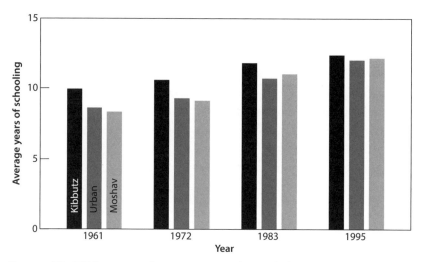

FIGURE 7.1: Kibbutz members are more educated than the non-kibbutz Israeli population. This figure shows the average years of schooling of kibbutz members ("Kibbutz"), the Ashkenazi Jewish city population ("Urban"), and the Ashkenazi Jewish population in other non-kibbutz rural areas ("Moshav"). The sample is individuals aged 25 to 64. Numbers are averages of categories rather than continuous variables. Data source: Population censuses of 1961, 1972, 1983, and 1995.

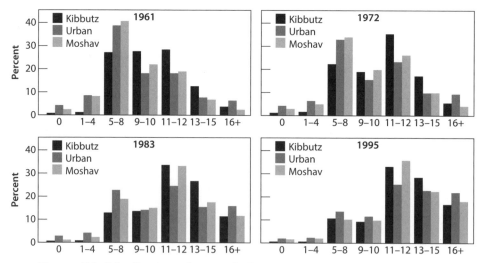

FIGURE 7.2: Distribution of years of schooling. Sample is limited to the Ashkenazi Jewish population aged 30 or older. Sample also excludes individuals who are currently students. Data source: Population censuses of 1961, 1972, 1983, and 1995.

levels of schooling (over sixteen years) is also relatively low. Overall, the variation between members of a kibbutz in years of schooling is lower than among the Jewish population as a whole, reflecting kibbutzim's incentives to reduce heterogeneity in the kibbutz population.

As education beyond high school was not free in Israel and kibbutz members did not have access to savings, kibbutzim had ample room for influencing the post-secondary schooling decisions of their members. For many years, kibbutzim discouraged higher education and even the attainment of the Israeli matriculation certificate (Bagrut certificate). As Inbari (2009, p. 206; my translation) put it, the Bagrut was not just redundant, but also dangerous, because "a kibbutz member who received a Bagrut certificate might end up using it: he would leave the kibbutz."

In early days, college education was discouraged and sometimes even prohibited. By the 1970s, kibbutz members were allowed to study fields that kibbutzim deemed necessary. Members wishing to pursue a college education could request a given course of studies, but kibbutzim made the final decision about whether and what a member could study. Kibbutz-specific human capital and fields such as agronomy were encouraged, while fields that represented more general human capital, such as law, were often not permitted. As a result, despite the fact that the overall proportion of students undertaking some sort of post-secondary education is higher in kibbutzim than in the rest of Israel, kibbutz members are underrepresented among those with academic degrees, which typically take sixteen or more years to complete (see figure 7.2). While the official intention was merely to serve the kibbutz's labor needs, this policy effectively limited members' prospects in the outside world.

Later on, at least since the 1990s, members demanded more individual freedom to choose their fields of study without having to bow to the collective needs. Increasingly, kibbutzim allowed members flexibility in higher education, with the idea that by living in a kibbutz and contributing to it, children of kibbutz members earned the right to study the subject of their choice. Nowadays, members are typically free to choose what and where to study, and the kibbutz finances their undergraduate studies if its budget allows. In return, children who study in college are sometimes required to work for the kibbutz during school breaks. Kibbutz children who attend university typically need to leave the kibbutz for the duration of their studies and live near the university, often in the city. Such a kibbutz student generally rents a small apartment with roommates or lives in the dorms, and work in the afternoons, weekends, or summers in order to finance her tuition (relatively low in Israel, around $2,500 per year in public universities and up to $10,000 per year in private colleges) and life outside the kibbutz. Children of kibbutz members today are often allowed to postpone their decision of whether to become members until after they graduate, which increases the incentives for the most educated members to leave.

While years of schooling are a conventional measure of educational achievement, they might not fully capture differences in human capital acquisition if kibbutz members put in different levels of effort while in school. Did kibbutz members shirk while in school by putting in only the minimum effort required to pass? I looked at this issue in more depth by analyzing a dataset with information on the schooling performance of high school students in Israel in the 1990s (I found no such data for earlier periods). This dataset contains detailed information on these students, including whether they graduated from high school, their mean score in the matriculation exam taken at the end of high school, whether they received a matriculation certification upon graduation, which requires passing a series of national exams in core and elective subjects taken between tenth and twelfth grade. In order to compare like with like, I focused on high school students in those schools that are actually attended by kibbutz students—which also means that the comparison focuses on students who face the same schooling environment, such as teacher quality and infrastructure. High school completion rates are also similar and close to 100 percent for both groups of students (figure 7.3). Likely reflecting the lower propensity of kibbutz members to complete academic studies, kibbutz members have tended to be on average less likely to receive a matriculation certificate, which is a prerequisite for admission in some post-secondary schooling

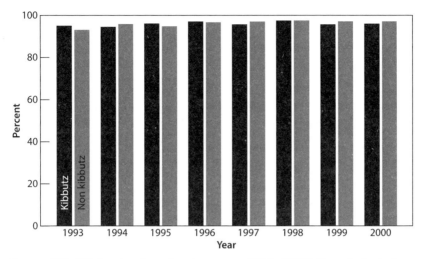

FIGURE 7.3: High school graduation rates, 1993–2000. Sample includes Ashkenazi Jews in schools with at least one kibbutznik in every entering cohort from 1993 to 2000. Students are assigned to years based on the year in which they started tenth grade. Data source: Administrative data files, Israel Ministry of Education.

institutions (figure 7.4). The mean matriculation exam score of kibbutz students is remarkably similar to that of the rest of students (figure 7.5), suggesting that, at least along these dimensions, kibbutz students are not underperforming relative to other Israeli students.

Why did kibbutz members study despite the lack of financial incentives? After all, academic study is hard work. It's easier to sit on the beach all day than to put in the many years and considerable effort required to complete an academic degree. There are several reasons. First, many people study for reasons other than just the financial returns. People could enjoy acquiring knowledge for its own sake. And, while it is hard to know the direction of causality, research suggests that more-educated people are happier, enjoy their jobs more, and are more patient and don't just live for today.[6] Second, members might complete higher degrees because they

[6] See Oreopoulos and Salvanes (2011).

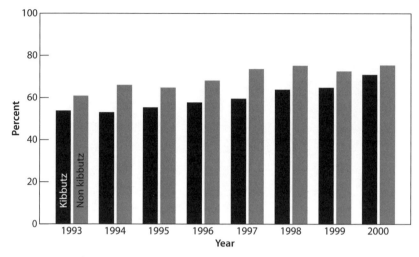

FIGURE 7.4: Share receiving a matriculation certificate upon graduation, 1993–2000. Sample includes Ashkenazi Jews in schools with at least one kibbutznik in every entering cohort from 1993 to 2000. Students are assigned to years based on the year in which they started 10th grade. Data source: Administrative data files, Israel Ministry of Education.

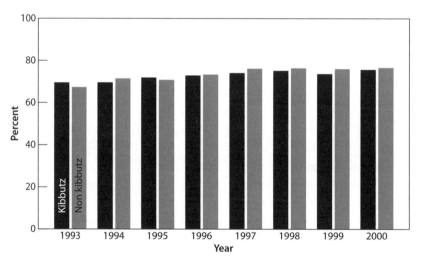

FIGURE 7.5: Mean matriculation exam scores, 1993–2000. Sample includes Ashkenazi Jews in schools with at least one kibbutznik in every entering cohort from 1993 to 2000. Students are assigned to years based on the year in which they started 10th grade. Data source: Administrative data files, Israel Ministry of Education in Israel.

want to keep open the option of leaving the kibbutz, and they know that with more education they will have better job opportunities outside.

While it is clear from the above discussion that kibbutz members invested in their human capital despite the absence of financial rewards, an interesting question is whether they would have invested more in their presence—that is, were kibbutz members at all responsive to financial incentives? The kibbutzim's shift away from equal sharing after the 1990s provides an opportunity to test the extent to which human capital in kibbutzim responded to changes in economic returns. I discuss this research in chapter 10.

OCCUPATIONS AND INDUSTRIES OF KIBBUTZ MEMBERS: CONCEPTUAL ISSUES

In principle, equal sharing does not require kibbutz members to work inside the kibbutz. At least in theory, it is possible to design a full-sharing arrangement in which members work outside the kibbutz and then contribute their earnings to a common pool. In practice, kibbutzim in early days were overwhelmingly based on internal labor: kibbutzniks worked inside the kibbutz and kibbutzim were reluctant to hire outside labor. One potential explanation for this fact is that internal labor works as a useful lock-in device. The internal labor principle locked in members because it makes it more difficult for them to compare their worth inside the kibbutz with their opportunity cost (their possibilities outside the kibbutz).[7] As previously discussed, members who consider exiting might find themselves with skills and work experience that are less easily transferrable to the general Israeli labor market. Moreover, this lock-in effect will be stronger if kibbutzim specialize in industries different from the rest of the Israeli economy, such as agriculture.[8]

[7] I hypothesize that members who worked outside their kibbutz were more likely to leave, but could not find data to test this hypothesis.

[8] Market forces that determine the profitability of different industries prevent kibbutzim from fully diverging from the rest of Israel in terms of their specialization.

Internal labor facilitates monitoring, and so reduces shirking. However, those working outside contribute their earnings rather than their labor directly to the kibbutz. Because earnings are much easier to quantify and attribute to specific members than the output of a factory or farm on which many people work, monitoring those working outside might be simpler to implement in practice. Overall, it is unclear which of these opposing forces will prevail.

Choosing the degree of specialization across industries also requires the kibbutz to balance conflicting forces. On the one hand, allowing members to perform a variety of different occupations in different industries makes the kibbutz more effective as a source of insurance: shocks that negatively affect certain occupations or industries will be "averaged out" by shocks that affect others positively, leading to less uncertainty in terms of total kibbutz income. On the other hand, a more diversified employment structure implies that the potential earnings of members outside the kibbutz will vary more, which increases the chances of brain drain of the more productive members. Moreover, monitoring is expected to be easier if the members work close to each other and in similar occupations. Members with an expertise in a given occupation are probably more proficient at judging the performance of their peers and hence can more easily identify those who shirk. Indeed, companies often take advantage of this by conducting peer-reviewed promotion processes.

OCCUPATIONS AND INDUSTRIES OF KIBBUTZ MEMBERS: IN PRACTICE

Historically, kibbutzim were largely based on agriculture. By 1961, about 35 percent of the kibbutz labor force—and 50 percent of working men—was employed in the agricultural sector compared with only 10 percent in the rest of Israel and 15 percent among men. Since the 1960s, kibbutzim have gone through a process of industrialization, which was accompanied by a marked reduction in the fraction of people working in agriculture. Manufacturing is now the largest sector in terms of employment, with more than double the agricultural workforce; the share of workers

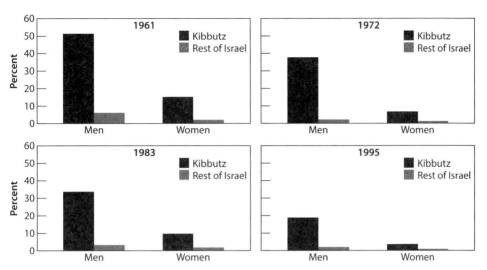

FIGURE 7.6: Share of workforce in agriculture, 1961–1995. Sample is limited to the Ashkenazi Jewish population aged between 25 and 64 years old. Data source: Population censuses of 1961, 1972, 1983, and 1995.

in manufacturing in kibbutzim has surpassed the share in the rest of Israel. However, the fraction of workers employed in the agricultural sector remains substantially higher in kibbutzim than in the rest of Israel, especially among men (figure 7.6). This is consistent with the economic logic that as GDP per capita increases, countries tend to shift from agriculture to industry and finally to services.[9]

Kibbutz members are underrepresented among academic and professional occupations (such as professors, medical doctors, and lawyers) and overrepresented among agricultural occupations, although there has been some convergence over time in this regard (figure 7.7). This difference in academic occupations reflects both the low propensity of kibbutz members to undertake academic studies and the low propensity of kibbutz members with academic degrees to work in academic occupations (illustrated in figure 7.8).

Although kibbutz members were concentrated in certain occupations, they had diverse occupations and worked in various

[9] This economic logic was developed in Fisher (1939) and Clark (1940).

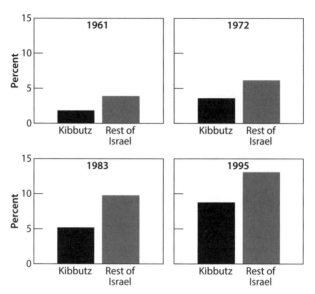

FIGURE 7.7: Share working as academics, scientists, or professionals. Sample is limited to the Ashkenazi Jewish population aged between 25 and 64 years old. Data source: Population censuses of 1961, 1972, 1983, and 1995.

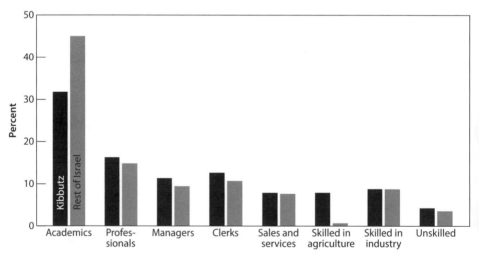

FIGURE 7.8: Occupation of individuals with academic diploma (1995). Sample is limited to the Ashkenazi Jewish population aged between 25 and 64 years old. Data source: Population census of 1995.

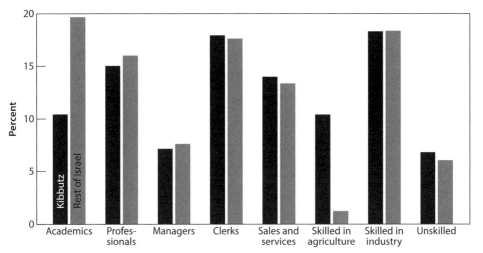

FIGURE 7.9: Workforce by occupational categories (1995). Sample is limited to the Ashkenazi Jewish population aged between 25 and 64 years old. Data source: Population census of 1995.

industries (figure 7.9). The differences between the education and occupations of kibbutz members and the Jewish population outside kibbutzim have narrowed over time, but substantial differences still exist. The large agricultural base of the kibbutz is rooted in its founders' ideology of "conquering labor" and their belief that only Jewish agriculture would buy the Jews rights in the land of Palestine, it also served as a lock-in device long after such ideology was gone.

Overall, the distribution of workers across industries in the kibbutz has largely converged to that of the general Israeli economy in recent years (figures 7.10 and 7.11), with the only exception being the relative expansion of the manufacturing sector in the kibbutz and its contraction in the rest of Israel. This convergence probably partly reflects market forces that operated similarly both in kibbutzim and outside them.

The education and occupations of kibbutz members are consistent with kibbutzim acting like families in providing their youngsters with a high level of education, while at the same time acting as employers by making the kibbutz more attractive for members

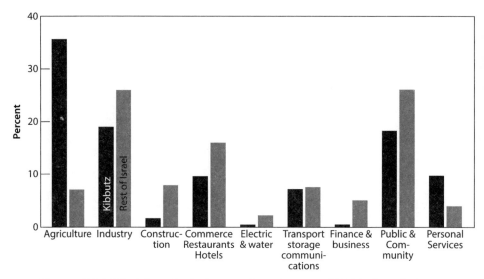

FIGURE 7.10: Workforce by industry of employment (1961). Sample is limited to the Ashkenazi Jewish population aged between 25 and 64 years old. These nine categories are the ones officially used by the census. "Public & community" includes people employed in the government, education, health services, and research institutions. Data source: Population census of 1961.

than their outside options. Moreover, to the extent that it is easier to monitor workers in agriculture and industry compared with academics and professionals, the occupational structure of kibbutzim also facilitates mutual monitoring among members. Notwithstanding the kibbutzim's attempts to lock in members, the industries and occupations of members are diverse, which allows the kibbutz to provide valuable insurance against shocks to member occupations.

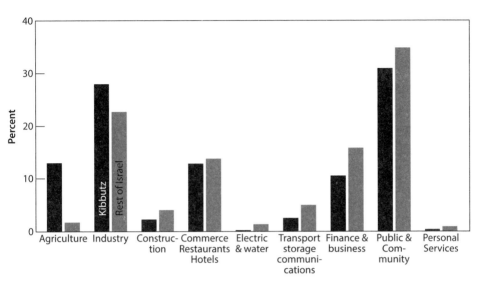

FIGURE 7.11: Workforce by industry of employment (1995). Sample is limited to the Ashkenazi Jewish population aged between 25 and 64 years old. These nine categories are the ones officially used by the Census. "Public & community" includes people employed in the government, education, health services, and research institutions. Data source: Population census of 1995.

PART III

THE FALL

CHAPTER 8

The shift away from equal sharing

PROCESSES THAT UNDERMINED THE KIBBUTZIM

> Much has been written about the rejection of socialism
> by major powers like China and the former Soviet Union.
> But nowhere is the failure of socialism clearer than in the
> radical transformation of the Israeli kibbutz.[1]
>
> —*Nobel Prize in Economics winner Gary Becker*
> *and Richard Posner, 2007*

Kibbutzim were established under circumstances favorable to their survival: their communal wealth was high; they received generous government support; their members had strong socialist ideology; the insurance they offered was very valuable in the pre- and early-state period; and employment opportunities outside were mediocre. These factors helped kibbutzim deal with brain drain and facilitated income equality for almost a century, but they didn't last forever. Gradually they diminished, eroding kibbutzim's ability to maintain income equality in an increasingly capitalist outside world.

In early years, the kibbutz movement enjoyed explicit and implicit governmental subsidies, which came in the form of land, water, and tax advantages. The kibbutz movement had been supported for many years by public institutions, such as the Israeli government

[1] Opening sentences of Becker-Posner Blog, 2 September 2007.

and the Jewish Agency, a Jewish organization that played a key role in building the state of Israel and supporting Jews who wanted to make aliyah. Kibbutzim also had a tax advantage over other Israelis. The taxes kibbutzim paid were based on the average incomes of members. Because of the progressive nature of taxation in Israel, this meant kibbutzim paid lower taxes than the sum of the taxes that members would have paid if they paid individually.

According to Near (1997, p. 317):

> Without the support of the Zionist movement and, later, the state of Israel, it is quite possible that the kibbutzim would have been no more than a handful of eccentric communities, eking out a living in a hostile or indifferent environment—like most communal societies the world over. That they were so much more than this stems from a contract between them and the Zionist/Israeli authorities, whereby they played a major part in the struggle for national objectives—primarily settlement, immigration and its absorption, and defense—and in return received various types of support. The contract was not always official or explicit, nor were the rewards consistent in character or quantity, but its existence was not in doubt.

Governmental support undoubtedly contributed to keeping kibbutzim from unraveling over time. However, it began to decrease in the 1960s, when the Labor Party started encouraging private investment. Such support weakened further with the election of the right-wing Likud government in 1977, which was a first in Israel's history. This election was a sign of a change in economic and social values in Israel, away from socialist ideals and toward a greater emphasis on free-market ideas and on settlement in the occupied territories. The new government viewed kibbutzim as the creation of the previous Labor government and stopped treating them as such important institutions. Kibbutzim's budgets became tighter, reducing living standards and making it less valuable for members to stay. Despite the decline in outside support, the late 1970s and early 1980s were probably the most prosperous decades in kibbutz history, thanks in part to their ability to borrow money cheaply, which would prove unsustainable.

For many years, kibbutzim faced a "soft budget constraint," whereby they knew that whenever they ran out of money the government would help them. With the decline in governmental support, kibbutzim began to face a "hard budget constraint," whereby they could only spend the money they had.[2]

For many years, collective provision of local public goods in the kibbutz might have been more efficient than the market, especially when government and markets were not well developed. Such public goods include education, health, welfare services, and insurance against the bad shocks of life.

As long as much of kibbutz consumption was in the form of public goods, kibbutzim were an efficient way of increasing consumption. For example, in the era when television was a luxury, the cultural center of a kibbutz might have a TV set and an auditorium where all members could watch TV. The nature of TV as a public good, namely that watching it can be enjoyed by many members at the same time, and the fact it was too expensive for any one family to purchase, gave kibbutzim an advantage in providing such luxuries. A similar argument can be made about other communal goods in kibbutzim, such as the swimming pool, basketball courts, and parks. These were all luxuries that most Israelis didn't have free access to, and all could be enjoyed by a member without reducing their use by other members, making kibbutzim attractive and stable. Over time, many TV-like goods became cheaper and many families could enjoy them in the comfort of their homes. Moreover, as more channels were added, families had the advantage that they could watch whatever channel they wanted, whereas kibbutzim had to coordinate among more people. Many kibbutzim did respond to these changes by buying a TV set for each member, and this reduced communal gathering, further contributing to kibbutzim's decline. One argument put forward was that as the share of consumption dedicated to public goods declined, living in a kibbutz became less attractive.[3] The incentives to exit of

---

[2] See Rosolio (1999) for detailed discussion of the shift from soft to hard budget constraint.

[3] This argument was first made by Keren, Levhari, and Byalsky (2006).

the most-educated and higher-skilled people increased, and brain drain became more severe.

The increase in hired outside wage workers in kibbutzim might have also made kibbutzim less stable, because it introduced an economic force whereby "expensive" kibbutz members were replaced with "cheap" outside workers.[4]

The founding generation of kibbutz members was filled with idealist zeal, inherently motivated to contribute to the common good, and didn't require economic incentives in order to work hard and stay. In contrast, later generation members were born into the kibbutz, rather than actively deciding to join it, and they didn't share the same level of idealism as their parents. Moreover, the decline in socialist ideology in the world as a whole, and in Israel in particular, might have trickled down to kibbutzim, weakening members' ideology.

As ideology declined, practical considerations took over, and members became more likely to shirk and to leave. In short, as kibbutz members stopped believing in kibbutz ideals, the economic problems of free-riding, adverse selection, and brain drain became more severe. This ideological decline weakened the egalitarian kibbutzim and set the ground for fundamental changes in the kibbutz way of life.

Finally, the economic opportunities for members outside of kibbutzim, their "outside option," improved substantially, especially for the most productive workers.[5] While talented members could always earn a wage premium for their ability, the returns to skill have increased substantially since the mid-1990s, when Israel experienced a high-tech boom. By that point, kibbutz members largely had the flexibility to study whatever they wanted: they could go to a university to study engineering, computer science, economics or

[4] See, e.g., Ben-Ner (1984); Satt (1991); and Satt and Ginzburg (1992).

[5] At the same time, inequality in Israel increased dramatically. Israel before the 1980s was considered a relatively egalitarian society. Inequality increased in the few years after the establishment of Israel with the huge wave of immigration, but decreased in the 1960s and 1970s. The main source of the recent rise in inequality was technology-oriented growth and the associated increase in the returns to education. This increased the wage premium high-ability workers in certain occupations could receive, encouraging skilled members to leave. Other factors contributed to the increase in income inequality, such as the increase in unemployment and the high inflation in the early 1980s.

finance. Furthermore, about one in five members worked outside her kibbutz. The rules and norms had changed so that a kibbutz member would no longer leave with her clothes only, without savings, with no idea how to deal with money, and with a sense of shame and guilt for abandoning the kibbutz and its values. Guilt and shame were long gone, and the kibbutz now often paid tuition and a stipend for the member, even if she would not return. In fact, members could take leave from the kibbutz, and decide only years later whether they wished to remain in the outside world or return to their kibbutz and become adult members. Even if the kibbutz budget did not stretch to tuition, members were now more independent and, just like many other city students, they worked in student jobs and learned to sustain themselves without kibbutz support. With the high return to skills, bright kibbutz students could now expect to earn a high wage upon graduating, and they could expect to start a new life outside the kibbutz and quickly catch up with their friends from the city even with limited savings and no parental support. This technology-oriented growth dramatically increased the premium high-ability members could earn for their labor in cities and thus increased brain drain, making equal sharing in kibbutzim less sustainable.

The general rise in incomes in Israel also improved the ability to accumulate assets and save for a rainy day outside the kibbutz. Overall, kibbutzim continued to provide more effective income insurance than living outside a kibbutz—but the gap narrowed.

Taken together, the incentive problems facing kibbutzim worsened, making equal sharing difficult to sustain. Indeed, over 20 percent of members left their kibbutz in the period between 1983 and 1995, and those who left were the most educated and skilled. It's impossible to know whether equal sharing would have survived had these factors been the only changes faced by kibbutzim. In the mid-1980s, kibbutzim were hit by a final straw: the kibbutz crisis.

THE FINANCIAL CRISES: THE FINAL
STRAW THAT TRIGGERED REFORMS

The financial crisis that became known as "the kibbutz crisis" dealt a serious blow to kibbutzim, leaving many with huge debts and dramatically lower living standards. In the words of Stanley Maron (1994),[6] a kibbutz researcher:

> At the beginning of the 1980s, the kibbutz economy had an annual turnover of U.S. $2 billion and a surplus of more than U.S. $120 million, with more assets than debts. Then came a crisis in the Israeli economy with soaring inflation, excessive interest rates, and a drop in exports. The productive sectors of the economy were hit especially hard because of their dependence on a high ratio of working capital that must be at low interest rates, particularly in agriculture.

In the decade before the financial crisis, kibbutzim borrowed on a large scale. They found it easy to raise capital by obtaining high-interest loans, which remained cheap to repay given inflation was running as high as 400 percent per annum. They borrowed to expand their industries; they borrowed to enlarge members' rooms and facilitate the move of children back into their parents' homes; they borrowed to improve their dining halls, swimming pools, and theaters. However, eventually the Israeli government decided to take action to slow the rampant inflation. It put in place a comprehensive stabilization program, which succeeded in bringing inflation under control. This made the high nominal interest rates faced by kibbutzim high in real terms too, and left many kibbutzim, like many other businesses in Israel, overwhelmed by debt.[7] Maron (1994) writes:[8]

> By 1984, [kibbutzim's] annual surplus had turned into an annual deficit of 165 million dollars, with the high interest rates creating a geometric increase in the debt load. Credit became more and more scarce, and that crippled the current operations, particularly in industry where factories had difficulty filling orders because they did not have the credit to buy raw

[6] Quoted in Mort and Brenner (2003, p. 27).
[7] The stabilization program included a combination of devaluating the shekel, reducing the ability of the central bank to print money, cutting government expenditures, and bargaining wage controls with the powerful union (Histadrut).
[8] See also Near (1997, p. 346).

materials. Within four years the debt loads almost quadrupled and reached 5 billion dollars.

A decline in the world price of cotton, a major source of income for kibbutzim, was another blow. The capital-intensive nature of kibbutz agriculture meant the high interest rates now required to borrow and invest in capital equipment were even more damaging. Kibbutzim were not alone in this. Many Israeli businesses went bankrupt, and the cooperative moshav villages were hit severely as well.

Kibbutzim were also hit by the fallout from the financial crisis in other sectors of the economy. The shares of the major Israeli banks crashed, and kibbutzim that had invested in them faced large losses. "Many kibbutzim, and the financial organs of the main kibbutz movement, had invested in these supposedly gilt-edged stocks—and, in some cases, also in highly speculative shares—in order to protect their assets from inflation, so they were very badly hurt" (Near 1997, p. 346). In addition, a financier who had been hired by many kibbutzim to guarantee their money against inflation went bankrupt and could not pay them back.

As a result of the sum of these factors, many kibbutzim faced loans that were impossible for them to repay. Although eventually some of these loans were erased and others rescheduled, it was evident by the early 1990s that kibbutzim were in crisis. They were forced to reduce the goods and services provided to their members. Living standards in many kibbutzim fell substantially, to the point that the newspaper *Haaretz* commented that "In the Israel of 2000, there are thousands of poor kibbutzniks," and that "More than 30 percent of all kibbutz members are living below the poverty line."[9]

The financial crisis also led to a pension crisis. Pension for old age in kibbutzim was a "pay as you go" system. Kibbutz members worked for many years and supported their parents' generation who retired. When they themselves got older, the younger generation was supposed to support them. Kibbutzim did not make use of external pension funds, because this seemed redundant given the system of mutual aid. However, as many skilled members started

---

[9] Quoted in Mort and Brenner (2003, p. 35).

to leave their kibbutz, there was no one left to support the older generation.

To get a sense of the magnitude of the problem—as of 2010 about 30–50 percent of kibbutz members were retired.[10] In an attempt to provide a decent standard of living for the retired population, in 2005 the government required kibbutzim to pay a pension of 35 percent of the average wage.[11] In addition, a retired kibbutz member also has access to an elderly stipend from Israel's Social Security,[12] and the post–WWII rents paid monthly by the Germans to Holocaust survivors.[13] However, many felt that this amount was too low and did not allow adequate living standards, especially because even retired members had to pay municipal tax for the kibbutz's services of 400–1000 NIS per month. In 2008 an organization named Pensions Ahead was established to advocate for the retired community, and in 2013 the kibbutz movement[14] increased the pension rate to 40 percent, which amounts to 3,738 NIS (US$968, in 2015 prices) per month.[15]

The crisis meant very low monthly allowances, no travel or special budgets, and no budget for communal enrichment activities. It also meant a strong sense of despair, and a huge loss of confidence, a similar feeling to what rich person would experience when she discovered she had lost everything. Gavron (2000) commented on the standard of living of kibbutzim before and after they had to deal with their huge debt crisis. Before the crisis, Gavron (2000, pp. 155–156) notes, "many of the kibbutz members continued to enjoy a middle-class standard of living while engaging in working-class occupations. Ideologically correct, this did not always make

---

[10] From the Israeli Congress's (Knesset) website: "discussion in the *work, welfare and health* committee on 10.27.10."

[11] The law was called the *Mutual Guarantee at the Renewing Kibbutz* (2005).

[12] This amounts to approximately 1,500 NIS a month.

[13] However, if a member is eligible for the rents, she is excluded from the kibbutz's retirement fund; this regulation is mandated by the Union's Registry and not the kibbutz. *Mutual Guarantee at the Renewing Kibbutz* (2005).

[14] Movement council decision regarding pensions [memo, in Hebrew], Dec. 18, 2013.

[15] Yet, to this day, a handful of kibbutzim are unable to sustain those levels of payments.

economic sense. Very often the kibbutznik lived at the level of the top deciles of Israeli society, while earning the wages of the lower deciles. Furthermore, as Helman pointed out, the standard of living on all the kibbutzim in Israel was very similar, regardless of the actual economic health of the kibbutz."

After the debt crisis, Gavron states, "Suddenly, kibbutz members, who had regarded themselves as partners in a more or less flourishing enterprise, discovered that in reality they had nothing. They had no old age pension, no social security, no house, no property of any kind, no rights of bequest—and in most cases not very much to bequeath. Kibbutzniks, who had felt themselves to be the most secure individuals on the planet, instead found themselves abandoned, naked, and buffeted by a savage storm. The trauma was extreme; the loss of confidence, crippling."

THE SHIFT AWAY FROM EQUAL SHARING

It became increasingly clear that the kibbutz system could not continue to work in the absence of fundamental changes. As early as in 1988, Yehuda Harel of Kibbutz Merom Golan called for a "new kibbutz", suggesting that kibbutzim should make substantial reforms if they wished to survive. Harel's idea was to separate the economy and the community. The economy would be run capitalist-style, whereas the community would continue to be run socialist-style. The income would still be based on need rather than work, but members would be free to spend it as they wished (Russell et al. 2013). In 1993, Harel formulated these ideas in a book titled *The New Kibbutz*. This proposal sparked widespread debate in kibbutzim and resonated with many, including those who didn't believe in the kibbutz way of life, those who long believed changes were needed, and those who were disillusioned by the collapse of communism in Central and Eastern Europe.

It took many years before kibbutzim adopted Harel's proposals, which were considered extreme at the time even though they proposed maintaining the full egalitarian model. When he formulated his proposals, Harel was still a socialist who devoted his life to the kibbutz idea. He was simply looking for ways to maintain socialism and improve the kibbutz economy. He later became a libertarian and published a book in 2010 in which he analyzes the reasons for the failure of the big ideologies in the twentieth century, and the kibbutz ideals in particular.

In the early 1990s, kibbutzim began discussing whether and how to adjust to the new times, and suggesting practical ways to implement changes. The talk became action, and so began the kibbutz transformations known as *hafrata* (Hebrew for "privatization") that continue today. Seventy-five types of reform occurred over the 1990s—ranging from reforms in the way kibbutzim make decisions and govern their economy, reforms that increase the role of nonmembers in the community and economy, and reforms in the relationship between the kibbutz and its members. The first wave of reforms was designed mainly to increase efficiency and reduce wastage, both in consumption and production. On the consumption side, kibbutzim had long felt that they lived beyond their means and that there was a lot of wastage. As Gavron (2000, p. 9) put it:

> [T]he kibbutzim were living beyond their means was an acknowledged fact, but there were also several endemic weaknesses in communal life, one of which was wastage. Food was "free," so members took more than they needed. Huge quantities were thrown away, and expensive items were fed to domestic animals. Electricity was paid for by the collective, so members left their air conditioners on all day in the summer and their heaters on all winter.

Eventually many kibbutzim, including Negba, Heftziba, and Ramat HaKovesh, privatized most services, meaning members had to pay for their food, laundry, and electricity. By 2001, 20 percent of kibbutzim had hired a contractor to run the kitchen.[16] In most cases, the kibbutz remained responsible for other services such as health care, daycare, roads, paths, gardening, and culture. A special fund was typically set up to help members in need, a reminder that mutual aid was still a fundamental principle.

---

[16] See Russell et al. (2013, table 2.3).

Under the reformed system, private allowances to members were extended, and members used these allowances to pay for their own electricity consumption. In 1990, less than 10 percent of kibbutzim had adopted this reform, but by 2001 about 80 percent had done so. Kibbutzim even started to turn their dining halls into cafeterias where members paid for their meals. Whereas in 1990, no kibbutz charged its members for meals, 70 percent did so by 2001. As Gavron (2000) made clear, the latter was a fundamental change because it touched one of the hallmarks of kibbutz life: the communal dining hall.

On the production side, kibbutzim started to privatize many of the kibbutz production and service branches by turning them into independent centers, whose goal was solely to reduce costs and maximize profits. Importantly, they were now able to make decisions without having to consult kibbutz members. This change was in part motivated by the 1989 negotiations between the government, banks, and kibbutzim to settle the debts of kibbutzim, which called for kibbutzim to increase accountability for costs and profits. The kibbutz federations required their member kibbutzim to introduce reforms but left it to the discretion of each kibbutz to pick which reforms to adopt. For that purpose, many kibbutzim set up "innovation teams" to identify appropriate reforms.[17] But kibbutzim went further in this process than simply improving the transparency of their balance sheets. Besides turning the dining hall into a restaurant and the branches into businesses, kibbutzim hired outside managers to run their economy and paid high salaries to these professionals. By 1997, more than half of the kibbutzim adopted this reform. These reforms achieved a clear separation between kibbutzim's economy and community. Outside managers, all with university degrees and considerable professional experience, were hired to run kibbutzim's economy without consideration of whether they cared about the kibbutz way of life; kibbutz members

---

[17] To document compliance, the kibbutz federations requested the University of Haifa's Institute for Research of the Kibbutz and the Cooperative Idea to conduct annual surveys from 1990 to 2001, asking about the reforms under consideration at the time. Shlomo Getz has been the key person in this nice effort.

in leadership positions, such as the kibbutz secretary, were in charge of running the kibbutz community.

Near (1997, pp. 352–353) explained that branches that turned into businesses indeed often identified pockets of wastage and inefficiencies. For example, kibbutzim located close to cities whose schools were underutilized opened up their kindergartens and schools to nonmembers, increasing both their profits and their reputation in the surrounding areas.

Kibbutzim also discovered the economic principle of comparative advantage: "A lawyer who was also a skilled cowman could be replaced relatively cheaply, and his monetary value to the kibbutz was much greater as a lawyer than as an agricultural worker" (Near 1997, p. 353). Kibbutzim began encouraging members to seek high-paying jobs outside the kibbutz and to establish small businesses within the kibbutz. Outsiders were hired to replace the kibbutz workers in the less-skilled work they had left. To be sure, since the 1960s the kibbutz had tolerated some kibbutz members who were professionals such as teachers, doctors, professors, painters, and designers working outside the kibbutz, but "until now [the late 1990s] it had been seen as a deviation from the norm, tolerated in order to ensure the self-fulfillment and happiness of the individual or the welfare of the neighboring town" (Near 1997, p. 353). Today, many kibbutz members work outside their kibbutz.

Sweeping though they were, these reforms were just the beginning. In the early 1990s, Kibbutz Ein Zivan proposed differential, market-based salaries. As a response, the kibbutzim federations threatened to expel any kibbutz that adopted such reforms. The federations did not permit changes that were inconsistent with the historic identity and legal definition of the kibbutzim (Russell et al., 2013). By the late 1990s, however, many kibbutzim started to discuss and implement differential wage reforms that abolished their most fundamental principle: income equality for all members. The wage reforms did not just reward extra effort and working hours by particularly motivated members, but they paid higher wages to members who brought high income to the kibbutz and lower wages to members who brought low income or who worked in less-skilled occupations.

Following the wage reform, members experienced a decrease or increase in their earnings, depending on their skills and occupations.

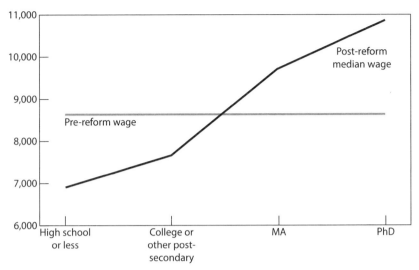

FIGURE 8.1: Wage by education, before and after the reform. The figure plots median wages by education of all working members in one particular kibbutz pre- and post-reform. Wages are measured in 2010 New Israeli Shekels (NIS) per month. In 2010, US$1 was equal to approximately 3.6 NIS. Note that the Y axis begins at 6,000 in order to zoom in on the differences in earnings by education before and after the reform.

Victor Lavy and I collected data on wages of all kibbutz members in one kibbutz; here I use them to show how the wage reform affected the wages of kibbutz members depending on their education. The gray line in Figure 8.1 reflects the equal wages of kibbutz members before the differential wage reform, and the black line reflects the wages after.

This change was also evident in kibbutzim as a whole. A survey of three thousand kibbutz members conducted by Pilat Institute in 2004 revealed huge wage differences by occupation and education. For example, a director of a kibbutz sector (e.g., the agricultural sector or industry sector) might earn close to 30,000 NIS (about US$8,000 per month), and members in leading positions such as the main secretary (chairman) and the treasurer of the kibbutz earned over 15,000 NIS (about $4,000). Over 80 percent of members holding such positions have academic degrees. In contrast, a member working as a menial laborer in the kitchen or in the laundry, without a post high school academic education, earned less than 4,000 NIS (about $1,000). A more recent survey in 2009 that included 180 kibbutzim that reformed their pay structures again revealed large pay gaps within kibbutzim. The survey looked only at members who worked inside kibbutzim; it provided data on the monthly wages of 120 different occupations. The highest gross monthly income recorded in the survey was 17,500 NIS ($4,600) and the lowest, 4,100 NIS ($1,080). This range suggests large income inequality, which would most likely be even higher if the wages of the members employed outside the kibbutz were taken into account.[18]

The wage reforms were a highly discussed topic in kibbutzim, and the new productivity-based sharing rules were hotly debated before being voted on by members. Needless to say, the pay reform caused a lot of stress. Yuval Albashan, one of the founders of Yedid, a nonprofit organization whose goal is to empower Israelis to become self-sufficient and civically engaged members of society, was quoted saying that in 2008 alone there were 746 requests for help by members in their fifties and sixties whose kibbutz privatized. "The new kibbutz has members with severe economic problems, including hunger," said Yuval.[19] The reform also caused envy—some members were extremely upset by the changes, and a few even sued their kibbutzim over it. Others were more understanding. A member of Kibbutz Gesher Haziv told Mort and Brenner (2003, p. 76): "You mean Pete [the factory manager] makes a lot more money than we do? Okay. That doesn't bother me. It bothers a lot of people, but not me. So some are adding on to their houses and others aren't. Okay." The pay reform also received a lot of attention in the media both in Israel and abroad, which took the line that the last socialist experiment was failing. The pay reform frustrated many kibbutz members, especially the older generation. Another member of Gesher Haziv said, "I had helped pay for their education, and they had much better jobs. Change was inevitable, but it could be

[18] This information is provided in the daily newspaper *Haaretz* [in Hebrew], Sept. 17, 2009, www.haaretz.co.il/hasite/objects/pages/PrintArticle.jhtml ?itemNo=1115205.

[19] From Arnon Lapidot, "There Are Hungry Members in the Kibbutz" [in Hebrew], an article in the online newspaper *ynet*, March 12, 2009, http://mynetkibbutz.co.il/article/140474.

a little fairer to everyone all around. I put thirty-two years into this place. I have nothing to show for it. I am a simple grunt in an assembly plant" (ibid., p. 78).

Booklets elaborating on the reforms were distributed to all members. Kibbutzim emphasized how, despite the fact that different members would earn different wages, they were still committed to mutual aid and assistance for weak members, and most of them still held their means of production and factories jointly. For example, in Kibbutz Ramat HaKovesh, the new bylaws (*amana hevratit*) stated, "members of Ramat HaKovesh hold jointly the assets of production, community and culture, and [they contribute to providing] mutual aid in education, health, social security, and nursing. At the same time, each individual is responsible for his own livelihood and the livelihood of his family, and has rights to private property, and to the development and fulfillment of his abilities."[20] Kibbutz Negba and Kibbutz Heftziba had very similar statements in their reform booklets. In practice, this meant that every kibbutz member or family was entitled to a "safety net," a minimum wage intended to ensure decent living. Members whose earnings were above the safety net amount would pay a "community tax" for the communal services she received and the mutual aid and assistance, as well as a progressive "balancing tax" to ensure "reasonable gaps in incomes." The member would keep the rest of her earnings for herself and her family. In reformed kibbutzim, members' wages reflected market wages. For members who worked outside their kibbutzim (about a quarter of all members), market wages were simply the wages they received from their employers. For members who worked inside the kibbutz, market wages were calculated based on the wages of non-kibbutz workers in similar occupations and with similar education, skill, and experience.

A number of kibbutzim introduced wage differentials without going all the way, retaining a wider safety net. More generally, the extent of the pay reform differed across kibbutzim. Kibbutzims' reforms can roughly be categorized into four models. A small number of kibbutzim abandoned equality altogether, privatized all services

[20] My translation from Hebrew.

and became almost like regular neighborhoods (*yeshuv kehilati*). Many kibbutzim introduced a full pay reform, moving to a "safety-net" model that reflected market forces. Kibbutz Negba, Kibbutz Heftziba, and Kibbutz Ramat HaKovesh all fall in that category. Other kibbutzim introduced only a partial pay reform, moving to a "combined" model (*meshulav*) that blended market forces with a more progressive tax and wider safety net for members. For example, Kibbutz Nir David (Tel Amal), earlier given as an example of an early kibbutz founded by Israel-born people, moved to that model in 2003. In these kibbutzim, salaries were differential, though less so than in the safety net model, and communal aspects such as the dining room and laundry were often preserved. Some sixty kibbutzim remained fully egalitarian.

Even kibbutzim that introduced a full pay reform still provided a safety net for weak and older members, as implied in the "safety-net" name they chose for this model. Kibbutzim that shifted to a combined model still probably provided more safety net to their members than welfare states like Norway and Sweden; Mort and Brenner (2003) suggested that standards of living in such kibbutzim varied by less than 20 percent, suggesting these kibbutzim were still very egalitarian. The same was not true for kibbutzim in the safety-net model, which were much less egalitarian and more free-market oriented. Many kibbutzim that first introduced a combined model eventually moved to the safety-net model, whereas the reverse didn't happen. Now that many kibbutzim are no longer based on equal sharing, the tax authorities are considering taxing each kibbutz member individually rather than based on the average kibbutz incomes, which would result in higher tax burdens on kibbutzniks.[21]

A few dozen kibbutzim that maintained full equal sharing established "the communal stream" (*hazerem hashitufi*) in 1999 as a reaction to the differential wage reforms. They sought to uphold the founding principles of the kibbutz: income equality, communal ownership of assets, complete mutual guarantees among members.

[21] See Koren Ora, "The Kibbutz Is Going for a Fight: The Mutual Guarantee Principle Might Break" [in Hebrew] *Marker*, August 2, 2016, http://www.themarker.com/news/1.3025767, for recent media coverage on the issue of taxing kibbutz members individually.

As a leader of Kibbutz Gan Shmuel of the communal stream told Mort and Brenner (2003, pp. 135–136): "The fact that I believe—not only me, all the leaders of those twenty-seven kibbutzim [that are part of Zerem Shitufi] believe—that any connection between your job, work, and your allowance will end kibbutzim." As we'll see in the next chapter, it was mostly rich kibbutzim that were able to maintain the socialist egalitarian model.

The third stage of the reforms touched another fundamental principle, private property. Members increasingly demanded that the kibbutz allowed them to purchase their own apartments and have the ability to pass their apartments on to their children when they died. This issue turned out to be complex. Most land in kibbutzim (and most land in Israel in general) belonged to the state of Israel, and whether a kibbutz member would be allowed to own his apartment was not just kibbutz business. This issue is still being resolved in many kibbutzim. Ramat HaKovesh, for example, came up with the concept of "residence stock," whereby members accumulate stocks in their apartment that depend on their seniority in the kibbutz, and after thirty-five years, a member owns 100 percent of her apartment. The member is able to bequeath the apartment to her spouse and children. If the member leaves, she cannot keep her apartment, and the kibbutz buys it from her. In contrast, kibbutzim today increasingly bring outside partners to their industries and sometimes even sell the entire ownership of their factories to outsiders.

For many years, members had trusted that their kibbutz would take care of them, and kibbutzim had trusted members to work hard even though this was not legally enforced. The financial crisis and corresponding reforms may have inadvertently and irreparably damaged this trust. Kibbutz members became more calculated and suspicious.[22] One member of Kibbutz Gesher Haziv told Mort and Brenner (2003, p. 74): "You felt secure. It wasn't a true life, but people met together in the dining room and elsewhere. Now, it's broken. No one has time. I don't have time myself. I don't feel secure now. I trust my family, not the kibbutz."

---

[22] See Near (1997), Gavron (2000), and Mort and Brenner (2003) for thoughtful discussions on trust and its decline in kibbutzim.

CHAPTER 9

Why some kibbutzim remained egalitarian and others did not

Only once in history did democratic socialists manage to create socialism. That was the kibbutz. And after they had experienced it, they chose democratically to abolish it.[1]

—*Joshua Muravchik*

THE EFFECT OF ABUNDANCE ON INCOME EQUALITY

As we saw earlier, kibbutzim face a trade-off. They would like to split all income equally, but in doing so might lose the brightest and most skilled members who find it in their best interest to leave the kibbutz and earn higher wages outside. Economic logic suggests that when kibbutzim have high wealth relative to the surrounding Israel, equal sharing is more viable.[2] Even skilled members who could earn somewhat more outside the kibbutz may choose to stay, given the high wealth and additional benefits such as insurance. When kibbutz wealth is lower, the benefits of living in a kibbutz may no longer be enough to keep highly skilled members from exiting; to control brain drain, the kibbutz will have to introduce

---

[1] From Joshua Muravchik, *Heaven on Earth: The Rise and Fall of Socialism* (2003, p. 344).

[2] For a formal theoretical model, see Abramitzky (2008a).

differential wages that reward skilled members and entice them to stay. The kibbutz financial crisis provides an opportunity to test this theory. Before the crisis, all kibbutzim were wealthy enough to maintain equal sharing. The crisis hit different kibbutzim to different extents, allowing me to test in the data whether kibbutzim that experienced greater decreases in wealth were more likely to experience higher exit and subsequently to shift away from equal sharing.

Of course, nonmonetary factors are also expected to matter for kibbutzim's ability to maintain equal sharing. Members with strong ideology experience large nonfinancial benefits from living in a kibbutz; they are less likely to exit even if they can earn more outside the kibbutz. A kibbutz where most members have strong ideology is thus expected to suffer less brain drain and be less likely to shift away from equal sharing even when it suffers a decrease in wealth. Members also differ in their costs of leaving the kibbutz and living outside. For example, older members and families with many children face high exit costs. We thus expect kibbutzim where members are older or families are large on average to suffer less brain drain and be less likely to shift away from equal sharing after the financial crisis.

To sum up, this simple conceptual framework yields five main testable predictions:

1. Under equal sharing, a kibbutz will experience brain drain, with highly skilled members more likely to exit and less-skilled members more likely to stay. In chapter 6, I showed that this was indeed the case.
2. Higher wealth leads to fewer exits. Kibbutzim that remained wealthier after the financial crisis are expected to experience lower exit.
3. The higher a kibbutz's wealth, the greater its degree of equality in the long term. Kibbutzim hit harder by the financial crisis are predicted to be more likely to shift away from equal sharing.
4. Kibbutzim whose members have stronger socialist ideology (which I will proxy by affiliation to socialist movement and voting for socialist parties in national elections) are expected to be able to retain greater equality.

5. When members are older or have larger families and thus find exit more costly, the kibbutz will maintain a higher degree of equality without losing members.

In this chapter, I use the data I collected on kibbutzim to test predictions 2 to 5.

Note that the conceptual framework and predictions are not limited to kibbutzim, but can be adapted to entities such as welfare states. Think of Norway, one of the richest countries in the world. Norway is an egalitarian country with a free public health care system, generous parental leave policies, high minimum wage, and relatively low wage differences between workers and mangers. Norway is richly endowed with natural resources. The natural gas discovered in the 1960s ensured high living standards to citizens. The conceptual framework helps link between Norway's high levels of wealth and its egalitarian policies. The high natural gas may have allowed Norway to support generous welfare policies while retaining high-skilled Norwegians.[3] Similarly, think of Sweden, where the income distribution is also quite equal. A highly educated Swedish citizen might have incentives to move to the United States, where income distribution is less equal. As long as Sweden is rich enough, bright and skilled Swedish might still stay, both because their average income is still quite high and because Sweden's welfare state provides them with a fabulous safety net. If Sweden suddenly faced a financial crisis whereby the citizens' incomes declined, skilled Swedes would have stronger incentives to move and earn a wage premium for their high skill. For Sweden to retain talent, it might be necessary at that point to reduce the level of equality (by reducing income tax rates) and increase the returns to skill, so that skilled Swedish citizens would want to stay. It would be interesting to test these predictions empirically for welfare states, but hopefully Norway and Sweden will not experience the financial crisis required to test this hypothesis.

---

[3] Of course, oil-rich countries are not always egalitarian, and natural resources often make only a few citizens rich, suggesting that translating wealth into more equality requires supporting institutions and norms.

Terrible as it was for many kibbutzim, the financial crisis of the late 1980s turned out to be useful for research. In economics, we are often interested in causal effects (e.g., the effect of minimum wages on employment, the effect of immigrants on locals). But, unlike epidemiologists, we are limited in our ability to use experiments. As economist Raj Chetty noted, "If we could randomize policy decisions and then observe what happens to the economy and people's lives, we would be able to get a precise understanding of how the economy works and how to improve policy. But the practical and ethical costs of such experiments preclude this sort of approach. (Surely we don't want to create more financial crises just to understand how they work.)" Instead, economists have developed ways to estimate causal effects in the absence of these experiments. One method is to use natural or quasi experiments in which circumstances outside the control of the researcher generate conditions similar to the random treatment that is used in true experiments. The kibbutz crisis is, in some respect, one such natural experiment.

Before the 1980s, members of all kibbutzim had roughly similar living standards, based on their movements' recommended per-member expenditure. A friend of mine who visited Israel in the early 1980s recalled that he was told to visit only one kibbutz, because "if you saw one, you saw them all." This was not entirely true. There have always been differences across kibbutzim in various dimensions, including wealth. But before the 1980s, most kibbutzim were doing quite well and differences in the living standards they offered members were small. To support a similar living standard across kibbutzim, assets and corporations were shared, and a system of guarantees dating back to the 1920s was in place. All kibbutzim were members of their movement funds, such that each kibbutz was liable for the total debt in addition to its private one.[4] In other words, the relevant variable for each kibbutz was the total wealth of all kibbutzim.

Events in the late 1980s and 1990s changed all that. The kibbutz crisis struck and the factors contributing to the crisis, discussed in the previous chapter, conspired more strongly against

---

[4] See, e.g., Rosner and Getz (1996); Near (1997); and Gavron (2000).

some kibbutzim than others. The system of mutual guarantees in place at the time would have made each kibbutz liable for the debt of all kibbutzim. However, something had to be done about all the kibbutz debt that could not possibly be repaid. The government, banks, and kibbutzim established an independent Kibbutz Arrangement Board, which conducted complex negotiations resulting in a series of agreements signed in 1989, 1996, and 1999. As a result of these agreements, the debt crisis was brought under control (see Near 1997 and Gavron 2000 for details). The conditions of the agreements included that the system of mutual guarantees be dissolved. As a result, each kibbutz became fully responsible for its own economic circumstances.

The fact that the crisis hit different kibbutzim differently, together with subsequent regulations, created for the first time large and unexpected variation between kibbutzim in wealth and living standards. These differences in economic conditions allowed me to test in the data the hypotheses discussed above, such as whether kibbutzim with lower wealth were more likely to shift away from equal sharing.[5]

It should be noted that very few natural experiments perfectly approximate randomized experiments, and the kibbutz financial crisis is no exception. For an ideal natural experiment, the extent to which each kibbutz was affected by the crisis would have been entirely random. However, the crisis was not entirely outside kibbutzim's control. For example, kibbutzim that remained ideologically committed were probably socially more united and suffered less than others from free-riding and brain drain, which made them richer; and according to their values, they remained committed to equality. The statistical analysis explicitly attempts to account for a kibbutz's ideology, but there is no perfect way to do so. Moreover, the causes of the crisis are still debated. Some observers claim that kibbutzim were victims of the government's recovery plan to fight inflation, and others claim that the kibbutzim are to blame for the

---

[5] Note that members' improved outside options does not explain why some kibbutzim remained equal and others didn't, because Israel is small, meaning that the direct costs for talented members of moving anywhere are similar.

huge loans they took and for unprofessional accounting. In reality, it was probably a combination of both. Events in the 1980s, and the financial crisis, did have substantial random elements, though, and thus provides useful variation to get one step closer to causal inference.

I tested whether kibbutzim that were hit harder by the financial crisis and whose living standards declined more saw higher exit rates and were more likely to shift away from full equality. To do so, I combined a census panel dataset of members exiting kibbutzim between 1983 and 1995 from the Israeli Bureau of Statistics with a range of data that I collected from various kibbutz archives and institutions.[6] Together, these datasets provided systematic data on kibbutzim.

My data cover 188 kibbutzim (about 70% of kibbutzim) and include elaborate demographic and economic information for the period 1930–2002, as well as data on recent reforms undertaken. I collected annual demographic information on each kibbutz: its population; the number of members and candidates exiting and entering;[7] the age distribution of the population; and average household size. I also collected the year of establishment, the kibbutz's movement affiliation and voting in national elections (which I use as a rough measures of a kibbutz's ideology), and information on recent reforms undertaken, including the level of equality chosen by each kibbutz. The Institute for Kibbutz Research (mainly through the efforts of Shlomo Getz) had classified kibbutzim into

---

[6] These variables were collected from several central archives of kibbutzim as well as from the Israeli Central Bureau of Statistics. Each kibbutz reports annually its number of members, number of members who exit, and the distribution of ages within the kibbutz, and these reports are kept in central archives of the kibbutz movements.

[7] Exit rate between 1987 and 2000 was calculated as total exit in years 1987 to 2000 divided by the number of members in 1987. Exit was recorded differently by kibbutzim from the Artzi and Takam movements, as kibbutzim from Artzi counted the children of members who exit. Thus, exit rates cannot be compared meaningfully between kibbutzim of the two movements. I include a dummy for whether the kibbutz belong to the Artzi movement to account for this level of difference. In Abramitzky (2008a), I also reported the estimation results of regressions run separately for the Artzi and Takam movements.

one of four categories that captured their degree of income equality.[8] Kibbutzim that have not yet decided on their degree of equality (about forty in number) were excluded from the analysis. I used data on reforms up to 2004, the most recent available when I first conducted this analysis in the mid-2000s. In the decade that followed, more kibbutzim shifted away from equality and introduced differential wage reforms. Nevertheless, I found that the events in the 1980s still predicted which kibbutzim had shifted away from equal sharing as of 2011 (the last year on which systematic data on the reforms are available). One difference between 2004 and 2011 was that the "sharing with differential pay only on the margin" seemed by 2011 to have largely disappeared.

For one year in the early 2000s, I gained access to the balance sheets of kibbutzim. Unfortunately, kibbutzim did not make economic data available for other years. I also collected economic data from two different sources: a credit rating company (Dun and Bradstreet, or D&B) and an elaborate report on the "economic condition" of the kibbutzim conducted in the mid-1990s by a large accounting firm. I collected economic variables such as the size and value of each kibbutz's land and the kibbutz credit rating that reflects its general economic condition, ability to repay its debt, risk of default, and so on. In the appendix to this chapter, I describe the analysis and findings in more detail.

RICHER KIBBUTZIM EXPERIENCED LESS EXIT AND CHOSE MORE INCOME EQUALITY

Because there is no single ideal measure of a kibbutz's wealth or living standards per member, I used several: the fixed capital per

---

[8] I used two alternative definitions of the degree of equality. The first, ranging from a low of 1 to a high of 4, assigns a value of 1 to kibbutzim in the "safety net" category, 2 to kibbutzim in the "sharing with differential pay" category, 3 to the "sharing with differential pay only in the margin" and 4 to the "full-sharing" category (see Appendix for definitions). My second alternative definition was an indicator variable that takes the value 1 if the kibbutz was based on equal-sharing ("full-sharing") and zero otherwise.

member as reflected in balance sheets; the assets per member;[9] the credit rating assigned by D&B;[10] and the economic status as assigned by the government.[11]

I found that wealthier kibbutzim saw lower exit rates and later maintained a higher degree of equality. Specifically, kibbutzim that remained economically stronger (measured two different ways) after

[9] The fixed capital and assets per member in 2000 are continuous measures of the post-crisis (2000) value of kibbutzim's fixed capital and total assets per member. The number of members is fixed at 1984. The fixed capital and assets were divided by a million for presentation purposes.

[10] After the crisis (in 1995), each kibbutz was assigned a credit rating by D&B. The credit rating was built to reflect how severely the kibbutz's economy was hit by the financial crisis and how wealthy the kibbutz was post-crisis. The credit rating was calculated by D&B in an attempt to evaluate the economic value of kibbutzim. It was based on the following parameters: economic strength, debt per member, ability to repay debt as reflected by economic forecasts of the Kibbutz Arrangement Board, type and diversification of industries, and kibbutz's land value. In Abramitzky (2008a), I used two measures: the first is the credit rating that was assigned to kibbutzim by D&B in 1995 (a number from 1 to 4), and the second is the credit rating assigned in 2002 (a number from 1 to 100). The measure from 1995 is appropriate because it reflects the economic position of the kibbutz after the debt crisis but before major differential reforms were implemented. The 2002 credit rating is more elaborate, but might reflect in part the initial effect of differential reforms on credit rating, since the reforms had already been underway by 2002. This potential reverse causality might introduce a bias. However, the direction of the bias works against the hypothesis that I test. That is, the shift away from equal sharing by a kibbutz is designed to keep productive members inside, thus improving the kibbutz's credit rating. This makes it more difficult to document a positive correlation between credit rating and degree of equality.

[11] Economic status/strength: as part of an attempt to resolve the crisis and to reach an agreement between the government, the banks, and the kibbutzim, kibbutzim were divided in 1994 into four groups, reflecting how severely they were hit by the financial crisis. The first group contained 31 kibbutzim that remained strong and did not need assistance. The second group contained 42 kibbutzim that were somewhat hit, but did not need assistance. The third group contained 104 kibbutzim that were hit harder but were expected to eventually be able to repay their debts in full. The fourth group contained 27 kibbutzim that were hit badly and could not repay their debts without assistance.

I also created a weighted average variable of all of these wealth measures using factor analysis, a statistical way of giving different weights to each wealth measure depending on fixed capital and how close it is to the other measures. There was a single dominant factor, which builds on all five measures and accounts for 60% of the variation between them. I called this (standard deviation–normalized) measure "wealth score" and used it as a sixth measure of kibbutz wealth per member.

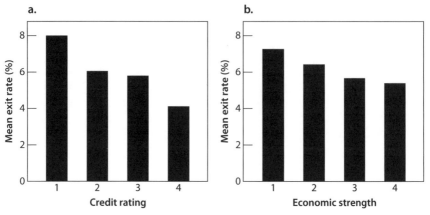

FIGURE 9.1: Wealthier kibbutzim experienced lower exit rates. (a) Kibbutzim with higher credit ratings experienced lower exit rates. (b) Kibbutzim whose economic conditions were stronger experienced lower exit rates. Each graph draws the mean percentage of members exiting each year (Y axis) by a different wealth measure. The first graph uses the credit rating (1–4), and the second uses the economic strength (1–4), which captures how severely a kibbutz was hit by the financial crisis. In both cases, a larger value indicates greater economic strength. The exit rates and the wealth measures are defined in the appendix. Both graphs depict kibbutzim in the Artzi movement; graphs are similar for the Takam movement. Data source: Abramitzky (2008).

the crisis experienced lower exit rates (figure 9.1a and b) and were more likely to remain egalitarian (figure 9.2a and b). And we already saw in chapter 6 (figure 6.5a and b) that members who left their kibbutzim in the equal-sharing period were more educated and skilled than those who stayed. As a member of Gesher Haziv put it, "the motivating factor for the change was the families that threatened to leave. They were in their mid-thirties and forties. I had helped pay for their education, and they had much better jobs."[12]

These patterns suggest that wealthier kibbutzim were able to maintain more income equality without losing the most educated and skilled members. A kibbutz that became poorer, on the other

[12] Quoted in Mort and Brenner (2003, p. 78).

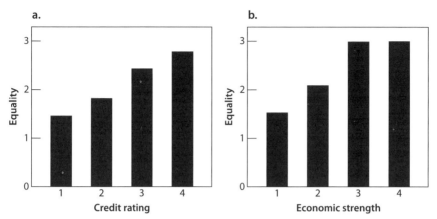

FIGURE 9.2: Wealthier kibbutzim remained more egalitarian. (a) Kibbutzim with higher credit ratings remained more egalitarian. (b) Kibbutzim whose economic conditions were stronger remained more egalitarian. Each graph draws the mean degree of equality (Y axis) by each of the (discrete) wealth measures. The first graph uses the credit rating (1–4), and the second uses the economic strength (1–4), which captures how severely a kibbutz was hit by the financial crisis. Higher values of the equality measure indicate a more equal society. The degree of equality and the wealth measures are defined in the text and the appendix. Data source: Abramitzky (2008).

hand, started to lose its most skilled members. Subsequently, poorer kibbutzim shifted away from equal sharing to retain talent.

Anecdotal evidence supports this finding that many kibbutzim that remained wealthy after the crisis, such as Hatzerim, Mishmar HaEmek, and Gan Shmuel, still functioned as traditional communes. Clearly for them full equality remained feasible and did not result in the exit of the most productive members.

Kibbutz Hatzerim, for example, is an economic success even today. Their highly successful factory, Netafim, discussed in Chapter 4, provides members of Hatzerim with comfortable lives. As of 2000, Hatzerim members had a large travel budget, freely available cars, fifteen years of education fully paid for by the kibbutz, large pensions, and yearly cash allowances. Yet Hatzerim is still a traditional commune and a strong opponent to the reforms. Members do not own their houses, nor do they have their own bank accounts. One member of Hatzerim claims that "in the final analysis, our ideology protected our economic interests" (Gavron 2000, p. 124). An economic interpretation of the kibbutz, and perhaps also of such welfare states as Sweden and Norway, suggests the opposite—the economic success of Hatzerim enables it to retain its egalitarian nature. As another member of Hatzerim said, "I have to be honest. At Hatzerim we buy equality with money. That's not cynicism; it's a fact" (ibid., pp. 128–129).[13]

Kibbutzim that found themselves poorer after the financial crisis, like Negba, Heftziba, and Ramat HaKovesh, were more likely to shift away from equal sharing, though the cooperative nature of these kibbutzim was not eliminated. A member of Kibbutz Kfar Ruppin, which moved to a capitalist model relatively early, remarked that it was important for the kibbutz to preserve cooperation and mutual aid even under the capitalist model, because "the capitalists have taught us that a worker who feels secure and who identifies with his company is more productive" (ibid., p. 222). Another member of Kfar Ruppin was asked whether it should still be called a kibbutz. He answered, "Call it what the hell you want. If people live together and help each other, I think that's a kibbutz!" (ibid., p. 227).

Here the religious kibbutzim are an interesting case in point. I excluded religious kibbutzim from the statistical analysis because they are different in nature and because I did not have sufficient quantitative information about them. In particular, most of the religious kibbutzim invested more conservatively.[14]

The Religious Kibbutz Movement, Kibbutz Dati, was founded in 1935 by religious Jews who immigrated from Europe. Today

---

[13] From a statistical perspective, one interpretation is that because there are so many kibbutzim—almost 300—some of them will be lucky enough to innovate something that makes them wealthier while others will not. According to such "law of large numbers," there is a normal statistical distribution of kibbutzim in terms of the realization of their innovation success, so that some kibbutzim will end up successful (on the right tail of the distribution) and others won't (left tail of the distribution). Note, however, that kibbutzim will not have this luck if they don't attempt innovation or take advantage of serendipitous discoveries.

[14] It is also fair to ask why socialist kibbutzim invested in the stock market to begin with.

there are close to ten thousand members living in sixteen religious kibbutzim (and seven other "cooperative moshavim," a combination of kibbutzim and moshavim, that also belong to the Religious Kibbutz Movement). The religious kibbutzim were similar in many ways to the secular kibbutzim. They too adhered to the key principles of equal sharing and communal ownership of property, and they had an important role in Israeli Zionism and nation-building. However, unlike other kibbutzniks, who were often very proudly secular and sometimes even anti-religious, kibbutzniks in religious kibbutzim were orthodox just as much as they were Zionists, and just as much as they believed in communal values. Their ideology is captured by the words "Torah VeAvoda" (Torah and work)—a commitment to combine Torah studies with Zionist and communal values. In fact, religious kibbutzim often saw their role in the broader Israeli society as promoting religious tolerance and bridging between secular Zionists and religious people.

Religious kibbutzim were less affected by the financial crisis, and their economic situation often remained stable. Consistent with economic theory that wealth supports equal sharing, many religious kibbutzim did not experience the same brain drain as the secular ones, and a higher fraction of them still maintain full income equality. Indeed, seven of the sixteen religious kibbutzim are still based on equal sharing. Wealthy religious kibbutzim such as Kibbutz Yavne and Kibbutz Sde Eliyahu were among the founders of the Communal Stream—kibbutzim that advocate for maintaining the founding principles of income equality and communal ownership of assets. While the experiences of religious kibbutzim are consistent with economic theory, in chapter 11 I discuss how religious communes have been more successful in other countries as well, so it is possible that religious kibbutzim were more successful for the same reasons. One member of Kibbutz Ein Tzurim put it this way: "Religious people are accustomed to living within frameworks, compulsory frameworks" (Gavron 2000, p. 235). Still, religious kibbutzim were just as involved in Israeli society, and they have had the same debates about whether and to what extent to introduce changes. A number of them have ended up shifting away from equal sharing.

IDEOLOGY, HOUSEHOLD SIZE, AND
MEMBERS' AGE MATTER FOR EQUALITY,
BUT KIBBUTZ SIZE DOESN'T

I tested (appendix, tables 9.A1 and 9.A2) the sociological conjecture that more ideological kibbutzim, or those whose ideology levels remained stronger, would be more likely to maintain equal sharing. I used four measures of the strength of a kibbutz's socialist ideology and ideological decline, acknowledging that ideology is more complex than what can be captured by observable measures. My first measure was an indicator variable for whether the kibbutz belonged to the Artzi movement, a standard measure of ideology used by sociologists of kibbutzim.[15] Artzi was viewed as a more ideological movement than Takam, the other major movement, and as such, more conservative in preserving kibbutz values.[16] On the other hand, such movement affiliation had no practical implications for life in kibbutzim (Near 1997). An alternative measure of a kibbutz's ideology is the percentage of members voting for the more

[15] See, e.g., Rosner and Tannenbaum (1987a), Rosner and Getz (1996), and Simons and Ingram (1997). The Artzi movement was formed by a leftist Eastern European group called Ha'shomer Ha'tzair. It was an independent political group but was supported by the Socialist League (a small party). The Artzi and Takam movements united in 1999, which itself is a sign of ideological convergence, but the historiography of the kibbutz suggests that kibbutzim affiliated with the Artzi group held a higher degree of socialist ideology.

[16] A more refined measure exploits the variation in ideology within the less ideological Takam movement, as was revealed in an ideological split during the 1950s into two submovements. In the early 1950s, the Kibbutz Meuhad movement, which would later reunite as Takam, was divided into Meuhad and Ihud. Ihud continued to support the dominant political party, Mapai. Kibbutz Meuhad supported the leftist Mapam, and was pro-Soviet during the Cold War (its supporters celebrated Soviet occasions such as Stalin's birthday). Forty-eight kibbutzim remained in the Kibbutz Meuhad movement, and twenty-three joined the Ihud. Kibbutzim and sometimes even families were split into Ihud and Meuhad supporters, and hundreds of individuals transferred between kibbutzim. In 1980, Ihud and Meuhad reunited to form Takam (Near 1997, pp. 210–215). I compared the degree of equality of kibbutzim affiliated with Ihud and Meuhad and found no significant difference between them.

socialist parties in national elections.[17] I measure ideological decline as the decline in the percentage of members voting for socialist parties over the twenty years before the reforms.[18] I found that kibbutzim whose members have a stronger socialist ideology maintained a higher degree of equality. Similarly, kibbutzim that experienced milder declines in socialist ideology after the 1980s maintained a higher degree of equality.

Smaller kibbutzim were not more likely to maintain income equality. As we saw in chapter 5, there are several reasons kibbutz size might affect ability to maintain equal sharing. Larger groups might be expected to be less effective in using social sanctions to alleviate free-riding. Thus, larger groups might find it more difficult to maintain a high degree of equality. On the other hand, larger kibbutzim can take advantage of returns to scale in production and in local public good provision. Moreover, purely because of the number of members, larger kibbutzim are more likely to give birth to a highly entrepreneurial person who might be all that was necessary to set up a factory that generated high living standards for all members.

I tested (tables 9.A1 and 9.A2) whether larger kibbutzim were more or less likely to maintain equal sharing, and found no strong relationship between number of members and degree of equality in either direction. This could mean that the two forces acting in opposite directions cancel out each other, or that none of these forces actually has an effect. It does suggest that group size did not substantially undermine the norms that determine the degree of equality. This could be either because kibbutzim were all sufficiently small that the free-rider problem could be solved even for

[17] Data on voting were assembled by the Israeli Central Bureau of Statistics. Socialist parties consist of (1) the labor party (Avoda), which is a social-democratic party that officially supports equality and, since the 1990s, has supported an economic policy of a free market "with a soul," and (2) Meretz, which is a leftist party formed from the Mapam (the Democratic Party for Change) and Ratz parties.

[18] The fourth measure—"ideology score"—is a weighted average of all these measures (calculated by factor component analysis). There is a single dominant factor, which builds equally on all the ideology measures and accounts for 70% of the variation among them.

the largest among them, or because the free-rider problem might not be a big deal.[19]

Household size matters.[20] Larger households might face higher exit costs, and also might benefit more from the kibbutz's local public goods, which were nonexclusive and could simultaneously be enjoyed by all family members. Therefore, kibbutzim whose households were bigger might be expected to maintain a higher degree of equality.[21] I included in the regression analysis a control for average household size to capture this possibility, and found that kibbutzim with larger families were slightly more likely to maintain equal sharing, but not substantially or significantly so.[22]

Members' age matters. One important determinant of equality appears to have been the kibbutz population's age distribution. The age distribution serves as a proxy for the different incentives faced by people at different ages. Old members might lose from the reforms as they no longer work and thus would earn less under pay-for-performance than under equal sharing. Indeed, it was usually older members who were opposed to the reforms. Moreover, the older generation might be more ideological and committed to kibbutz values of equality. These factors are expected to make kibbutzim with a higher proportion of older members more likely to keep a higher degree of equality. On the other hand, the compensation of older members largely depended on the younger members, even more so for those of retirement age. Thus older members would lose

[19] Another economic reference is the seminal paper by Alchian and Demsetz (1972), which suggests that profit sharing is more appropriate for small teams.

[20] Average household size was assembled from data collected by the Central Bureau of Statistics on kibbutzim in 1995.

[21] Recall that in the past, when children used to live in special residences outside parents' homes, most households consisted of only the parents. Nowadays, children live with their parents.

[22] I also controlled in the regressions for the land area of the kibbutz (in thousands of square meters) per member, with the idea that more land per member may reflect more wealth per member. However, land value varies across kibbutzim and this measure also reflects both residential and agricultural land; thus, its coefficient does not have a clear predicted sign. The results suggested that kibbutzim with more land per member were more likely to maintain a higher degree of equality, suggestive but not conclusive additional evidence for how wealth supports equality.

more from a brain drain process whereby talented and motivated younger ones exited. Furthermore, the exit option was unrealistic for most older members, because they couldn't save much and it is hard for older people to find new jobs and start new lives. This consideration is expected to make kibbutzim with a higher share of older members more likely to implement the pay reform in order to avoid brain drain. The regression analysis suggested that the latter effect is stronger. That is, the higher the average members' age, the lower the degree of equality.[23] The appendix below presents these findings more formally.

APPENDIX: ECONOMETRIC TESTS

The Higher the Kibbutz Wealth, the Higher the Degree of Equality

This section tests the prediction that wealthier kibbutzim and more ideological kibbutzim maintained higher degrees of equality. Because wealth and ideology are measured after the crisis but before the reform, reverse causality is not an issue. However, I cannot rule out omitted variables that affect both a kibbutz's wealth and its degree of equality that would generate a relationship between wealth and equality that is not causal.

The correlations between the degree of equality and all measures of wealth are high and range from 0.32 (for credit rating) to 0.42 (wealth score per member). Figure 9.2 illustrates the unconditional relationship between the two discrete measures of wealth and the degree of equality. It shows that higher wealth is associated with a higher degree of equality.

To test the determinants of the degree of equality more formally, I performed a regression analysis, where the dependent variable was the degree of equality and the main explanatory variable was the kibbutz's wealth, as well as other factors that might affect

---

[23] The regressions presented in tables 9.A1 and 9.A2 use the average age of members who are over 29, but the same negative effect holds when instead using average age over 21; percentage of members over 40; percentage members over 56; and percentage of members over 60.

the degree of equality, including group size, year of establishment, average household size, land per member, and the average age of members.

Formally, the regression equation is:

$$Equality_i = \alpha + \delta_1 \cdot Wealth_i + \beta' \cdot X_i + \varepsilon_i \tag{5}$$

Where $Equality_i$ is kibbutz i's degree of income equality, $Wealth_i$ is the post-crisis wealth per member of kibbutz i, and X_i are other controls that might affect the degree of equality of kibbutz i.

To evaluate the role of ideology in maintaining a higher degree of equality, I included measures of socialist ideology and ran the following regressions:

$$Equality_i = \alpha + \gamma_1 \cdot Ideology_i + \gamma_2 \cdot Wealth_i + \beta' \cdot X_i + \varepsilon_i \tag{6}$$

where $Ideology_i$ is the level of socialist ideology (or the decline in kibbutz i's socialist ideology).

As mentioned earlier, I used two definitions of the degree of equality $Equality_i$. The first dependent variable is discrete and can be ranked from high (4) to low (1), so I performed an ordered probit regression analysis to test the determinants of the degree of income equality.[24]

---

[24] The ordered probit regression treats outcomes as ordinal rather than cardinal. A kibbutz is assumed to have its "preferred" degree of equality D_{2i}^* and choose the equality-level category $Equality_i$ closest to its preferences. Let D_{2i}^* be the (unobserved) preferred level of equality of kibbutz i:

$$D_{2i}^* = \alpha + \delta_1 \cdot Wealth_i + \beta' \cdot X_i + \varepsilon_i$$

Where $\varepsilon_i \sim N(0,1)$. Although D_{2i}^* is not observed, we do observe to which of the four categories it belongs. In particular:

$$D_{2i}^* = \begin{cases} 1 \ if \ D_{2i}^* \le 0 \\ 2 \ if \ 0 \le D_{2i}^* \le \mu_2 \\ 3 \ if \ \mu_2 \le D_{2i}^* \le \mu_3 \\ 4 \ if \ \mu_3 \le D_{2i}^* \end{cases}$$

The marginal effects in the ordered probit regression are

$$\frac{\partial Prob(D_{2i}^* = 1)}{\partial x_1} = -\phi(-\beta' \cdot x_1), \quad \frac{\partial Prob(D_{2i}^* = 2)}{\partial x_1} = [\phi(-\beta' \cdot x_1) - \phi(\mu_2 - \beta' \cdot x_1)]\beta$$

$$\frac{\partial Prob(D_{2i}^* = 3)}{\partial x_1} = [\phi(\mu_2 - \beta' \cdot x_1) - \phi(\mu_3 - \beta' \cdot x_1)]\beta, \quad \frac{\partial Prob(D_{2i}^* = 2)}{\partial x_1} = \phi(\mu_3 - \beta' \cdot x_1)\beta$$

Each of columns 1–6 of table 9.A1 reports a regression, each using a different measure of wealth and the same set of controls. Column 7 reports a regression without controls, and columns 8–11 introduce the various ideology measures to the ordered probit regressions.

The second dependent variable is a dummy that equals 1 if the kibbutz implemented equal sharing, so I performed a probit regression analysis to test the determinants of equal sharing. Columns 1–11 of table 9.A2 report the probit regression results using the same regressors as in table 9.A1.

Table 9.A1 and table 9.A2 show that the wealth measures in all regressions are strongly positively and significantly associated with a higher degree of equality. For example, a one standard-deviation increase in the wealth score increases the probability of equal sharing by 60 percent, the probability of a medium/high degree of equality by 36 percent, and the probability of a medium/low degree of equality by 16 percent. It reduces the probability of a low degree of equality ("safety-net" category) by 36 percent.

The Association of Ideology, Group Size and Age Distribution with the Degree of Equality

Table 9.A1 and table 9.A2 show that the ideology measures are positively and significantly associated with a higher degree of equality (besides % of voting for socialist parties, which is not statistically significant). For instance, a one standard-deviation increase in the ideology score increased the probability of equal sharing by 58 percent, the probability of a medium/high degree of equality by 31 percent, and the probability of a medium/low degree of equality by 14 percent. It reduces the probability of a low degree of equality by 28 percent.

Other findings related the degree of equality to the variables: group size (the number of kibbutz members) before the crisis, average household size, land per member and the age distribution. One finding was that a smaller group was not more likely to maintain equal sharing. This might come as a surprise, since economic theory suggests that larger groups might be expected to be less effective in alleviating moral hazard by social sanctions. Thus, larger groups might find it more difficult to maintain a high degree of

TABLE 9.A1 The Higher the Wealth, the Higher the Degree of Equality

	(1)	(2)	(3)	(4)	(5)	(6)	(7)	(8)	(9)	(10)	(11)
Estimation method	Ordered probit	Ordered probit	Ordered probit	Ordered probit	Ordered probit	Ordered probit	Ordered probit	Ordered probit	Ordered probit	Ordered probit	Ordered probit
Dependent variable	Degree of equality	Degree of equality	Degree of equality	Degree of equality	Degree of equality	Degree of equality	Degree of equality	Degree of equality	Degree of equality	Degree of equality	Degree of equality
Wealth:											
Credit rating (1–4)	0.397*** (0.111)										
Economic strength (1–4)		0.377*** (0.103)									
Credit rating (1–100)			0.019*** (0.005)								
Fixed capital per member				4.459*** (1.569)							
Assets per member					2.032*** (0.613)						
Wealth score						0.479*** (0.107)	0.476*** (0.097)	0.453*** (0.108)	0.490*** (0.110)	0.471*** (0.111)	0.462*** (0.112)
Ideology:											
Most socialist movement (Artzi)								0.446** (0.214)			

	(1)	(2)	(3)	(4)	(5)	(6)	(7)	(8)	(9)	(10)
% votes for socialist parties								0.026		
								(0.021)		
Ideological decline:										
Decline in % votes for socialist parties									-0.036**	
									(0.016)	
Ideology score										0.317**
										(0.130)
Controls:										
Group size	0.001*	0.001*	0.001*	0.001	0.0008		0.0008	0.0004	0.0001	0.0002
	(0.001)	(0.001)	(0.001)	(0.001)	(0.0009)		(0.0009)	(0.0009)	(0.0010)	(0.0010)
Year established	-0.012	-0.014	-0.019	-0.020	-0.025**	-0.013	-0.015	-0.016	-0.017	-0.017
	(0.012)	(0.012)	(0.012)	(0.012)	(0.013)	(0.013)	(0.013)	(0.014)	(0.014)	(0.014)
Average household size	-0.858	-0.875	-0.863	-0.767	-0.903	-1.205*	-1.067*	-1.081*	-1.163*	-1.016
	(0.555)	(0.556)	(0.543)	(0.586)	(0.597)	(0.620)	(0.625)	(0.632)	(0.633)	(0.635)
Land per member	0.022**	0.020**	0.019**	0.022**	0.021**	0.019*	0.020**	0.019*	0.020**	0.020**
	(0.009)	(0.009)	(0.009)	(0.009)	(0.010)	(0.010)	(0.010)	(0.010)	(0.010)	(0.010)
Members' average age	-0.083***	-0.081**	-0.085***	-0.061*	-0.074**	-0.060	-0.068*	-0.051	-0.046	-0.052
	(0.032)	(0.032)	(0.031)	(0.035)	(0.035)	(0.037)	(0.038)	(0.038)	(0.038)	(0.038)
Observations	188	188	184	159	156	147	151	142	142	142

Note: The dependent variable is the kibbutz's degree of equality (the higher, the more equal). t-test significant at ***1% **5% *10%. Standard errors are given in parentheses.

TABLE 9.A2 The Higher the Wealth, the More Likely Is Equal Sharing

	(1)	(2)	(3)	(4)	(5)	(6)	(7)	(8)	(9)	(10)	(11)
Estimation method	Probit	Probit	Probit	Probit	Probit	Probit	Probit	Probit	Probit	Probit	Probit
Dependent variable	Equal sharing	Equal sharing	Equal sharing	Equal sharing	Equal sharing	Equal sharing	Equal sharing	Equal sharing	Equal sharing	Equal sharing	Equal sharing
Wealth:											
Credit rating (1–4)	0.118*** (0.032)										
Economic strength (1–4)		0.101*** (0.030)									
Credit rating (1–100)			0.005*** (0.002)								
Fixed capital per member				0.801* (0.490)							
Assets per member					0.366* (0.190)						
Wealth score						0.115*** (0.033)	0.134*** (0.031)	0.099*** (0.032)	0.106*** (0.033)	0.089*** (0.032)	0.087*** (0.031)
Ideology:											
Most socialist movement (Artzi)								0.189*** (0.078)			
% votes for socialist parties									0.008 (0.007)		

Ideological decline:

Decline in % votes for socialist parties

	(1)	(2)	(3)	(4)	(5)	(6)	(7)	(8)	(9)	(10)
Ideology score									−0.014***	0.110***
									(0.005)	(0.036)
Controls:										
Group size	0.0004*	0.0004*	0.0004*	0.0006**	0.0005*	0.0004	0.0004	0.0003	0.0002	0.0002
	(0.0002)	(0.0002)	(0.0002)	(0.0003)	(0.0003)	(0.0003)	(0.0003)	(0.0003)	(0.0003)	(0.0003)
Year established	−0.008**	−0.008**	−0.009***	−0.011***	−0.012***	−0.009**	−0.010**	−0.011**	−0.012***	−0.012***
	(0.003)	(0.003)	(0.004)	(0.004)	(0.004)	(0.004)	(0.004)	(0.004)	(0.004)	(0.004)
Average household size	0.015	0.007	−0.035	−0.032	−0.044	−0.118	−0.056	−0.035	−0.075	−0.018
	(0.157)	(0.159)	(0.158)	(0.192)	(0.196)	(0.191)	(0.183)	(0.183)	(0.173)	(0.171)
Land per member	0.003	0.003	0.003	0.004	0.004	0.003	0.003	0.003	0.002	0.002
	(0.003)	(0.003)	(0.003)	(0.003)	(0.003)	(0.003)	(0.003)	(0.003)	(0.003)	(0.003)
Members' average age	−0.032***	−0.032***	−0.034***	−0.035***	−0.037***	−0.029**	−0.035***	−0.027**	−0.028**	−0.031**
	(0.010)	(0.010)	(0.010)	(0.012)	(0.012)	(0.013)	(0.012)	(0.012)	(0.012)	(0.012)
Observations	188	188	184	159	156	147	151	147	142	142

Note: The dependent variable is a dummy for whether the kibbutz is based on equal sharing. The marginal coefficients are presented. t-test significant at ***1% **5% *10%. Standard errors are given in parentheses.

equality. At the same time, larger kibbutzim have higher returns to scale in production and in local public good provision.

Table 9.A1 and table 9.A2 suggest that larger kibbutzim were even slightly more likely to maintain a high degree of equality. This probably reflects the fact that even large kibbutzim were small enough to make social sanctions effective, and thus moral hazard in kibbutzim was mitigated similarly in kibbutzim of all sizes.

I included in the regressions a control for average household size to capture the possibility that larger households might face higher exit costs, and also might benefit more from the kibbutz's local public goods, which were nonexclusive and could simultaneously be enjoyed by all family members. Therefore, kibbutzim whose households were bigger were expected to maintain a higher degree of equality. Nevertheless, the empirical analysis suggested that the coefficient on the variable "average household size" generally had the expected sign but it was often not statistically significant.

The land size (in thousands of square meters) variable reflected both residential land and land for agriculture; more land either for agriculture or residential might mean greater wealth and higher standard of living. At the same time, this is a very imperfect measure because the value of land across kibbutzim varies substantially, so it is important not to overinterpret this variable. As expected, the regression suggested that kibbutzim with more land per member were more likely to maintain a higher degree of equality.

Under Equal Sharing, Exit Rates Decrease with Wealth

This section uses the kibbutz-level data to test the prediction that under equal sharing, wealthier kibbutzim experienced lower exit rates. Figure 9.1 illustrated that under equal sharing, higher after-crisis but before-reform wealth led to fewer exits.

To test whether wealth affected exit rates above and beyond other factors, I regressed (OLS) exit rates on wealth and a set of controls for the period when all kibbutzim were based on equal sharing:

$$ExitRate_i = \alpha + \beta_1 \cdot Wealth_i + \beta_2 \cdot Ideology_i + \gamma' \cdot X_i + \varepsilon_i \quad (7)$$

where *ExitRate$_i$* is kibbutz *i*'s exit rate, *Wealth$_i$* is the after-crisis wealth of kibbutz *i*, and *X$_i$* are control variables that may affect the degree of equality such as group size, year of establishment, average household size, land per member, and age distribution. Because Artzi, the more socialist movement, and Takam, the less socialist movement, defined exit somewhat differently, I controlled for Artzi in all regressions. Hence, unlike in the previous regressions, affiliation with Artzi cannot be interpreted here as a measure of ideology. In regressions where I allowed the coefficients in all variables to differ across Artzi and Takam, I found that whereas exit rates decrease with wealth in both groups, the effect is stronger in Takam.

The regression results, presented in table 9.A3, suggest that when kibbutzim all practiced equal-sharing, the wealthier kibbutzim experienced lower exit rates. Each of columns 1–12 reports the coefficients from an OLS regression using a different measure of wealth. To avoid reverse causality, I use only the two wealth measures that reflect the wealth immediately following the crisis. Columns 1 and 3 report the results from a regression with a set of controls and columns 2 and 4 report the results from a regression without controls. Columns 1 and 2 suggest that when credit rating increases by one unit, exit rates decline by 0.78 percentage points with controls and 0.89 percentage points without controls. Columns 3 and 4 suggest that when a kibbutz's economic strength measure increases by one unit, exit rates decline by 0.49 percentage points with controls and 0.56 percentage points without controls. Columns 5–12 introduce measures of ideology to the regressions. The regressions suggest that ideology, as measured by the percentage of votes to socialist parties, does not play a role in determining exit rates. However, a bigger decline in voting for socialist parties is positively associated with exit rates. Larger kibbutzim experienced lower exit rates, and a higher average age of members was associated with fewer exits.

TABLE 9.A3: The Higher the Wealth, the Lower the Exit Rates

	(1)	(2)	(3)	(4)	(5)	(6)	(7)	(8)	(9)	(10)	(11)	(12)
Estimation method	OLS	OLS	OLS	OLS	OLS	OLS	OLS	OLS	OLS	OLS	OLS	OLS
Dependent variable	Exit rate	Exit rate	Exit rate	Exit rate	Exit rate	Exit rate	Exit rate	Exit rate	Exit rate	Exit rate	Exit rate	Exit rate
Wealth:												
Credit rating (1–4)	−0.779***	−0.887***			−0.729***	−0.773***			−0.691***	−0.731***		
	(0.182)	(0.179)			(0.191)	(0.189)			(0.194)	(0.193)		
Economic strength (1–4)			−0.494***	−0.558***			−0.425**	−0.435**			−0.383**	−0.379**
			(0.168)	(0.168)			(0.178)	(0.176)			(0.180)	(0.181)
Ideology:												
% votes for socialist parties					−0.016	−0.019	−0.018	−0.022				
					(0.015)	(0.016)	(0.016)	(0.017)				
Ideological decline:												
Decline in % votes for socialist parties									0.039*	0.041*	0.045*	0.050**
									(0.023)	(0.023)	(0.023)	(0.024)
Controls:												
Artzi movement	−3.510***	−3.727***	−3.586***	−3.818***	−3.470***	−3.723***	−3.546***	−3.802***	−3.354***	−3.610***	−3.400***	−3.652***
	(0.290)	(0.307)	(0.297)	(0.317)	(0.305)	(0.319)	(0.311)	(0.328)	(0.318)	(0.331)	(0.325)	(0.340)
Group size	−0.002*	no	−0.003**	no	−0.002*	no	−0.003*	no	−0.002	no	−0.002	no
	(0.001)		(0.001)		(0.001)		(0.001)		(0.001)		(0.001)	
Year established	−0.024	no	−0.018	no	−0.025	no	−0.018	no	−0.023	no	−0.015	no
	(0.018)		(0.018)		(0.018)		(0.018)		(0.018)		(0.018)	

	(1)	(2)	(3)	(4)	(5)	(6)	(7)	(8)	(9)	(10)	(11)	(12)
Average household size	-0.457		-0.627		-0.408		-0.594		-0.359		-0.538	
	(0.896)		(0.918)		(0.927)		(0.948)		(0.920)		(0.939)	
Land per member	0.029*		0.031**		0.030**		0.033**		0.030**		0.034**	
	(0.014)		(0.015)		(0.015)		(0.015)		(0.015)		(0.015)	
Members' average age	-0.137***		-0.133**		-0.127**		-0.121**		-0.133**		-0.128**	
	(0.052)		(0.054)		(0.054)		(0.056)		(0.054)		(0.056)	
	no	no	no	no	no	no	no	no	no	no	no	no
Observations	184	187	184	187	178	180	178	180	177	179	177	179
R-squared	0.58	0.50	0.56	0.46	0.58	0.50	0.56	0.47	0.58	0.51	0.56	0.48

Note: The dependent variable is exit rate (%). Since exit rates are recorded differently in Artzi and Takam movements, a dummy variable for Artzi is included. t-test significant at ***1% **5% *10%. Standard errors are given in parentheses.

CHAPTER 10

The consequences of rising income inequality

In the early 1970s, the Chinese premier Zhou Enlai was asked about the impact of the French Revolution that took place nearly two centuries earlier. His answer—"It is too early to say"—has become a famous cliché about the long view of history.[1] In the context of kibbutzim, though, it is certainly too early to say what the full long-term consequences of the recent rising inequality are. Will kibbutzim continue to care for weak members and provide a safety net, or will kibbutzim turn into regular towns, villages, and neighborhoods in Israel? Will the next generation continue to believe in kibbutz life, will they complete the shift to capitalism, or will they maybe turn back to equality? Can a kibbutz that shifted away from equal sharing still be called a kibbutz?

Twenty years after kibbutzim began instituting major reforms, it is clear that the "privatization" process has already changed kibbutzim substantially. On the positive side, the economic situation in many kibbutzim appears to have improved, and the economies of many are thriving. Living standards, once looked down on as a bourgeois consideration, have become a key aspiration and have improved substantially in many reformed kibbutzim. Many young people who could not have tolerated life in a traditional kibbutz now stay and raise their families in a community that better serves their needs and preferences. On the negative side, many kibbutzniks have

[1] Of course, it is possible he misunderstood the question.

seen their social status decline, and some struggle to find work. As we already saw, there was a lot of frustration, especially among the older generation. Many felt that the dream they had devoted their lives to was broken, and that the kibbutz was reneging on all the promises it had made when they had joined many years earlier. Some members even committed suicide.[2] A kibbutz was once a community where everyone sat together around a large table in the dining hall; today neighbors in some privatized kibbutzim don't even say hi to each other. Nevertheless, few members question that the reforms were necessary for the revival of their kibbutz, even those who found the transition stressful and disheartening. Kibbutzniks have turned their helpful and supportive energy from their kibbutz to their family.

While we cannot test empirically all consequences of the shift away from income equality in kibbutzim, I will next describe some quantitative research that empirically tested some of the impacts of privatization. Beyond kibbutzim, the shift away from income equality allows a rare opportunity to test economic logic about the effects of income equality and redistributive policies.

Specifically, as we discussed, economic theory predicts that strong redistributive policies will reduce people's incentives to work, reduce their incentives to invest in schooling (because higher income equality implies lower returns to schooling), and increase the incentives of the most talented to move to a society that will not redistribute away from them. Strong redistributive policies are also expected to encourage people to have more children. Yet, despite their centrality in modern economics, these fundamental predictions are challenging to test empirically, both because of data limitations and because sharp changes in the redistribution schemes, which are necessary to test these predictions, are rare.

We saw that during the late 1990s, changing external pressures and internal circumstances caused many kibbutzim to abandon the equal sharing that had been in place for decades by introducing

---

[2] See, e.g., Shlezinger Liat's article, "The Kibbutzim Dealing with the Privatization" [in Hebrew], *nrg*, June 27, 2009, http://www.nrg.co.il/online/1/ART1 /908/011.html.

compensation schemes based on members' productivity.[3] This change created a link between productivity and earnings in kibbutzim for the first time, providing an opportunity to empirically test these important economic predictions. We expect this decrease in redistribution to decrease shirking by kibbutz members, increase the education acquired by kibbutz children, and increase the propensity of highly skilled members to stay.

In the next section I show how Victor Lavy and I tested whether kibbutz high school students decided to take school more seriously once their kibbutz shifted away from equal sharing. In the following section, I present research findings on the effect of the shift away from equality on kibbutz members' decisions on how many children to have.[4] I then present some preliminary evidence on how the pay reform affected the use of money in kibbutzim, work ethic, and happiness.

THE EFFECT OF RISING INCOME INEQUALITY ON EDUCATION

The Increase in the Financial Return to Education

When all kibbutzim were based on full income sharing between members, and each member of a kibbutz was paid an equal wage regardless of her contribution to the community, the individual financial returns to education and effort were low. A member of Kibbutz Gesher Haziv told Mort and Brenner (2003, p. 75): "I studied art and have a degree in graphic design. I didn't finish university before coming to the kibbutz, because I knew I was coming to the kibbutz and you didn't need a degree for kibbutz."

As we already saw, in reformed kibbutzim, members' wages reflected market wages. Members who worked outside their kibbutzim (about a quarter of all members) largely kept the wages they received from their employers. Members who worked inside received wages

---

[3] See also Abramitzky (2008a, 2011a).

[4] I hope in the future to be able to obtain the data required to study how the pay reform in kibbutzim affected members' labor supply decisions, marriage decisions, and the decision of whether to stay or leave the kibbutz.

based on the wages of non-kibbutz workers of similar occupation, education, skills, and experience. A kibbutz "tax" was deducted from these gross wages to guarantee older members and very low-wage earners in the kibbutz a safety net (i.e., a minimum wage). The pay reform was essentially a sharp decrease in the income tax rate. Before the reform, the income tax rate in kibbutzim was close to 100 percent. Post-reform, the tax rates in kibbutzim were more similar to the Israeli tax rates. Specifically, kibbutz members faced a progressive tax system, with marginal tax rates ranging from 20 to 50 percent.

To gain a better sense of how big the reform was in terms of an increase in the return to education, note that the pre-reform monetary return to education was zero and the post-reform return to education became similar to the rest of Israel, which is estimated at about an 8 percent increase in income per year of schooling. In actuality, while the reform resulted in a big increase in the return to schooling, it likely increased the return to education by less than this amount for several reasons. First, monetary rewards are not the only reason people acquire education.[5] Indeed, as we saw in chapter 7, members of kibbutzim have never been uneducated even before the pay reform, despite the absence of monetary returns to schooling. Nonmonetary incentives such as prestige and care about the collective encouraged members to pursue education in the pre-reform period. Peer pressure and collective bargaining may also have played a role. Such nonmonetary benefits of schooling cause us to overstate the size of the increase in return to schooling.

Second, the exit option meant that the pre-reform return to education was higher than zero, and some members might have acquired education to improve their wages upon exit.[6] If a high

[5] See Oreopoulus and Salvanes (2009) for a recent paper that makes this point convincingly.

[6] As noted, a kibbutz-born individual could always choose to leave her kibbutz and earn the market rate of return on her education outside. At the same time, a range of mechanisms was in place to limit the attractiveness of this option. Note that Israel is a small country, meaning the outside market return to education was similar for members of all kibbutzim, specifically in kibbutzim that reformed both early and later. Moreover, we show in the paper that exit rates during the period we study were relatively low and nearly identical in kibbutzim that reformed early and late.

school student knew for sure that he was going to leave in the future and if he was fully aware of the return to education, his perceived return to schooling was high even pre-reform, and the pay reform did not change his perceived return to schooling. However, because in practice the reform likely increased awareness about the return to education, his perceived return to education increased. On the other hand, a high school student who planned on staying faced no monetary returns to schooling, and the pay reform increased his return by the full amount. For an average high school student who had not yet decided whether to stay, the reform increased the perceived returns by less than the full amount. Third, for kibbutzim that only reformed partially, the post-reform returns are smaller, so that their pay reform increased the returns by a lower amount.

To understand the effect of the reforms on schooling decisions, it's useful to understand a bit about the Israeli school system. When entering high school (tenth grade), students choose whether to enroll in the academic or nonacademic track. Students enrolled in the academic track obtain a matriculation certificate (Bagrut) if they pass a series of national exams in core and elective subjects taken between tenth and twelfth grades. Students choose to be tested at various proficiency levels, with each test awarding one to five credit units per subject, depending on difficulty. Advanced-level subjects are those subjects taken at a level of four or five credit units; a minimum of twenty credit units are required to qualify for a Bagrut certificate. About 52 percent of all high school seniors received a Bagrut in the 1999 and 2000 cohorts (Israel Ministry of Education, 2001). The Bagrut is a prerequisite for university admission, and receiving it is an economically important educational milestone.

The Challenge of Testing the Effect of the Increase in Returns to Schooling

A word on methodology for readers interested in how we try to get at causality and not just correlations in the context of a natural (rather than randomized) experiment. For that purpose, here I take the reader through the research in more detail: the research question; why it might be informative about more than just kibbutzim; the research design and how we used this natural experiment to distinguish causality from correlation; how we collected and analyzed the data; what we found; and what we concluded from the findings. The data in isolation can tell us only about correlation, not causation. This is a well-known problem and can be obvious. For example, people who go to a hospital are more likely to die than people who don't, but this is simply because sicker people are more likely to go to a hospital, not because going to a hospital kills you. At other times, this problem is present but not so obvious. For example, consider the typical finding that more-educated people earn higher wages. It might be tempting to conclude that acquiring education makes one earn higher wages. Intuitively, this seems likely to be true, but this simple correlation definitely doesn't prove it. One alternative story is that smarter or more motivated people are more likely to both acquire higher education and earn higher wages. This will generate a positive correlation between education and earnings that has nothing to do with causality. Another possibility is that the children of more-educated, richer parents who can afford to send their kids to university would earn higher wages even if they didn't get degrees. There are plenty of other stories that would generate a correlation between education and wages that is not causal. This problem is described in most econometrics textbooks.[7]

We set up to test the extent to which this policy change induced high school students in kibbutzim to invest more in their educations, as reflected by their academic achievements during high school and in adulthood. We aimed to contribute to two strands of the economics literature. From a public economics perspective, this research sheds light on the extent to which redistributive policy influences long-run labor supply, as mediated through educational choices. While it is well known that changes in taxes affect labor supply decisions in the short run (Saez, Slemrod, and Giertz 2012), much less is known about the long-run effect, because it is difficult to identify empirically how such tax changes affect educational choices. This research fills this gap by studying how responsive

---

[7] Angrist and Pischke have written two particularly nice and accessible such textbooks: *Mastering Metrics* (2014), for undergraduate students, and *Mostly Harmless Econometrics* (2009), for graduate students.

educational choices are to tax changes. From a labor economics perspective, economic models of optimal human capital investment (Ben-Porath 1967) suggest that the level of investment in schooling is expected to increase in the perceived rate of return to education. However, despite its centrality in modern labor economics, this fundamental assumption has hardly been tested empirically, both because differences across individuals in the rate of return to schooling are rarely observed and because sharp changes in this return seldom occur.[8] You can find the technical details of the estimation and findings in Abramitzky and Lavy (2014).

How We Tested the Effect on Education

The empirical analysis is based on a sample that includes students who live in kibbutzim at the start of tenth grade, and on information drawn from several administrative data files obtained from the Ministry of Education in Israel. We obtained data for six consecutive cohorts (from 1995 to 2000) of tenth-grade students. Each record contains an individual, a school identifier, student date of birth, gender, parental education, number of siblings, year of immigration, ethnicity, and schooling outcomes (graduating high school, receiving a Bagrut, receiving a Bagrut that meets university entrance requirements, and the average score in the matriculation exams). We link these student-level data with additional data

---

[8] Note simple models of investment in education, such as presented in Eaton and Rosen (1980), show that when the only cost of education is the opportunity cost of forgone earnings, a proportional change in the income tax rate does not affect private incentives to invest in education. However, because education inevitably involves effort costs and likely other costs besides, theory predicts that the change in income tax rates that we study will affect investment in education. Freeman (1976) and Kane (1994) find a positive response of schooling investments to increased returns. However, the limitation of these studies is that they are primarily based on a coincidence of time series, namely the similar timing of a rise in returns to education and a rise in college entry. Therefore, a causal interpretation of the association between returns and college enrollment is difficult to establish. Several studies estimate the perceived rate of return to schooling, and then assess its effect on schooling (Betts 1996). Jensen (2010) finds that students who were better informed (experimentally) of higher returns were significantly less likely to drop out of school in subsequent years. Attanasio and Kaufman (2009) find that college attendance decisions depend on expected returns to college.

collected by the Institute for Research of the Kibbutz and the Cooperative Idea (Getz 1998–2004) on the date at which each kibbutz reformed. We also use data on post–high school educational outcomes that we obtained from the National Insurance Institute of Israel.

One research approach would be to test whether, in kibbutzim that reformed, cohorts of students after the reform had better schooling outcomes than cohorts of students before the reform. We found that they did. However, this research approach couldn't tell us whether the improvement in schooling outcomes was caused by the pay reform or by any number of other factors that might have changed over time. To get at the causal effect of the pay reform, we needed a comparison group of students who were not affected by reforms, but who faced the same changes in other factors over time. One comparison group could be students who lived outside the kibbutz but went to the same schools. However, non-kibbutz students faced very different incentives to perform in school and grew up in a very different environment, making it difficult to interpret differences as resulting from the pay reform. Students in kibbutzim that did not reform were another possible comparison group. However, these students might not have faced the same changes in other factors because kibbutzim that never reformed differ from those that did, in that they had different experiences in the decade leading to the reform period. There are reasons to believe kibbutzim that did not reform strengthened their group identity and social norms, which may have improved educational outcomes through a different channel.[9] We thus decided to compare students in kibbutzim that reformed early with students in kibbutzim that reformed late, and see how their outcomes changed when the early-reforming kibbutzim had their reforms.

[9] Specifically, kibbutzim that reformed experienced a deeper financial crisis and higher exit rates in the decade leading to the reform. Subsequently, kibbutzim that never reformed formed the "egalitarian/communal wave" (*zerem shitufi*) that revived the traditional egalitarian norms by instilling communal and equality norms in members, opposed the reforms in other kibbutzim and proudly became "the only kibbutzim like in the good old days". These kibbutzim have often become even more successful economically and socially.

We used an econometric approach called a difference-in-differences (DID) to compare educational outcomes of high school students in kibbutzim that reformed early (1998–2000) versus late (2003–2004), before and after the early reforms (but before the late reforms). We cannot rule out that members in kibbutzim that reformed later observed the reforms in other kibbutzim, and anticipated that at some later date their kibbutz would reform too. However, three relevant things are worth noting. First, conceptually, any anticipation effects that were present make it more difficult for us to find an impact of the reform. Second, our choice to compare kibbutzim that reformed at least four years apart makes such anticipation effects less likely and less prominent if they exist (that is, we excluded kibbutzim that reformed in 2001–2002 to avoid anticipation effects). Third, empirically, we did not find evidence of anticipation effects, in the sense that educational outcomes in kibbutzim that reformed later are similar for the earlier and later cohorts. These timings are illustrated below.

The underlying assumption of our research strategy is that the exact timing of the reform is unrelated to potential outcomes of students. This assumption implies that older cohorts of early- and late-reforming kibbutzim should have had similar high school outcomes on average. We provided evidence in support of the research strategy and this assumption. The first question that came to our minds was whether kibbutzim that reformed later were otherwise similar to kibbutzim that reformed earlier. This is necessary for one to make a good comparison group for the other. We showed that students in kibbutzim that reformed early and late had very similar

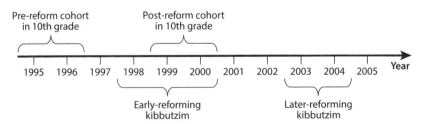

FIGURE 10.1: Comparing cohorts of students in kibbutzim that reformed early and late.

background characteristics and schooling outcomes before the reform took place. While students from kibbutzim that reformed earlier and later appeared similar, we were concerned that they could have been on different time trends. Perhaps students from early-reforming kibbutzim were on a path to improve their educational outcomes and would have continued on that good path even in the absence of the reforms. We found that the trends in outcomes in the five years before the reforms were similar for kibbutzim that reformed early and late, and that exit and entry rates of high school students were low and similar in kibbutzim that reformed early and late. We concluded that both groups were on similar time trends of educational matriculation outcomes.

Kibbutzniks Took School More Seriously Once Their Kibbutz Shifted Away from Equal Sharing

We next tested how the shift away from equal sharing affected educational outcomes. We found that students started to take school more seriously when their kibbutz reformed. They were 3.3 percentage points more likely to complete high school, 6 percentage points more likely to receive a university-qualified Bagrut certificate, and scored an average of 3.5 points higher on their matriculation exams. Multiple requirements must be met for a student to receive a university-qualified Bagrut; the improvement in the proportion of students receiving these could thus be driven by two particular improvements. The first is an increase in the proportion of students who enroll in and pass the English matriculation program at higher than a basic level. The second is an increase in the proportion of students who pass the matriculation program in at least one advanced-placement subject. These two criteria are an admission requirement for all universities and most colleges in Israel. It is likely that post-reform, more students put effort into receiving university-qualified Bagrut because more intended to enroll in post-secondary schooling.

Because our interest was in estimating the effect of the change in returns to education on schooling decisions, we wanted to rule out other potential causes of the estimated effect we found. One possibility was that the pay reforms affected schooling outcomes by changing social incentives more broadly. Under equal sharing, members might have felt indebted to their kibbutz for everything it provided, and so invested in education for the common good. Such social norms would be reduced following the pay reform. As we discussed, the 1990s saw a number of other reforms in kibbutzim that are likely to have changed social incentives to invest in schooling without changing the financial returns to education. We collected information on the precise years in which four relevant reforms were implemented: the introduction of user fees for (1) meals in the common dining room, (2) electricity at home, (3) personal laundry, and (4) private health insurance. Our main findings were not sensitive to the inclusion of controls for these social reforms, and we concluded that the social incentives channel was unlikely to be a major driver of our estimated effect of the pay reform.

As we saw, the pay reform was not identical across kibbutzim. Some kibbutzim introduced a full pay reform, moving to a safety-net model that reflected market forces. Other kibbutzim introduced only a partial pay reform, moving to a combined model (*meshulav*) that was still based on market forces, but kept a more progressive tax system and wider safety net for members. We took advantage of the variation over time in the degree of pay reform, which was present because some kibbutzim changed immediately from an equal-sharing system to a full differential pay system, while others introduced a partial differential pay system initially but later changed to a complete differential pay structure.[10] We showed that students who spent their entire three years of high school in a fully reformed kibbutz improved their educational outcomes the most.

---

[10] We could exploit these changes to define "treatment intensity" because some of these kibbutzim made the second change within the period of study. Specifically, of the 37 kibbutzim that reformed in 1998, 17 introduced a full pay reform and 20 a partial reform; and of the latter group, only 6 changed to a full reform within the study period (before 2003). Of the 14 kibbutzim that reformed in 1999, 7 introduced a full pay reform and 7 a partial reform; of the latter group, 6 kibbutzim changed to full reform by 2002. Of the 22 kibbutzim that reformed in 2000, 13 introduced a full pay reform and 9 a partial reform; of the latter group, 4 kibbutzim changed to full reform by 2002.

Kibbutzniks Whose Parents Were Less Educated Improved Their Schooling More

Next, we looked at whether the pay reform affected students with different social backgrounds differently. Conceptually, it is not obvious who will be affected more by the reform. On the one hand, we might expect students with less-educated parents, who likely faced a decrease in parental income and were expected to have lower personal income on average, to be more affected by the decrease in the income tax because a future dollar increase in earnings was more valuable for them. Moreover, one might expect students from lower social backgrounds to take school even more seriously following the change in return if they were less likely to have inherent motivation to invest in schooling and would only do so when given external incentives. On the other hand, students whose parents were more educated might receive more help at home or elsewhere, because their parents were better able to help them or pay for private tutoring, and thus be in a better position to improve their schooling when given the incentive. We split the sample into two groups as follows: students whose mothers have thirteen or more years of schooling (50% percent of students) and those whose mothers have less than thirteen years of schooling. Alternatively, we stratified by the father's years of schooling and found similar results.

One issue was that student attainment might have increased not because students expected their schooling to gain them more future income but because of the changes in income experienced by their parents. In particular, more-educated parents experienced pay increases with the reforms, which could have caused them to invest more in their children's educations. However, we found that the total effect on educational outcomes was largely driven by students with *less*-educated parents.[11] This finding rules out the possibility that such an income effect was driving our main result.

---

[11] Interestingly, these results by parents' education level are the opposite of Jensen's (2010) study of educational response in the Dominican Republic. We note that the less-educated parents in the kibbutz are on average more educated than the more-educated parents in the Dominican Republic, meaning that financial constraints are likely to be less important in our context.

Our result that children from less-educated families responded more strongly to the reduction in the income tax rate could reflect a higher rate of return to schooling perceived by this group. A growing body of evidence suggests that, indeed, individuals who are more credit constrained, have greater immediate need to work, or have greater distaste for school have a higher rate of return to schooling.[12]

Male Kibbutzniks Improved at School More than Female Kibbutzniks

Next we tested whether males or females were affected differently. Male and female students have been shown to respond differently to incentives, with females typically being more responsive. We find that, if anything, male kibbutzniks responded more.

Our finding that the effect of the pay reforms on females is not significantly larger than the effect on males stands in contrast to Schultz (2004), who found that girls' school completion responded more to the incentives introduced by Progresa in Mexico. Our finding is also different from those of Angrist and Lavy (2009), who concluded that females' Bagrut diploma attainment is affected by conditional bonus payments, whereas boys do not react to this monetary incentive. In these papers, females respond more to an increase in incentives designed to directly increase educational outcomes. In our context, the pay reform does not increase such short-run incentives to perform better in school. In contrast, the pay reform we studied operates through affecting the future rewards in the labor market. It is possible that females perceive a lower return to education in the labor market, and expect to work in lower-paying jobs on average, perhaps because they do not expect to become the main earner (possibly because they plan to play a bigger role in raising children or because they expect to be discriminated against in the labor market). Indeed, in regression analyses we ran using the 1998–2000 Israeli labor force surveys

---

[12] See Card (1993, 1999, 2001). Brenner and Rubinstein (2011) showed evidence of higher returns to schooling for individuals in poor families in the United States.

and matching occupations to their mean earnings using income surveys, we found that females (both within kibbutzim and outside them) were substantially more likely to work in lower-paying occupations; they sorted into occupations and industries that paid around 20 percent less on average.

Kibbutzniks Also Increased Their Post-Secondary Schooling

Did the reforms affect education decisions beyond high school, as theory would predict? We tested whether the shift away from equal sharing had long-term consequences, by looking at the post-secondary schooling outcomes of these students by age twenty-eight to twenty-nine (in 2010–2011).[13]

The post–high school academic schooling system in Israel includes seven universities (one of which confers only graduate degrees), over forty-five colleges that confer academic undergraduate degrees (some of these also give master's degrees), and dozens of teachers' colleges that confer bachelor of education degrees.[14] All universities require a Bagrut for enrollment. Most academic colleges and teachers' colleges also require a Bagrut, though some look at specific Bagrut components without requiring full certification. For

[13] In assessing this exercise, we should note that, unlike high school outcomes, post-secondary schooling could be affected by the pay reform through two channels. The first channel operates through the effect of the improved high school outcomes and the higher educational aspirations while in high school, which could make higher education easier to pursue. The second channel is an additional effect where individuals may respond as adults to the higher rate of return to schooling, regardless of their attainment in high school. The early-reforming kibbutzim are exposed to both effects while the late-reforming kibbutzim are exposed only to the second because their kibbutzim reformed after they completed high school. In this research, we cannot cleanly distinguish between these two potential channels because the effect of an increase at adulthood in the rate of return to schooling on the decision to pursue higher education could be different for individuals in early- and late-reforming kibbutzim. If these two effects are similar, then the estimates reported below capture mainly the first channel of effect on post–high school education.

[14] A 1991 reform sharply increased the supply of post-secondary schooling in Israel by creating publicly funded regional and professional colleges.

a given field of study, it is typically more difficult to be admitted to a university than to a college.[15]

Our information on post-secondary enrollment came from administrative records provided by Israel's National Insurance Institute (NII). The NII is responsible for Social Security and mandatory health insurance in Israel; it tracks post-secondary enrollment because students pay a lower health insurance tax rate. Postsecondary schools are therefore required to send a list of enrolled students to the NII every year. For the purposes of our project, the NII Research and Planning Division constructed an extract containing the 2001–2011 enrollment status and number of years of post-secondary schooling of students in our study. This file was merged with the other information in our sample, and we used it for analysis at the protected research lab with restricted access at NII headquarters in Jerusalem.

We coded three indicators for enrollment in post–high school education. The first indicator identifies if the person ever enrolled in one of the seven universities (at any time from 2001 to 2011); the second identifies if she ever enrolled in one of the certified academic colleges; and the third identifies if she ever enrolled in a teachers' college.[16] We found that for many students, the increase in high school outcomes translated into increased enrollment in academic and teachers' colleges and practical engineering schools (possibly at the expense of university enrollment).

[15] The national enrollment rates for the cohort of graduating seniors in 1995 (through 2003) was 55.4 percent, of which 27.6 percent were enrolled in universities, 8.5 percent in academic colleges, 7 percent in teachers' colleges, and the rest in nonacademic institutions. These data are from the Israel Central Bureau of Statistics, Report on Post Secondary Schooling of High School Graduates in 1989–1995, available at http://www.cbs.gov.il/publications/h_education02/h_education_h.htm.

[16] The overall ever-enrolled rate in any post-secondary schooling in our sample is 69%, of which 31 percentage points are in one of the seven universities, 32 percentage points are in an academic college, and 2.3 percentage points are in a teachers' college. Note that very few students ever enroll in more than one type of post-school educational institution. The average number of post–high school years of schooling completed until the school year 2010–2011 in our sample is 2.7, of which 1.21 are in university schooling, 1.25 are in college education, and 0.05 are in teachers' colleges.

There are several possible reasons why the reform increased enrollment and attainment in colleges but not in universities. First, we showed that the effect on high school outcomes was largely driven by the subgroup of students whose parents were less educated, and such students are more likely to enroll in colleges, for which admission requirements tend to be less strict than for universities.[17] Second, the number of academic colleges has expanded dramatically since the mid-1990s, making them more accessible than universities, since these colleges are located in all regions of the country. The proximity of many kibbutzim to these new colleges made it possible for kibbutz members to enroll in higher education without having to move to a big city, where the universities are located. Third, the decline in university enrollment may reflect a shift in preferences of kibbutz students among different tracks of higher education following the pay reform. For example, kibbutz members may now find university education, especially in the humanities and social sciences, to be less attractive and less practical in terms of financial rewards in the "new" kibbutz in comparison with law and business education, which are now available in almost all the academic colleges. Such a shift in preferences may have been more relevant to women, who tended to enroll in larger proportions in humanities at universities, and now may be shifting to more financially rewarding subjects.

Consistent with this idea, we found that the reform induced a shift of females away from university enrollment and toward colleges. Regrettably, our data do not allow a more rigorous examination of this conjecture. However, we note that the net effect on females is close to zero, consistent with a smaller effect of the pay reform on females' high school outcomes. For males, on the other hand, the effect was positive on both university and academic college enrollment (although results could not always be measured precisely).[18]

---

[17] We also estimated the effect of the pay reform on post–high school education separately for students of low and high parental education. The results obtained from the sample of students with low parental schooling indicate mainly an increase in studying in colleges to become teachers.

[18] The effect on males' academic college years of schooling is quite large, over a quarter of a year of schooling, which is about a 28% increase.

In summary, we viewed this episode of shift away from equal sharing in kibbutzim as a useful natural experiment to estimate the responsiveness of investment in education to changes in the returns to education. We found students were indeed responsive to changes in redistribution: when their kibbutzim reformed, they considerably improved their educational attainment at school. Students who spent their entire three years of high school in a kibbutz that reformed to a greater extent improved their educational outcomes more. Males seem to have reacted more strongly than females, and students with less-educated parents appear to have reacted more strongly than those with more educated parents.

Implications of These Findings for Kibbutzim and Beyond

Our findings have implications beyond the Israeli context. They show the educational responses that could result from a decrease in the income tax rate, thus are informative on the long-run labor-supply responses to tax changes. They also show the educational responses expected when the returns to education increase. For example, such changes might be occurring in many countries as technology-oriented growth increases the return to skills.[19] While the pay reform in kibbutzim is likely larger than many other policy changes aiming to reduce the income tax rates or increase the rates of return to education, the kibbutz serves as a microcosm for learning about other important episodes with similarly large reforms. Examples of such episodes include the transitions of Central and Eastern European countries from centrally planned to market economies after the fall of the Iron Curtain, the abolition of village collectives in China in the 1980s, and Vietnam's labor market liberalization in the mid-1980s.

Our findings also inform the debate on the increase in earnings inequality in the United States and many other developed countries over past decades, which perhaps is one of the most important aggregate phenomena in labor markets since World War II (known as "skill-biased technological change"). A large body of research

---

[19] See, e.g., the discussion in Autor, Katz, and Krueger (1999); Card and Dinardo (2002); and Goldin and Katz (2008).

focuses on the implications of technological advancement for the demand for skill,[20] yet no attention is given to estimating the impact of the returns to education on the supply of educated workers. This is a key factor for understanding the longer-run consequences of changes in the demand structure in today's technological landscape. The experience of the kibbutzim communities provides a unique setting for estimating the causal impact of the returns to education on school choices and the supply of educated workers.

From the perspective of a traditional egalitarian kibbutz, however, these results are both optimistic and pessimistic. On the pessimistic side, financial incentives matter. Once kibbutzim shifted away from equal sharing, high school students started to take school more seriously, implying that under equal sharing they put less effort into their educations. On the optimistic side, kibbutzniks did treat school seriously under equal sharing and acquired considerable education before the reforms, despite the lack of individual financial returns. Yes, kibbutzniks improved their matriculation average from 70 to 74 percent, a substantial improvement, but if this is all the improvement that takes place when a society moves from full income equality to a much higher degree of income inequality, perhaps the main takeaway is how little financial incentives matter in the decision to acquire education and excel in school.

HOW INCOME INEQUALITY AFFECTED THE NUMBER OF CHILDREN

In modern times and in developed economies, there is typically a negative correlation between parental education and number of children. But when Ben-Porath analyzed data from kibbutzim in 1974, he found that higher-educated kibbutz women did not have fewer children. Avraham Ebenstein, Moshe Hazan and Avi Simhon (2015) showed these findings using the 1995 census (see figure 10.2). This was hardly surprising to the economists. In kibbutzim, all incomes were shared equally and parents did not face the usual

[20] See Autor, Katz, and Krueger (1998); Autor and Katz (1999), and recent updates of this survey, e.g., Autor, Katz, and Kearney, 2008.

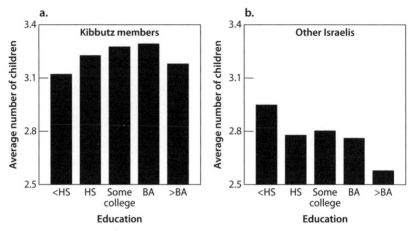

FIGURE 10.2: More-educated kibbutz members had more children. Sample comprises Jewish women born in Israel between 1930 and 1945. Note that the Y axis begins at 2.5 in order to zoom in on the differences in the number of children by education level. Source: Ebenstein et al. (2016), based on data from the Israel Central Bureau of Statistics (1995).

trade-off between earning more and spending more time with their children. Moreover, the kibbutz provided education, health care, food, and clothing for children. Parents thus did not bear the full financial costs of raising their children; the cost of having more children was lower than it was outside kibbutzim. That kibbutz children lived in special residences outside of their parents' homes further reduced the cost of raising children.

It is thus not surprising from an economic perspective that when kibbutzim were all based on equal sharing, women in the kibbutz had, on average, half a child more than other Jewish women in Israel.[21] Even after children moved to their parents' homes, parents with more children typically received bigger apartments. Cramped living quarters, a potential consequence of having additional children, were thus avoided. In short, kibbutzniks did not bear the full cost of raising their children, generating free-riding behavior whereby they had more children than city dwellers.

---

[21] See Ben-Porath (1974) and Ebenstein, Hazan, and Simhon (2016).

Did kibbutzniks start to have fewer children once their kibbutzim shifted away from equal sharing? Ebenstein, Hazan, and Simhon addressed this question in their 2016 study. They focused on parents and prospective parents who were most affected by the financial crisis and the subsequent shift away from equal sharing. Specifically, they focused on women aged thirty to forty at the time of the 1995 Israeli census, who were of prime childbearing age after the financial crisis and the shift away from equality.

The authors found that the reform reduced the number of children of kibbutzniks substantially. To be sure, the number of children per woman declined over this period in both kibbutzim that reformed and those that did not. But figure 10.3, which displays how the number of children vary with mother's birth year, shows the number of children in reformed kibbutzim declined by much more than the number in non-reformed kibbutzim.

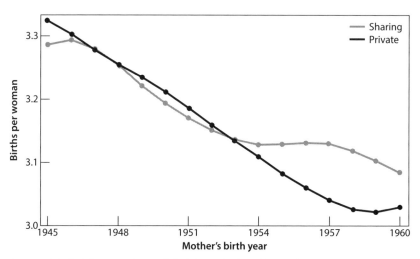

FIGURE 10.3: The number of children declined in reformed kibbutzim relative to ones that maintained equal sharing. The plot reports the fertility among Israeli Jews born between 1945 and 1960, restricted to ever-married women who were living in a kibbutz in 1995. The sample is stratified by whether the woman was observed at a kibbutz that retained sharing or eventually privatized. The X axis refers to the birth year of the mother. *Source*: Israel Central Bureau of Statistics (1995, 2008). I would like to thank Avi Ebenstein for providing this figure.

Ebenstein, Hazan, and Simhon found that the number of children declined the most for parents with less education (less than a college degree), who were likely to experience a decline in their incomes following the shift away from equality. They also found that the decline in the number of children was larger in bigger kibbutzim. This is consistent with the idea that free-riding by having more children was more prevalent in bigger kibbutzim. In smaller kibbutzim, social sanctions might have been stronger before the reform and helped limit the number of children.

Parents with many children who lived in egalitarian kibbutzim were more likely to stay in their kibbutz, because giving up living in a kibbutz was more costly for large families. Even in reformed kibbutzim, child services were offered at a discounted price relative to cities, so parents with many children stayed. Consistent with this idea, when I analyzed the linked 1983–1995 census, I found that kibbutzniks with bigger families in 1983, the eve of the financial crisis, were more likely to stay in their kibbutzim in the following decade.

HOW THE RISE IN INCOME INEQUALITY AFFECTED OTHER OUTCOMES

The shift away from income equality may have affected other outcomes, including free-riding, brain drain, and adverse selection. There is currently no systematic quantitative evidence on these, and the existing research is not able to distinguish causality from correlation; the evidence I discuss below should be considered indicative only. Anecdotally, the reforms improved the economic situation of many kibbutzim. For example, Mort and Brenner (2003) conducted an in-depth study of Kibbutz Gesher Haziv, a kibbutz that had always struggled and was one of the earliest to shift away from equal sharing. They reported, "In 2001, for the first time since its establishment as a kibbutz, Gesher Haziv turned a profit and dedicated most of it to care for the founding generation and to an economic safety net for those members who can't adequately support themselves." The second half of this sentence illustrates how providing a safety net nevertheless remained an important objective.

It became clear that most members wanted to work and earn for their families. As one member of Kibbutz Gesher was quoted saying: "[M]ost strong members said that they actually don't want to carry on their back those who don't earn, that they want to take care of themselves."[22]

Kibbutz members, as it turns out, are not immune to economic incentives. As one member of Kibbutz Hasolelim put it, "One couple, who worked reduced hours, refused to apply for national insurance benefits (i.e., welfare benefits). Two years ago, when they saw their paychecks under the new system, you should have seen them running to the National Insurance Institute!" (Gavron 2000, p. 101).

How did the rising inequality affect work ethic in kibbutzim? Mort and Brenner (2003, p. 43) quote Halperin, the trustee for the Israeli government on the Kibbutz Arrangement Board, as saying in 1997, at the height of the crisis, "We are witnessing the erosion of the kibbutz work ethic and the collapse of the labor system, both of which are taking a toll on kibbutz life. The kibbutz work ethos was as integral to kibbutz ideology as the ethos of cooperation and equality. Lacking the work ethos, the kibbutz community cannot survive."

One way to shed light on motivation and work quality would be to compare survey data on the perceived work ethic of kibbutz members with those of city natives. Unfortunately, such data exist only for kibbutzim. Surveys of public opinion conducted in kibbutzim in 2003 and 2005, which was after many kibbutzim had already shifted away from equal sharing, asked kibbutz members about the work ethic in their kibbutz. These survey data identify whether the respondent lived in a full equal-sharing kibbutz or in a reformed kibbutz,[23] and thus can be used to compare perceived work ethic in kibbutzim with different degrees of equal sharing.[24] If

---

[22] Shlezinger Liat, The Kibbutzim Are Dealing with the Privatization, *nrg*, June 27, 2009, http://www.nrg.co.il/online/1/ART1/908/011.html.

[23] The scale for the kibbutz degree of equality is 1–4, where 4 is the full equal-sharing category and 1 is the least equal safety-net category (which still involves more redistribution than outside kibbutzim).

[24] Perceived work ethic is not a perfect measure of work quality, both because it is subjective and because we cannot ensure that members classify their kibbutz's work ethic in the same way.

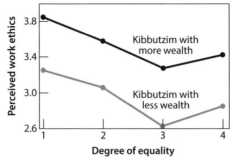

FIGURE 10.4: Kibbutzim with greater equality had lower work ethics. The black line gives average reported work ethic for kibbutzim with high levels of wealth; the gray line gives average reported work ethic for kibbutzim with low levels of wealth. Kibbutz members were asked about how they perceive the level of work ethic in their kibbutz. The graph shows the average response to this question (1 is the lowest and 4 is the highest), by kibbutz compensation scheme and economic condition. The X axis gives the degree of equality in the kibbutz, where 1 corresponds to a low level of equality (safety-net model) and 4 corresponds to full equal sharing. Data source: "Survey of Public Opinion in the Kibbutzim" (Palgi and Orchan 2005).

equal sharing encouraged shirking as incentive theory predicts, we expect work ethic in kibbutzim with higher degrees of equality to be lower. Figure 10.4 illustrates that this is the case, to some extent.

One possibility is that kibbutzim with different degrees of equality might have different levels of wealth and that kibbutz wealth rather than degree of equality may have driven shirking behavior. Indeed, figure 10.4 suggests that wealthier kibbutzim reported higher work ethic. But figure 10.4 also shows that even when comparing kibbutzim with similar wealth levels, reported work ethic was somewhat lower in kibbutzim with more income equality.

One member of Kibbutz Hasolelim, which shifted away from equal sharing, defended the reform: "Was Hasolelim more of a kibbutz when each member thought he was doing all the work and the other members were living on his back? I ask myself: Was it more of a kibbutz when we were forced to stop calling volunteer work days because no one turned up?" (Gavron 2000, p. 89).

Another question to ask is whether the shift away from equal sharing reduced wastage, inducing members to squander fewer communal resources such as food, electricity, and water. Anecdotally, it seems to have. The secretary of Hasolelim noted, "[T]he introduction of individual electricity meters cut consumption by almost a third . . . even though members were not at first asked to pay for their electricity" (Gavron 2000, p. 92). This could suggest that making actions observable and the threat of social shame, rather than the financial incentives, did some of the trick. That being said, financial incentives were clearly important too.

Anecdotal evidence and official reports also suggest that the shift away from equality seems to have been successful in keeping members inside. For example, David Koren, a former member of the Knesset (Israeli parliament) and a member of Kibbutz Gesher Haziv, commented, "Since we started with the privatization, no one has left (the kibbutz)."[25]

The rising income inequality also affected the use of money in kibbutzim. Following the crisis and reforms, money started to play a bigger role in kibbutzim, and kibbutzniks opened personal bank accounts. Inside the kibbutz, members could still get by without using money, instead paying with credit that would be deducted from their monthly allowances. But there was more interaction with the outside, especially for members who worked outside their kibbutz. Some kibbutz members had difficulty adjusting to the various aspects of a money economy. Kibbutzniks attended financial literacy workshops that taught them how to write checks, use credit cards, and so on.

Azarnert, Goldberg, and Franck (2014) used quarterly macro data over the 1989–2005 period to indirectly estimate the effect of the shift away from equality on kibbutz members' demand for money. They found that "the entrance of kibbutz members into the monetary system affected only aggregate cash but not checkable deposits or the sum of cash and deposits." They concluded that kibbutz members tended to prefer cash to deposits. In their words: "Being unfamiliar with the intricacies of banking, partial reserves, deposit insurance, checks, and credit cards, kibbutz members kept their money under the mattress, so to speak."

---

[25] As quoted in the Israeli newspaper *Yedioth Aharonot*, May 22, 2002. A good avenue for future research would be to test quantitatively whether kibbutzim that shifted away from equal sharing experienced a decline in exit rates.

Despite improved incentives, at least some members miss their traditional egalitarian kibbutz. One veteran of Kibbutz Hasolelim commented, "[T]hey have stolen the kibbutz away from me" and, "I came here to live a certain way of life, and it has been turned on its head. If the others want a non-kibbutz, so be it, but at least they should give me—and anyone else who wants it—the option of living the old way" (Gavron 2000, p. 101). The frustration is, of course, understandable, but it is also understandable that kibbutzim could not offer such a choice because it would have invited adverse selection into the "old way" group.

More generally, while in surveys members of more equal kibbutzim reported being less happy about the work ethic in their kibbutzim, they seemed happier about some other important aspects of their kibbutzim. Specifically, they reported better social atmospheres and better cultural activities in their kibbutzim, as shown in figure 10.5. These patterns suggest that equality in kibbutzim had certain benefits, even if work ethic suffered. As is usually the case in economics, everything involves a trade-off.

At the same time, figures 10.4 and 10.5 suggest that kibbutzim in the full-equality range (4's) do better in terms of both work ethic and quality of life than kibbutzim in the high- but not full-equality range (3's), which is opposite to expectations. I do not wish to make too much of this finding, because it is impossible to tell how much it is real and how much is statistical noise. To the extent that this pattern is real, it might tell us something important and subtle about the nature of the kibbutz—that kibbutzim that were able to maintain full equality were somehow able to solve the free-rider problem without sacrificing the social atmosphere and quality of life. This is an interesting avenue for future research.

To sum up, some evidence supports that the shift away from equal sharing improved incentives. The shift away from income equality increased the return to schooling in kibbutzim. As a result, kibbutz-born high school students whose kibbutz reformed started to take school more seriously, received better grades, were more likely to matriculate, and completed more years of university education. Kibbutz members also had fewer kids following the reform, because raising children was now the financial responsibility

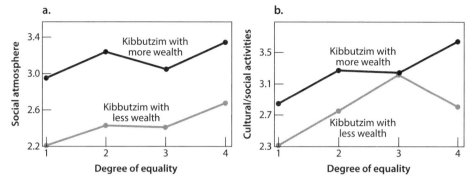

FIGURE 10.5: Social atmosphere and cultural activities in kibbutzim increase with level of equality. The left-hand panel (a) shows the reported quality of the social atmosphere in kibbutzim with high and low wealth levels by their degree of equality. The right-hand panel (b) shows the reported quality of cultural and social activities. In each case, the black line gives averages for kibbutzim with high levels of wealth, and the gray line gives averages for kibbutzim with low levels of wealth. The response scale ranges from 1 (the lowest) to 4 (the highest). The X axis gives the degree of equality in the kibbutz, where 1 corresponds to a low level of equality (safety-net model) and 4 corresponds to full equal sharing. Source: "Survey of Public Opinion in the Kibbutzim" (Palgi and Orchan 2005).

of the family rather the entire kibbutz. Anecdotal evidence suggests that the reforms alleviated brain drain, although more evidence is needed on this question. Compared with members in kibbutzim that remained egalitarian, members in kibbutzim that shifted away from income equality reported higher work ethic in their kibbutz. However, such members also reported lower levels of satisfaction from social life. More generally, anecdotal evidence suggests a revival of kibbutzim, with reduced exit and increased entry that reverses the recent demographic trends. It will be interesting to test these more systematically and to test the effects of the shift away from equality on a range of other outcomes, such as mortality and the marriage market.

CHAPTER 11

On the (lack of) stability of communes: an economic perspective

COMMUNES IN ECONOMIC PERSPECTIVE

While this book is about kibbutzim, I hope I have been able to convey that its insights apply much more broadly than to kibbutzim alone. The lessons from kibbutzim apply to any society and organization striving for even some degree of income equality and redistribution. Examples of such societies and organizations include welfare states, villages in developing countries, firms, and insurance schemes. This chapter aims to illustrate some lessons from and for other communes.

There are striking parallels in the structural and incentive problems faced by the kibbutzim and by North American communes, though many of the latter did not last as long or adapt as well. Specifically, this chapter uses the economic perspective developed in this book to shed light on the conditions under which communes that strive for equality and cooperation are stable, how they persist, and why they often collapse.[1] It presents a view of communes as communities striving for internal equality while mitigating the inherent problems associated with a high degree of equality: the tendency of more productive members to leave (brain drain); the

---

[1] See also Abramitzky (2011b).

tendency to shirk (free-riding); and the tendency of less-productive individuals to join (adverse selection).

The inherent problems associated with equal sharing of resources mean most communes in history have been short-lived. Communes that were better able to structure themselves to solve these problems lasted longer and were more successful (e.g., Oved 1993). We will pay particular attention to the Hutterites, whose long-lived communities still exist today. The Hutterites have maintained equality and mutual aid for many years, despite changes in their surrounding environment that have forced other communes to disband.

Attempts to solve these problems explain many of communes' shared key features, such as their constant struggle between isolation from and adaptation to outside influences,[2] the homogeneity of their members, their reliance on ideology and religion, their rituals, their small sizes, their communal ownership of property, and the commune-specific nature of the human capital of their members.

I will discuss how ideology and religion play important roles in alleviating brain drain, adverse selection, and free-riding. As we saw in figure 6.3 of chapter 6, ideological members are more likely to stay even if they are very skilled, because ideology increases members' perceived value of living in the commune (their inside option). The same argument holds for very religious members. Ideology and religion thus help alleviate the brain drain problem. They also serve as hard-to-fake signals of commitment to the commune, thereby alleviating both adverse selection (by preventing free-riders from entering)[3] and free-riding (by promoting loyalty and norms of cooperation).[4] Furthermore, because it seems plausible that religious rituals are typically more difficult to fake than socialist rituals, religious communes have generally been more successful than socialist ones. They are better at screening out applicants who seek to enter for the wrong reasons, and are better at encouraging out the door people with weak religious beliefs, who would shirk because they have no religious zeal telling them not to.

---

[2] This struggle also reflects some communes' aspiration to influence the outside world with their ideology.

[3] See, e.g., Iannaccone (1992) and Berman (2000).

[4] See, e.g., Sosis (2000) and Sosis and Bressler (2003).

The focus is on communes in North America since the mid-1700s and comparisons with Israeli kibbutzim, mainly because these are better documented than communes in earlier periods. It would be impossible to comprehensively discuss other communes in a single chapter, and here I do not attempt to do so. Furthermore, much research on these communes is yet to be done. My purpose in this chapter is rather to briefly suggest how the insights from kibbutzim that I laid out in earlier chapters might apply to other communes. I refer the reader who wants to learn more about these communes to other books, some of which are referenced in this chapter. I found two books particularly helpful for the purpose of this book: Oved's comprehensive work, *Two Hundred Years of American Communes* (1993) and Pitzer's collection of essays in *America's Communal Utopias* (1997).

LONG-LIVED COMMUNES FROM AMERICA'S HISTORY

This section discusses some significant historical American communes that are well documented in the literature and from which I draw lessons later in this chapter. American communes have existed continuously since the mid-1700s, founded largely by immigrants from Europe. Freedom of religion in the United States provided an opportunity for many sects that were religiously persecuted or oppressed in Europe to form communities in which they could freely practice their beliefs. In addition, the abundance of land was ideal for communes that needed to acquire land at low prices in regions where they could maintain their isolation.[5]

The Shakers, a protestant Christian sect that originated in England, formed the first long-lived communes; as a large-scale movement, they survived for seventy years.[6] The Shakers initially immigrated to the American colonies in 1774 as a group of nine

[5] Communes in the United States have been geographically dispersed. However, many communes formed in more isolated regions, even when settling in the more populated East Coast, and some (Harmony, Amana) actually relocated to the West, motivated by their desire for greater isolation.

[6] By 1920, only twelve Shaker communes were left.

members. By 1850, the sect consisted of close to four thousand adherents. During a history of over two hundred years, eighteen separate Shaker communities have been established from Kentucky to Maine (Pitzer 1997), all under communal principles. Most Shaker communes were relatively prosperous through the nineteenth century until membership began to dwindle in the twentieth century. Natural increase was not an option, as the Shakers lived according to the principle of celibacy.

Another early commune was the Woman in the Wilderness, a religious commune established in 1694 on the northern shore of the Chesapeake Bay by forty male immigrants from Germany. The commune's life was centered around the expectant arrival of the kingdom of heaven. After the kingdom of heaven was repeatedly postponed, the commune began its disintegration and in 1741 the commune was dissolved. The religious commune Ephrata was established in 1732 in near present-day Lancaster, Pennsylvania. The commune's main defining features were celibacy and observance of many customs of Jewish origin, such as the Sabbath and circumcision. At its peak, the commune numbered around one hundred members. The commune lasted until the 1790s.

In the beginning of the nineteenth century, a number of other communes were formed. For example, Harmony, a Lutheran Christian sect originated near Stuttgart in Germany, under the leadership of George Rapp. The first group of about five hundred members arrived in America in 1804 and within a year organized the Harmony Society in Pennsylvania (Oved 1993). By 1810, the commune's population had reached nine hundred. To manage an increasing population and escape rising costs and unfriendly relationships with neighbors, the commune relocated to New Harmony, Indiana, less than ten years later; in 1825, this time for religious reasons, to live closer to German-speaking neighbors, and to improve access to markets, it returned to Pennsylvania. The Harmony colony was mostly prosperous during its existence, even after George Rapp's death in 1847. However, due to celibacy and limited member recruiting, its numbers diminished significantly until it dissolved in 1916 (Pitzer 1997). Robert Owen purchased New Harmony in Indiana from the Harmony Society in 1825, when the Harmonites relocated to Pennsylvania, and used the existing infrastructure to construct a socialist commune. The commune accepted members without selective criteria, and expanded rapidly to a population of nearly one thousand. Members' heterogeneity caused many schisms and a number of factions departed to establish their own communes. In addition, the commune was burdened by debt to George Rapp. This social experiment came to an end in 1827 (Oved 1993).

Another commune was Zoar, a communal society established in 1817 by German religious dissenters called the Society of Separatists of Zoar in Ohio. Their immigration to the United States was a result of religious oppression from the Lutheran Church in Germany. Their leader, Joseph Bimeler, was known to be charismatic, but his death in the 1850s lead to a disintegration in the cohesion of the commune, and members voted in 1898 to dissolve the communal society.

Amana was a group of colonies in Iowa established by a religious sect originating from the Community of True Inspiration in Germany. The sect had existed since the early 1700s, but it wasn't until the 1840s that several hundred members immigrated to the United States in the hopes of establishing independent communal settlements. They initially established settlements near Buffalo, New York, but as the city expanded they decided to relocate further west to Iowa, where they established the Amana colonies. By 1865, the transfer was complete and the sect numbered 1,200 members (Oved 1993). For a time the communities, which dealt mostly with agriculture and farming, prospered. Amana's decline resulted both from its younger generation calling for revision of the strict religious rules and communal system and from the economic impact of the Depression. In 1931, the members voted to reorganize the commune and abolish it as an economic entity.

A little later in the nineteenth century, other communes joined these. One was Oneida, a religious commune in upstate New York, established in 1847 under the leadership of John Humphrey Noyes. Prior to settling in Oneida, members of the group resided for a decade in Putney, Vermont. The group practiced a complex marriage system, with the goal of moving beyond the "egotism for two" implicit in monogamous family life and creating an "enlarged family" in which all loyalties, including sexual loyalties, would eventually be raised to the level of the entire community (Pitzer 1997). In order to prevent unwanted births, male continence was promoted and expected as a measure of birth control. The commune was successful in its agricultural and manufacturing activities, and at its peak reached 250 members. In 1879, the complex marriage system was abandoned, due to mounting public pressure. With the retreat from the complex marriage system and the return to the monogamous family, commune members began to lose their conviction. In 1880, members agreed to dissolve the commune.

Another commune was Bishop Hill, established 1846 in Illinois by a Swedish religious group led by Eric Jansen. Nearly all Eric Janssen's 1,400 followers emigrated from Sweden to the United States between 1846 and 1854 (Pitzer 1997). Just four years after the founding of Bishop Hill, Jansen was murdered in a dispute with one of the commune's new members. In 1854, the new leader forced the commune to adopt celibacy, and members who objected were expelled. In 1857, a recession hit agriculture and industry. The younger members used this financial undermining to rebel against the spiritual stagnation of the trustees and in 1859 came a demand to dissolve the commune. In 1862, the group disbanded (Oved 1993).

In addition to the religious communes, socialist communes began to appear in the United States in the 1820s, many established by European migrants. Icaria was a socialist movement led by Etienne Cabet and originally established in France. In 1848, Cabet guided a group of emigrants to found a new society in the United States. Icaria movement members settled in several locations throughout the United States (Illinois, Missouri, Iowa, and California). All the Icaria communes ended up dissolving, due to limited membership as a result of language barriers and economic struggles.

Another example is Fourierism, a utopian socialist doctrine, which influenced the establishment of twenty-one secular communes throughout the United States primarily in the 1840s. Its originator was Charles Fourier, a French utopian visionary who spread his ideas during the early nineteenth century. In Fourierist communes, there was no common ownership, only common use of resources, and members earned according to the work they invested. However, housing, food, health services, and education were promised to everyone (Oved 1993). The most prominent Fourierist commune was Brook Farm in Massachusetts. Life on Brook Farm centered around its local educational institution, which attracted students from all over New England. With the exception of one last attempt at a Fourierist commune in Kansas in 1869, all Fourier communes had dissolved by 1859, mostly due to economic struggles.[7]

THE HUTTERITES

The only communes in the United States that were established before the twentieth century and still exist today are the Hutterites. A number of important principles characterize the Hutterites: communal ownership of all property, equality in the distribution of resources, strong religious ideology, reluctance to absorb new members unless candidates demonstrate strong commitment to the commune, education and socialization entirely within the commune, maintenance of the appropriate membership size for the communal framework, and many children. The Hutterites adhered strictly to these principles and incorporated mechanisms to relieve pressure and accommodate the needs of young members. In addition, their economic prosperity and openness to adopting the newest technologies for their agricultural practices brought stability to commune members.

It is interesting to note that some of these factors were also key to the survival of Israeli kibbutzim in the twentieth century. Kibbutzim, too, were established by European immigrants who wanted to establish a more just society based on the principles of equal sharing and communal ownership of resources. They, too, have been reluctant to absorb outsiders unless candidates demonstrated strong commitment to the commune's way of life. Like the Hutterites,

---

[7] Two short-lived communes are the Kaweah Cooperative Colony and Llano del Rio. Kaweah Cooperative Colony was a socialist communal settlement established on the western slopes of the Sierra Nevada in central California in 1887. Llano del Rio was another socialist commune established in 1914 outside of Los Angeles. It lasted only four years, and at its height—three years after its establishment—its population approached 900 (Pitzer 1997).

kibbutzim had their own education system, where they tried to instill their values in their children, and traditionally few members pursued higher education. I next discuss the Hutterites in more detail, how they dealt with various challenges, and how they compare and contrast with kibbutzim.

The Hutterites emerged from a sect that had been living in European communes for 350 years prior to their arrival in the United States. Their history involves a series of migrations in search of religious freedom. After hundreds of years of persecution throughout Europe, these migrations eventually led them to North America. Although World War I displaced many Hutterites from the United States into Canada, many Hutterite settlements stayed put in the United States. Hutterite colonies today are located throughout the two countries.

Modern-day Hutterites can attribute their continued success to a few factors: an uncompromising belief system, strong socialization of members from a young age, a high birth rate, and proper management of innovation. We will see how these attributes, alongside some other contributing factors (expansion guidelines, difficult application process, avoiding work specialization), helped both the Hutterites and kibbutzniks mitigate problems within their communities.

The first and most important way that the Hutterites survive to this day, as well as avoid problems like brain drain, is through their uncompromising belief system. Being a community rooted in religious ideology, their beliefs "prove the foundation for the Hutterites' willingness to die rather than change their social institutions" (Hostetler 1997, p. 286). Even though they practiced forms of privatized farming during times of persecution, the Hutterites managed to persevere through these periods and continue to live communally today.[8]

---

[8] At various times in their history, the Hutterites were unable to withstand the problems that their surrounding environments placed on them. During their stay in Europe, there were moments when persecutions against the Hutterites led to a breakdown in harmony. Some of the sects ended up completely breaking down, as their communities had taken too much damage from wars and attacks. That being said, not all Hutterite sects were destroyed; those that survived relied on factors like their uncompromising belief system to persevere through these tough times.

This uncompromising belief system is a quality shared by the kibbutz movement at the outset, as they were both built on similar premises: each rejected current authority and wanted to start a community based on socialist/communal values. Members in kibbutzim pushed selfish instincts aside and worked for the greater good of the community as a whole. A strong ideology enhanced members' loyalty to their community and gave them a reason to continue abiding by communal practices regardless of the enticing incentive to shirk and free-ride.

To preserve an uncompromising belief system requires comprehensive socialization of members beginning from a very young age. Without strong ideology imparted through socialization, there is no guarantee that as members age and are increasingly exposed to the outside world, they won't reject communal principles. The Hutterites use their education system to instill Hutterite values in young children, and ensure that as adults they would be dedicated members. Children of school age (ages six to fifteen) are taught unquestioning obedience to Hutterite authority—such as teachers, parents, and adults—as well as to the specific practices and teachings of the Hutterite community (Hostetler 1997). Although English school is required, the Hutterites view this as a mandate instead of a learning opportunity, and discourage students from furthering their knowledge in subjects such as math and science. By not permitting further learning in these subjects, Hutterites reduce brain drain by limiting the outside opportunities available to their members. Like the Hutterites, kibbutzim used education to instill desired values into their members. Education within the kibbutzim promoted altruism and caring more about the collective than about oneself. Additionally, kibbutzim, too, encouraged members to learn skills that were more valuable within kibbutzim than in the outside world.

Another method that the Hutterites use for long-term survival veers away from ideology and focuses on the importance of families.[9] Hutterites place high value on having children; families are

---

[9] Benham and Keefer (1991) also emphasized governance, such as restrictions on who could place items on the agenda and limits on the number of voting members.

assured support for all the kids they decide to have. Demographers report that the average Hutterite family has over ten children, with an average interval between births in a family of two years (Hostetler 1997). The motivation behind encouraging families to have many children is fairly straightforward: the higher the population, the more people the colony has for expansion to ensure its success in the future. Reproduction rates in kibbutzim were not nearly as high as they were in Hutterite colonies—kibbutzim hovered around three children per family. The difference may relate to the lower level of security enjoyed by the Hutterites, which was exacerbated by hostility from surrounding civilizations. For many years the future of kibbutzim seemed secure, whereas the survival of future Hutterite generations relied on multiplying from within.

With a higher reproduction rate for Hutterites, however, come greater problems such as free-riding and brain drain. Among the numerous children born, it is more likely that some will pursue outside options, and some will endeavor to hide behind the work of others. The Hutterites combat these problems by continually expanding their territory. Once a colony hits its maximal population of around 130 to 150 members, it looks to expand and create a new colony. By not allowing colonies to get too large, the Hutterites ensure that each able-bodied member in the colony has a role and no members are left idle, minimizing free-riding since each individual has a responsibility to the community. New colonies are built within a few miles of existing colonies, and ideally about thirty miles away from their parent colony (Hostetler 1997). By creating a dense network of colonies, they lessen the risk of interactions with the outside world.

The Hutterites carefully manage their adoption of innovations to preserve their values. Some subcultures in North America failed to survive through periods of industrialization, as they were unable to retain their social bonds while managing the modernization (Hostetler 1997). The Hutterites differ, however, in that they introduce only new technology that benefits them economically as a community, rather than benefiting individuals. For the Hutterites, "the crucial consideration in mechanization, aside from large risks in investments, is whether the change will introduce too many elements of personal convenience" (Hostetler 1997, p. 299). When young men began to wear belts instead of suspenders, for example, there was no problem. However, when these belts became embellished, they turned into a sign of individuality, and were thus banned from Hutterite society. Other examples of innovations adopted by Hutterites that aided the community at large rather than individuals include automatic thermostats that were used in hog barns before they were used in dwellings; floor coverings that appeared in the communal kitchen before they were allowed in family apartments; electric floor polishers that were first used in some of the wealthier colonies and are still not permitted in others. Even the trend to install plumbing in family apartments is for some Hutterites a concession to convenience, but is ultimately justified on the basis of sanitation and health (Hostetler 1997). By pursuing the greater good of the community at large, rather than an individual's convenience, the Hutterites maintain a high level of communal ideology while still benefiting from innovation.

The Hutterites use many other lock-in devices to ensure the longevity of their communities, some of which are similar to the lock-in mechanisms used by kibbutzim. Most Hutterites are born into the colony, rather than entering from the outside. Those who do attempt to enter from the outside are given a one-year probation period to prove their worth to the community. Since the selection process is so competitive, only around fifty to a hundred new members have been admitted during the Hutterites' century-long stay in the United States (Oved 1993, Hostetler 1997). The tough selection process ensures the ideological zeal of new members, thus reducing adverse selection into the Hutterite colonies. Kibbutzim also were reluctant to take members in from the outside, but were not opposed to those with a strong desire to enter. Applicants were required to go through a lengthy application process as well (completing multiple forms and interviews, submitting a handwriting sample, etc.) to be considered for entry. Both kibbutz and Hutterite members knew the appeal that their communities could have for low-income and/or lazy workers who craved the economic protection. Both also had to make sure the select members they brought in did not end up returning to the outside world; neither allowed members much private property (including money), which greatly increased the difficulty of exit.

Lastly, from a business standpoint, the Hutterites have not always focused on maintaining enterprises that generated the most profit, but rather favored multiple smaller enterprises with lower profit margins. They traditionally placed a strong emphasis on ensuring constant work, which increased stability within the commune, because a "lack of work could mean the breakdown of harmony" (Hostetler 1997, p. 182). Constantly having work also kept adults from having much free time to pursue other activities that may lead to brain drain (learning English, developing other agricultural skills, etc.). The importance of work was just as stressed within kibbutzim. Members within kibbutzim were taught to have a strong work ethic, and kibbutzim had a reward/punishment system to ensure that members were not free-riding off others.

Hutterites still practice equal sharing today, but of a less strict variety. In Hutterite communities, as in kibbutzim, the shift away from traditional equal sharing came in response to advancements made in their surrounding environment. However, the Hutterites stuck more closely to their core values and traditions than did kibbutzim. Additionally, both communities dealt with a diminishing strength in ideology: over generations, ideology becomes more difficult to maintain, and outside options continue to improve and pull members away.

PROVIDING EQUALITY WHILE MITIGATING FREE-RIDING AND ADVERSE SELECTION

Consider a commune that desires equality in the distribution of resources, say, because it wants to provide members with insurance or because it has preferences for redistribution. The commune chooses a sharing rule (degree of equality) and a set of internal rules and norms to mitigate three problems: brain drain, adverse selection, and free-riding. A higher degree of equality makes these problems more severe. Thus, the commune, like almost every modern society, faces a trade-off between equality and incentives, and it needs to design its rules and norms while accounting for both. As already discussed, this simple conceptual framework rationalizes many of the key principles of kibbutzim, the timing of their recent shift away from equal sharing, and the differences among kibbutzim in the degree of this shift. Here I illustrate that this framework also rationalizes the factors that are believed to have affected the stability of US communes over the past two centuries. Furthermore, I discuss in more depth the roles of ideology and religion in the stability of communes.

As in the kibbutz, more-productive members have stronger incentives to leave their communes because they are forced to share their earnings with less productive individuals. Indeed, Murray (1995) shows that literate members of the Shaker communes in nineteenth-century America were more likely to exit, and I earlier showed a brain drain process in kibbutzim in the 1980s and 1990s in which more-educated and higher-skilled members were substantially more likely to leave.[10] Hutterite members complained that "those who worked outside the commune . . . did not maintain a modest life style. They were attracted by luxurious ways and kept some of their income in order to equal their standard of living to the one prevailing outside the communes" (Oved 1993, p. 344). Pitzer (1997) also mentions that those leaving Bishop Hill were primarily men, who had a greater chance to manage on their own outside of the commune. Oved (1993) explains that in Woman of the Wilderness the first to leave were intellectuals. Such a brain drain process threatens to leave communes with only the least productive members, resulting in a low standard of living for everyone.

Similarly, less-productive individuals living outside communes are expected to be the first to seek to enter them, because inside they expect to be subsidized by more-productive individuals (adverse selection). Murray (1995) shows that illiterate individuals were more likely to enter the Shaker communal societies, and I earlier showed that individuals who earned lower wages were more likely to enter kibbutzim.

---

[10] See also Coşgel and Murray (1998).

Brain drain and adverse selection are aggravated when economic conditions outside the commune improve, because this is generally accompanied by an increase in the return to skills outside. Indeed, when Israel's economy became more focused on advanced technology, which offers greater returns to skills, exit from kibbutzim increased. Equality, a socialist commune established in Washington State at the end of the nineteenth century, lived a similar story. This was a period of economic expansion for the region, and the more-talented members and professionals who could earn better livings outside the commune were tempted to leave (Oved 1993). Communes' economic activity often forced them to integrate into the market in a way contrary to their original intentions. The decline of Sunrise, an anarchist commune in Michigan established during the Depression era, was partially attributed to its close proximity to Detroit, which experienced a great resurgence in the auto industry as the Depression came to an end (Oved 1993).[11]

COMMUNES' INSTITUTIONAL DESIGN

The exit option threatens the stability of communes because it exposes them to possible brain drain. This may explain why in systems like the Russian kolkhozes and the Chinese household registration system (*hukou*), exit was prohibited. When members are not permitted to exit, brain drain is a nonissue, and equality is easier to maintain. It should also be noted that when exit is restricted and power is unequally spread among the individual members, an equal-sharing rule could be more prone to corruption,

[11] Sunrise was a Jewish anarchist commune established in 1933 in Michigan. Their main source of income was the farm on which the commune was established. Several months after its establishment, the commune had 216 inhabitants, and most of them were Jews from various states in the East and Midwest. The founders were mainly anarchists, but those who joined later came from a more heterogeneous background, including union activists, communists, or members of Poalei Zion, a Jewish religious socialist movement (Oved 1993). This heterogeneity caused internal strife, and when the 1934 crops failed due to a drought, many members started to leave the commune. As the financial instability and the frictions continued, more members left until the summer of 1939, when the community was dissolved.

which in turn increases inequality (e.g., as in formerly communist countries). However, communes have always been based on voluntary participation and so have had to deal with the problem of brain drain.

As already discussed, to deal with the related problem of adverse selection, successful communes were generally very selective in their admission of outsiders (Oved 1993; Abramitzky 2009) or were more likely to admit individuals who were young adults (e.g., kibbutzim) or children (e.g., Shakers), and thus who were homogeneous in their expected productivity. The Hutterites had many barriers for entry that deterred most candidates. These barriers included the language spoken by the Hutterites (Hutterisch), differences in culture, and rules against accepting divorced people.[12]

The few communes that were less selective, such as New Harmony and Christian Commonwealth, did not survive for long. New Harmony in Indiana, discussed previously, accepted members without selective criteria, and expanded quite rapidly to a population of nearly one thousand. Members' heterogeneity caused many schisms, and many groups departed to establish their own communes. In total, this social experiment lasted only a couple of years (Oved 1993). The Christian Commonwealth, a commune established in 1896 in Georgia, had a similar experience. Its founders had come from among Christian socialist circles, and they intended to create an open, nonselective communitarian society (Oved 1993). In its first years, the colony was characterized by optimistic enthusiasm. However, this receded in 1899 when a number of social, personal, and economic calamities struck. Extreme weather patterns in 1898 and 1899 destroyed their crops, and a former member wrote a book

[12] Although some colonies offered membership to outsiders, there were many barriers for entry that deterred most candidates. The first barrier for many outsiders was Hutterisch, the Carinthian-Tirolean dialect spoken by the Hutterites, which is difficult for outsiders to pick up. Second, large differences in culture and traditions proved too foreign for many outsiders. Third, outsiders who were divorced and remarried were ineligible for membership. The divorcés who became members were allowed to marry only their original partner. Lastly, similar to the culture shock, most outsiders could not sacrifice their free will, career, and personal belongings to become members.

presenting the colony as a free-love community for the purpose of discrediting it. In 1899, members decided to dissolve the colony and sell its assets.

Before entering many communes, potential members had to signal their serious intentions by demonstrating support of the key religious or socialist principle of the commune. Adverse selection can be in terms of ability or in terms of belief or ideology. Ideally, the commune would like to attract members of high ability and high belief or ideology. It seems reasonable that someone who is serious about his or her belief would also be more likely to work hard and vice versa, but this is not necessarily the case; there could be adverse selection along one of the dimensions but not the other. For immigrant communes, such as Icaria, Amana, Zoar, and Bishop Hill, members could signal their commitment by migrating from Europe to America. The requirement for new members to first signal their commitment mitigated adverse selection and free-riding while creating a positive externality for other members, who got to enjoy living among people who shared their belief system.

The adverse selection problem may be aggravated when the commune's population is more diverse. With more heterogeneous candidates and members, overlap between the candidates' background and the backgrounds of current commune members who will make the admission decision tends to be less, and thus members have more difficulty identifying the candidates who are good fits. Israeli kibbutzim chose new members mostly from among Israelis of European descent, which characterized most kibbutz members as well. These mutual backgrounds enabled better recognition of certain traits in a relatively brief trial period and relieved some of the adverse-selection problems. Immigrant communes also managed to limit the heterogeneity of applicants and new members by focusing on immigrants, especially those from their own country. In Zoar, for example, the vast majority of new members were immigrants, primarily from Germany (Oved 1993). In the Icarian commune of Speranza in California, new members had to speak fluent French. In Bishop Hill, most new members were of Swedish descent.[13] Such requirements served as barriers to entry and might have alleviated adverse selection.

Celibacy in communes such as the Shakers, Ephrata, and Harmony is expected to contribute to stability because it eliminates the alternative loyalty to the family unit. Moreover, children are differentiating: families might have different number of children of different ages and needs. Celibacy is a way to keep the commune homogeneity of preferences, which increases stability. At the same time, celibacy is expected to increase the adverse-selection problem because such communes need to admit all new members, rather than gaining some naturally.

To deal with brain drain, communes instituted various lock-in mechanisms that increased the cost of exit and alleviated brain drain. The Hutterites, for example, built new colonies within a few miles of existing colonies to reduce contact with the outside world. Additionally, although many provided high levels of basic education, as did kibbutzim, communes often limited members to commune-specific education that was of little use in the outside world. Many also discouraged higher education[14] and held all property communally. These strategies all increased the cost of exit and mitigated brain drain. When these lock-in mechanisms were stronger, we expect to have seen less brain drain and a higher degree of equality. I earlier discussed these mechanisms in the context of the Israeli kibbutzim.

Another lock-in mechanism used by immigrant communes in the United States was limiting the amount of English taught. Oved (1993) discusses complaints of Harmony Society's dissenters that their leader, George Rapp, made withdrawal extremely difficult by refusing to let them learn English and by not allowing

---

[13] In fact, even the murderer of Bishop Hill's leader, one of the new members of Bishop Hill, was an American soldier of Swedish descent (Pitzer 1997).

[14] This was not true in all communes. In Oneida, for instance, children and adults were taught geometry, trigonometry, biology, chemistry, and physics, and five young members who were studying medicine, engineering, and law at Yale University came home during summer vacations to teach and expand the curriculum (Oved 1993, p. 180). In Brook Farm (a Fourierist commune), life was centered around the educational institutions, which served as a prep school for those who wished to continue to Harvard University (Oved 1993, p. 145).

them "knowledge of the liberal institutions of our country." In Amana, education for most members was only provided through the eighth grade. A few young men were sent out of the community to receive training in medicine, dentistry, pharmacy, or education, but Amana's elders chose to do this because it was deemed beneficial for their society (Pitzer 1997). Amana is an example of a society that did not limit the language training of its younger generation, and as a result suffered from greater exit rates among the younger generation in the late nineteenth century. Most members who left during this period were sixteen to forty years old (Pitzer 1997).

Financial liabilities also served as lock-in mechanisms in various US communes. In Harmony, a "book of debts" was created to record all members' contributions on joining, but this was only done because Pennsylvania state law required it. Members joining Bishop Hill gave over their money and assets; those who left got neither back (Pitzer 1997).

I earlier showed that higher total communal wealth is associated with a lower exit rate and a higher degree of equality in kibbutzim. Oved (1993) notes that some of the key characteristics of communes that were short-lived are that they settled in difficult agricultural areas and had poor land. For these communes, the smallest shock, such as a fire, drought, or quarrel between members, could bring their commune to collapse. In contrast, long-lived communes often were located on fertile land and thus could accumulate wealth.

When output is shared equally, individuals are likely to shirk and free-ride on others, which decreases the wealth of everyone in the commune. In the context of teamwork, Holmstrom (1982) shows that when only the group's (rather than each individual's) effort is observed, individuals have an incentive to free-ride. When effort is observed, peer monitoring and social sanctions can prevent free-riding even under equal sharing (Kandel and Lazear 1992).[15]

---

[15] Note that social sanctions are naturally less effective in solving participation constraints, because a member is less likely to care what the group thinks about her once she has left the commune.

I discussed how social sanctions and monitoring were used in kibbutzim to mitigate the free-rider problem. In US communes, members used diverse mechanisms to observe each other's work effort. In Icarian communes, women rotated between occupations every week, and they always worked in pairs (Pitzer 1997); in Bishop Hill, the harvest was always done in groups of two hundred (Pitzer 1997). In addition, communes set up punishment systems for kids starting at a very young age. The Hutterites socialized their children through strict education, and used social sanctions to teach them the importance of the community at large. By socializing from a young age, the Hutterites hoped to guarantee members' future motivation (Hostetler 1997).

This need for social sanctions could explain various internal practices common to communes, such as communal dining, repeated interactions between members, the efficient transmission of information between members that is facilitated by the lack of privacy, and the ubiquity of gossip. In the US context, many communes, including the Icarian communes in Illinois and Iowa, some Shaker communes, the Fourierist North American Phalanx, and Bishop Hill, built their living quarters as "apartments" in one building. As a result, members of these communes had frequent interaction with each other, even in their own living quarters. In religious communes, frequent congregational religious worship also facilitated monitoring and transmission of information.

Smaller groups are likely to be more effective in facilitating social sanctions and mutual monitoring. In fact, longer-lived communes often display an active concern about becoming too big, and some such as the Hutterites, Shakers, and Amana even split so as not to exceed a few hundred members.

Too small a group size may also be bad for stability if there are increasing returns to scale in the commune's economic activity, especially if production takes place inside the commune and the commune is isolated from the outside world. In kibbutzim, which range from about one hundred to one thousand members, group size does not seem to be correlated with the degree of equality within the commune. The optimal size of communes likely trades off returns to scale with the need for social sanctions and monitoring.

THE TRADE-OFF BETWEEN
ISOLATION AND INTEGRATION

In the literature about the history of the communes in the United States, the prevailing opinion was that most of them strove to cut themselves off from society ("the outside world"), to go into seclusion and isolation in order to practice their faith and way of life undisturbed.

—Oved 1993, p. 447

A key feature shared by all communes is that they struggled to find a balance between isolation and integration/assimilation. American communes typically started out with some degree of isolation, either geographical (as in the case of many socialist communes) or in their establishing principles and beliefs. In contrast to the Hutterites, for example, kibbutzim tended over time to become more similar to the society around them. This tension between isolation and assimilation is common to all surviving communes (Kanter 1972; Oved 1993). The framework developed in this book helps explain this tension and rationalizes the communes' choices of increased isolation or increased assimilation as a response to changes in their environments.

The historical literature suggests that religious communes desired isolation to allow their members to practice their religious beliefs, which were distinct from those of the outside world. The Harmony Society migrated from Pennsylvania to Indiana due to the sect's desire to live a life of seclusion (Oved 1993); Amana colonies were originally founded near Buffalo, New York, but as the city expanded, the members decided to relocate farther west to Iowa. Similarly, socialist communes desired isolation to create "ideal" societies, free from the influences of the rest of the world. According to Kanter (1972), the outside world imposed a threat to communes, and they strove to minimize contact with it. According to Oved (1993), communes actually preferred to isolate themselves from society to protect their way of life; isolation was not merely forced on them because of their inherent differences from the rest of society. For example, one of the Shakers' key principles was to withdraw from what was believed to be a sinful society. Sin was a justification for isolation of the group. The Shakers set up rules that restricted contact between members and outsiders to avoid "contaminating" contact with the world. Similarly, Oneida instilled in its members a sense of superiority toward the outside world and required members who worked outside their commune to receive "purification." When peddlers returned from their business (which generally would not last for more than a week), they were "cleansed from the worldly spirit by a thorough scrubbing and criticism of their comrades." (Oved 1993, p. 176). Isolation was a similarly important value for communes such as Harmony, Zoar, Amana, and the Hutterites. However, for the socialist communes, there was an ongoing conflict between assimilation and spreading their ideology—in particular, with respect to isolation versus recruiting new members for the commune.

I suggest an additional explanation for communes' desire for isolation, namely, that isolation alleviates the problems of brain drain (by increasing the cost of exit), adverse selection (by creating a hard-to-fake costly signal for entrants), and free-riding (by increasing cohesion and loyalty). If isolation were absolute, then members would not know about the outside world and their outside option, so the brain drain problem would disappear. Isolation also removes members from the outside labor market, causing them to lose skills that would make them more productive in the outside world, and thus reducing the brain drain problem.

However, even the most successful communes could never isolate themselves completely from the rest of society. First, they couldn't avoid relationships with their neighbors (e.g., mutual aid between Hutterites and nearby farmers), and they naturally attracted curiosity from outsiders (e.g., Shakers and Amish). Second, being on good legal and political terms with the state authorities aided survival. Third, despite the intentional isolation in terms of their values, ideology, and religion, the economic activity of stable communes could only function if it was integrated with the markets, especially after the shift from agriculture to industry. An agriculture-based economy may be largely self-sufficient; an industry-based economy, on the other hand, is much more likely to rely heavily on trade even for basics such as food.

The Amish are an interesting case in point here. The Amish are not classic communes: although members' lives are controlled by numerous prohibitions, they do own private property. However, they share many similarities with other American communes. Like the Hutterites, the Amish were a sect of Anabaptists who rejected the current religious teachings. Like other communes, they faced persecution in Europe, which eventually pushed them to the United States and Canada. Additionally, Amish communities provide each other with mutual aid and insurance. Each Amish district has a deacon—an officer who is responsible for managing a fund for less fortunate members. Other rules are also in place to help alleviate the financial burden for poorer members, such as interest-free loans to start businesses in wealthier districts (e.g., Choy 2016).

Although many factors have led to the continued survival of the Amish, their reliance on isolation is likely one of the most important reasons. Amish theology, which advocates humility and simplicity, emphasizes separation from the outside world, which is viewed as overly materialistic and corrupt. Many Amish districts opt to limit the use of technology and Internet access for their members (perhaps the aspect of Amish culture best known to outsiders). They speak a dialect unique to them[16] and have limited contact with the outside world. They are also required to wear a certain set of clothing to further isolate themselves from outsiders. Additionally, since the Amish are not required to adhere to mandatory state education laws, many districts only school children until they are fourteen years old.[17] This ensures members have equal education, and also helps alleviate brain drain by limiting members' outside options. Being able to devise their own education system also allows the Amish to instill their own values in their children, teaching them the importance of family and community over individual desires. This control over their education systems helped alleviate

[16] Although most also speak English, the Amish speak a dialect of German called Pennsylvania German. Church services are in German, and Amish children are taught German.

[17] The Amish are exempt from following mandatory state education, as well as Social Security and government-provided health insurance. These exemptions give the Amish free rein to live their lives with little intervention from the state.

free-riding. Lastly, the Amish avoid adverse selection by restricting entry to their community; it is said that acceptance of an outsider into an Amish community seldom occurs. Many districts also have their own rules and norms about punishment for rule breakers, a norm which Choy (2016) views as a way for parents to commit to punishing children who misbehave.

Today, Amish districts have been forced to change their surrounding environments. Rather than being rural, isolated areas, present-day districts have become more suburban in nature, as urban development has encroached on Amish settlement areas. Additionally, rising land prices have led members to abandon their traditional farming roles for other trades. In the Holmes County settlement, for example, many Amish men work as artisanal craftsmen in trades such as woodworking and masonry, or as small-business owners in areas such as retail or construction. Other Amish men work as unskilled or semi-skilled laborers, including for non-Amish employers (Choy, 2016). Nevertheless, they continue their efforts to remain isolated from the outside world and maintain their strong connection to their traditional values, which has helped them survive despite the changing environment.

Exposure to the outside world has obvious economic benefits, but it also threatens a commune's stability. Exposure increases brain drain, both because members' knowledge of outside options is greater and because their ideology may be weakened. The latter could also worsen free-riding because members with less ideology are more likely to shirk. One example of the tension between isolation and assimilation appears in the question of whether to hire outside workers. This is believed to threaten the stability of communes (Oved 1993; Simons and Ingram 1997) for three possible reasons: it is contrary to their ideology; outside workers earn a wage, which might provoke envy; and outside workers could also increase members' knowledge of their outside option.[18] Nevertheless, most communes (e.g., kibbutzim, Oneida, Harmony, and Amana)

---

[18] In religious communes, those hired laborers were nonbelievers. In socialist communes, the hired laborers put the commune into an employer-employee relationship, which was against socialist ideology.

eventually hired outside workers because it greatly improved their financial situations, which reduced the incentives of the most talented members to leave.

Most communes faced external environments that evolved so as to increasingly provide higher returns to skill, which threatened the stability of the communes by worsening the various incentive problems.[19] The framework suggested in this book implies that to survive, communes needed to respond either by increasing the difference between them and the rest of society (isolation) or by decreasing that difference (assimilation). Indeed, as their environment changed, communes either gradually became more isolated (e.g., the Hutterites) or gradually assimilated by introducing reforms that decreased the difference between them and the outside world (e.g., Amana, Zoar, Oneida, and kibbutzim). Which of the two options is chosen could be a function of whether the outside world is supportive, whether the ideology dictates avoidance of high living standards, and so on.

We saw that increasing isolation is one possible response to higher returns to skill outside the commune and the brain drain they cause. Alternatively, the commune could increase assimilation—for example, by reducing the level of equality, which also alleviates brain drain because it gives high-ability members a premium for their ability even inside the commune. Kibbutzim, for example, shifted away from equal sharing when members' outside options relative to their inside options increased in the late 1980s. Kibbutzim faced the choice of either experiencing massive brain drain or introducing reforms and shifting to some extent away from equal sharing. Many chose the latter, despite the fact that this reform was counter to their founding principles.[20]

---

[19] Kanter (1972) suggests that the changing external environments, together with the deaths of their founders, eventually brought about the collapse of communes. The problem of the aging and death of founders was naturally more severe in communes that practiced celibacy, such as Ephrata and the Shakers.

[20] Pitzer's (1997) idea of "developmental communalism," the idea that communalism is just a phase in a community's life, would suggest that this shift from equal sharing to greater inequality is a natural progression for a commune to undergo.

Similarly, when norms of cooperation erode, the free-rider problem worsens. One response of the commune could be to increase isolation by intensifying the social sanctions and education in the commune's values. Alternatively, the commune could increase assimilation by shifting away from equality and introducing monetary rewards for effort.

THE ROLE OF IDEOLOGY IN THE STABILITY OF COMMUNES

A High Level of Ideology Enhances Stability

All communes have a certain ideology that is a core founding principle. In religious communes, this is a set of religious beliefs, such as the belief in the arrival of the kingdom of heaven. In secular communes, such as nonreligious kibbutzim, it is often a set of socialist ideologies. The ideologies and belief systems of communes are different from those of the outside world and set communes apart from the rest of society. These ideologies are usually the defining features of communes, at least at the outset.

Ideology serves to both increase the value of the inside option, thereby alleviating brain drain, and enhance cooperative norms within the group, thereby alleviating free-riding.[21] Indeed, the erosion of ideology is often believed to be a key reason for the collapse of communes. Ephrata, Shakers, and Harmony started their declines once they lost their faith in the coming of the kingdom of God during their lifetimes (Oved 1993). Oneida's ideology focused on the complex marriage system and a critique of the monogamous family as harming members' loyalty and commitment to the community. Nonexclusivity in romantic relationships was encouraged, and any two members could have sex with one another if both agreed; free love was encouraged, and exclusive relationships were frowned upon. Oneida's decline began with its retreat from the

---

[21] The idea that ideology enhances cooperative norms within groups was advanced by Putterman (1983), Oved (1993), Sosis (2000), Sosis and Bressler (2003), Sosis and Ruffle (2004), and Ruffle and Sosis (2006).

complex marriage system and return to the monogamous family (Pitzer 1997).

A member with a high level of ideology is inherently less likely to leave or shirk than a member with a low level of ideology; thus, the presence of ideologically motivated members is important for the stability of communes. When ideology is high for all members, the commune can maintain a high degree of equality while avoiding brain drain and free-riding.[22] However, especially in later generations, typically the core group of ideologically motivated members is accompanied by other members who lack strong ideology and just focus on their daily lives. The latter are less intrinsically motivated. They will only stay in the commune if the insurance value of equal sharing is sufficiently high and their outside option is less attractive; they will only work hard if social sanctions are effective.

It is interesting to note that the exit mechanism, although threatening to the stability of communes because of the brain drain problem, may be somewhat self-limiting. As members with weak ideology or religious beliefs leave the commune, the average level of members' ideology increases by definition. After the departure of the least ideological and committed members, the commune will consist of only the more ideological members, who are less likely to free-ride. Thus, future brain drain may be dampened.

A High Degree of Homogeneity in Ideology and in Ability Enhances Stability

Founders of kibbutzim often shared ideological training in youth movements in the diaspora before moving to Palestine and founding their communes. This was not accidental; members' homogeneity in background and ideology tends to enhance the stability of a commune. One characteristic of short-lived communes is that members did not share ideological training and had different backgrounds. Many communes that collapsed early were formed in haste, with little ideological or practical preparation. A majority of

---

[22] Note that ideology without a costly signal for commitment does not solve the adverse selection problem. As we saw in figure 6.3 of chapter 6, less-skilled people have incentives to enter an equal-sharing arrangement even if they have no ideology.

their members came from diverse backgrounds and geographical regions, and many were just attracted to communes for the security they provided (Oved 1993). The Brotherhood of Cooperative Commonwealth began its program for colonization with settlers who were unfamiliar with each other, and it failed within five years. In New Harmony and the Christian Commonwealth, an open policy toward new members created ideological heterogeneity and significantly affected the ideological component of these communes. In contrast, members in most long-lived communes had shared ideological training prior to establishing the commune. For many American communes, such as the Hutterites, Zoar, and Amana, the members arrived in the United States following persecution in Europe, which strengthened their internal cohesion. Additionally, in long-lived communes, new applicants underwent tests to ensure that they shared the same ideological background as other commune members prior to acceptance. In Ephrata, new candidates had to pass severe spiritual and physical tests spread over a year. Icarian communes required candidates to have thorough knowledge of the writings of Étienne Cabet, their leader. Another advantage of having members with shared ideology is that homogeneous members are more likely to cooperate with each other than are members who do not share their ideology (see Ruffle and Sosis 2006 in the context of Israeli kibbutzim).

Besides heterogeneity in ideology, heterogeneity in members' skills worsens brain drain (Abramitzky 2008a, 2009). If a commune's members were homogeneous and all contributed the same, equal sharing would not encourage exit. As soon as members differ in skill or ability, this ceases to be true. When forced to share their earnings with less-productive members, more-productive members have incentives to leave the commune and earn a premium for their skill. This logic can explain why communes strive for homogeneity: by encouraging conformity and discouraging excellence, they minimize brain drain (Oved 1983; Gavron 2000).

Heterogeneity is also likely to be higher for members of later generations. While first-generation members made an active choice to join the commune and share their resources with people with similar expected productivity, second-generation members were born into the commune and were more likely to differ in ability. It is thus expected that heterogeneity in the ability of members will increase over time, making brain drain more likely. This could also explain why few communes survive more than a generation.

I discussed above how the exit of less-ideological members may make brain drain somewhat self-limiting because it increases the average ideology of remaining members. At the same time, it increases the homogeneity of remaining members, at least in terms of ideology, which is also beneficial for the stability of the commune.

Rituals Enhance Stability

Just like Shavout and other holiday celebrations in kibbutzim, social rituals such as prayer, arts, music, and other shared celebrations have always been an important part of life in both socialist and religious communes.[23] Even in the Protestant religious communes such as Zoar, Amana, and Ephrata, which avoided all luxury and decorative arts, rituals of prayer meetings and special festivals were important. Frequently, these rituals were ingrained in the commune's everyday life: in Amana, members attended eleven church services a week; in Oneida, religious and business meetings were held every evening and attended by all adult members of the community; and in Bishop Hill, two-hour morning and evening church services were held daily. In secular communes, dance, music, parties, and other cultural activities replaced religious rituals.

Social rituals enhance social bonding between commune members and encourage togetherness, which increase members' perceived value of the inside option and thus alleviate brain drain. Rituals also mitigate adverse selection by demanding a hard-to-fake, costly signal of commitment to the commune. Iannaconne (1992), Berman (2000), and Sosis (2000) emphasize this role of rituals as signals of commitment to belonging to the group and as measures that help prevent free-riders from enjoying the public goods without contributing. Rituals also mitigate free-riding because they enhance loyalty in members and instill caring about their peers. Note, however, that the costliness of these signals may face an upper limit

---

[23] For a good account of communist rituals, see Froese (2008) and Pfaff (2011).

because rules that are too taxing or inconvenient to follow may encourage exit of even committed types. Lastly, social rituals generally increase the social interaction among commune members and therefore serve as a mechanism to create a tighter community. This in turn enables more efficient monitoring and creates greater social dependence on acceptance among the commune members. These factors mitigate the free-rider problem.

The Roles of Instrumental and Noninstrumental Ideology in Communes' Stability

As I mentioned in chapter 4, political philosophers distinguish between noninstrumental egalitarianism, which values equality as an end in itself, and instrumental egalitarianism, which can be thought of as equality as means to an end. When founders talked about equality as a sacred principle to create a more just society, this is an example of noninstrumental egalitarianism. In contrast, when they mentioned how great income equality was in providing safety net in a world that lacked job security, or how great communal life was in avoiding duplication and providing cheaper services, these are examples of instrumental egalitarianism. It is easy to see how the distinction between instrumental and noninstrumental is relevant to ideological features beyond egalitarianism. For example, when discussing how the children's residences in kibbutzim freed women from their traditional role as main child-care givers and facilitated the core value of gender equality, this can be thought of as noninstrumental ideology. However, when thinking about how the children's residences allowed a kibbutz to provide child care more cheaply and increase women's labor force participation, then children's residences have an instrumental ideology component—they are a means to an end (making child care cheap) rather than an end in themselves (promoting gender equality). The distinction between instrumental and noninstrumental ideologies matters in part because noninstrumental ideology tends to diminish over time and is often insufficient for institutions to survive. Whereas the origins of institutions often contain a noninstrumental element, institutions that persist manage to do so because they are an equilibrium choice for their members. That is, they have instrumental value.

Like ideology and insurance, rituals practiced by communes may be instrumental or noninstrumental. They may be hard-to-fake signals used to avoid adverse selection in entry (instrumental) or manifestations of the communes' desire to practice its religious or ideological beliefs (noninstrumental).

Noninstrumental ideology is often a key establishing principle of communes, and it facilitates a high level of equality at the outset. However, it tends to decline over time because the first-generation members, who consciously chose this way of life, are more committed to the pure ideology than members of later generations, who were born into the commune (e.g., Rosner 1990).

Noninstrumental ideology helps to overcome the problems of free-riding, adverse selection, and brain drain, because members intrinsically care about the collective and its goals. As noninstrumental ideology declines and instrumental ideology becomes the main driving force, the problems of brain drain and free-riding become more severe. The principle of equality is still desired and pursued, but the motives for it have become more practical. That is, members of second and third generations in communes tend to have weaker ideological zeal (weaker noninstrumental ideology), and they often make their decisions of whether to leave and work hard more selfishly, based on the value of equality as a risk-sharing device and the effectiveness of social sanctions (instrumental ideology). Similarly, when members' instrumental ideology is low, rituals are still used, but their purpose increasingly becomes instrumental, that is, a way to avoid adverse selection.

Communes (and other religious groups such as the Mormons) are aware that noninstrumental ideology declines with each generation, which might explain why long-lived communes put emphasis on creating their own institutions to instill their beliefs and ideology in the younger generations. However, even long-lived communes, such as Amana, Zoar, Icaria, Oneida, and kibbutzim, often failed to fully pass their ideology and values to their children. Thus, in Oneida, as in kibbutzim, it was the younger generation who demanded an abolition of the commune (for Oneida, see Oved 1993, p. 185). Similarly, in Amana, it was the younger generation that broke the rules set by the elders (e.g., playing sports and wearing the color red, which was forbidden) (Pitzer 1997).

Instrumental ideology is still useful for the stability of communes in that it promotes the founding principles of equality and communal rituals, and it coordinates expectations of how members should behave (e.g., cooperate and work hard). However, material factors that increase and decrease the attractiveness of the commune relative to the outside option (e.g., the commune's wealth, hiring outside labor) become more important as instrumental ideology comes to dominate noninstrumental ideology.

Religious Ideology Enhances Stability
More than Socialist Ideology

Religious and socialist communes existed side by side in collaboration. The socialist communes regarded the religious ones as their "older sisters," acknowledged their seniority, and admired their survivability. The religious communes were happy to assist them in any way, be it advice or material aid. In practice, there were wide areas of mutual fertilization.

—*Oved 1993, p. 375*

Religious and secular communes have many similarities: voluntary membership, an attempt to create an alternative and better society, isolation, high moral norms, and the abolition of private property. Indeed, despite often being atheists, secular communes showed great respect for the religious communes and the two types maintained good relationships with each other. Both practiced mutual aid and possessed all property in common; both aimed for moral perfection so that altruism would replace selfishness. Besides their noninstrumental aspect, such ideals have the instrumental purpose of overcoming free-riding.

However, religious communes have typically been more successful. In a study of US utopian communes in the nineteenth century, Sosis (2000) found that religious communes tended to survive longer. Similarly, religious kibbutzim have been more successful than secular ones (Fishman 1992, 1994). Moreover, Ruffle and Sosis (2007) found that members of religious kibbutzim, and especially those who were more observant of their religion, cooperated more with other members of their group than did members of secular kibbutzim. Interestingly, religious kibbutzim members were not more cooperative with just anyone; the higher cooperation of religious kibbutzim members (and kibbutz members relative to city people) was mainly toward other members of their own community.

There are a few potential reasons that religious communes have been more successful. First, religious beliefs seem more difficult to fake than socialist beliefs, perhaps because feigning religious beliefs involves more daily routines, restrictions on behavior, and group rituals. It is more costly to pray and live according to a strict religious code than it is to convey sympathy to the socialist idea. Thus, commitment to a religious commune is harder to fake, and so adverse selection and free-riding tend to be less prevalent in these communes.

Second, religious ideology, unlike socialist ideology, is not necessarily dependent on the principle of equality. This is helpful for survival because changes in the utopian nature of the commune can be made without threatening its founding religious principles. Consistent with this idea, religious communes (e.g., Oneida) often were created to facilitate the practice of religious beliefs rather than create a utopian commune, per se (Oved 1993). This is not true for socialist communes, in which the utopian ideal came first (in both the United States and kibbutzim).

Third, religion often has a value in itself for members, which, like noninstrumental ideology, may increase the attractiveness of the religious commune to its members. Moreover, when religion is thought of as a club good, religious acts practiced together among commune members who know each other well could also increase the value of the members' inside option.

Lastly, in the absence of a theoretical authority, general meetings often turn into endless trivial debates that an efficient set of rules or authoritarian figure could have prevented (Oved 1993, p. 382). Leaders within communes not only allowed for decisions to be made quicker, but gave members a figurehead to follow. When analyzing the success of various American communes, many of those that lasted for a longer period of time had strong leaders for many of their years.[24]

[24] Another factor that enhanced stability in religious communes relative to socialist communes is a charismatic leader, who coordinated expectations and

To summarize, I discussed the factors that affect the stability of communes in North America and Israel in light of a framework that views communes as organizations that strive for equality while dealing with their inherent problems of brain drain, free-riding, and adverse selection. Communes' internal organization is designed to mitigate these problems by facilitating social sanctions; enhancing commitment, loyalty, and cooperation; and creating lock-in devices. Ideology, especially when religion-based, is helpful in mitigating brain drain, adverse selection, and moral hazard, and it facilitates a high degree of equality. As members' outside options increase and their ideology declines, communes' stability is threatened because these problems become more severe. To survive, communes such as the Hutterites increased their isolation, which strengthened their ideology and reduced members' knowledge of their outside options. Other communes such as kibbutzim increased assimilation, that is, reduced the difference between them and the outside world, by shifting away from equal sharing. This shift helped solve these problems because it reduced the incentives both for less-productive members to shirk and for the most-productive members to leave.

It is interesting to note that both the Hutterites and kibbutzim survived for long periods and still exist today. While the Hutterites have done so by sticking to their establishing principles, kibbutzim have gone through reforms that shifted them away from their establishing principles. They reflect two alternative ways to deal with a changing economic environment. Nevertheless, both Hutterites and kibbutzim seem to share an understanding of the economic forces that threaten them. Both have demonstrated flexible and creative ways to mitigate these threats and maintain a higher degree of equality than the rest of society, even in an external environment that has changed in destabilizing ways.

---

enhanced ideology and norms. Most religious communes had one at the outset, though a replacement was not often found on the leader's death. Communist communes usually did not have such a leader, because having a leader was inconsistent with the socialist idea of equality.

CHAPTER 12

Economic lessons in a nutshell

―――――――――――――――――――

AN ECONOMIC INTERPRETATION OF THE RISE AND FALL OF THE EGALITARIAN KIBBUTZ

Kibbutzim were created in the early twentieth century in modern-day Israel by Jewish Zionist immigrants who rejected capitalism and formed a socialist society. All property in a kibbutz belonged to the community, which acted as a substitute for the nuclear family. Each member received an equal share of everything available regardless of her contribution, based on the Marxist principle "From each according to his abilities to each according to his needs." Members worked in agriculture on communally owned land and in the communal kitchen and dining hall, rotating jobs as instructed by the kibbutz work organizer. They ate together in a communal dining hall, and children lived in separate residences from their parents, who were only permitted short daily visits to see their kids. The ideal was to create a new and improved human being who cared about the common good. At the very least, the hope was that income equality and mutual aid would lead members to work for the common good, even when this conflicted with their selfish goals.

The kibbutz movement played an important role in nation building, and kibbutzniks were considered elite. At the community level, kibbutzim promoted and supported Zionism, and in return enjoyed governmental support; at the individual level, kibbutz members played prominent roles in Israeli society: they accounted for a disproportionate number of Israel's political and military leaders and intellectuals. Beyond idealism and ideology, economic reasons can rationalize the creation of an egalitarian kibbutz. Income equality in kibbutzim provided valuable insurance to young people who came to a new land full of uncertainty. Economic theory can also explain why the early kibbutzim were founded by immigrants and not by people already living in the region. The explanation is the adverse selection problem—the tendency of the least productive workers to be attracted by equal sharing arrangements. Kibbutzim were viable in their early days, and adverse selection less of a problem, partly because they were founded by homogeneous groups of migrants starting over in a new country, with similar economic prospects and similar social, ideological, and vocational training.

The ideological zeal of the kibbutz founders could have overcome members' tendencies to put their immediate families' needs before the needs of the community, but early generations did not rely solely on human kindness. Instead, they developed various rules and norms that would help sustain income equality in kibbutzim even after the initial idealism had faded.

In order to provide full insurance without losing the members who turned out to be particularly productive, kibbutzim required entrants to post a bond, by giving all their property and earnings to the kibbutz. A member who left forfeited his share in the kibbutz property. This meant even members who could make a better living outside the kibbutz lacked the savings required to start a new life in the city. This effective lock-in ensured that only exceptionally productive members (and those who couldn't stand the lifestyle) left the kibbutz. Notably, the Israeli high-tech sector is full of former kibbutz members.

Kibbutzim's rules and norms also helped them deal with incentive problems. The kibbutz has always been concerned about members who lived off the efforts of others. Free-riding was alleviated by mutual monitoring and peer pressure. Members dined, worked, socialized, and gossiped together, which helped support the peer pressure and made social sanctions more effective. Although expulsion from the kibbutz was rare, poor workers could be assigned miserable jobs, while stellar workers were rewarded with prestigious leadership roles. The relatively small size of each kibbutz ensured that the social sanctions and rewards were effective, and allowed kibbutzim to sustain income equality. The education system taught cooperation and ideology, which helped sustain equal sharing by making members more committed.

In the 1960s and 1970s, kibbutzim industrialized, building factories and large service sectors alongside their traditional agricultural base. Kibbutz members became less homogeneous and began working in a wide range of occupations and industries, which may have decreased the effectiveness of monitoring. At the same time, idealism was waning. The founders of kibbutzim had been selected for their idealism, but later generations were born to the kibbutz rather than actively choosing to join, and each generation had weaker ideology than the last.

As long as kibbutz property was valuable and the kibbutz was wealthy, full equality could be sustained without serious brain drain even in the absence of strong ideology. Other rules and norms, such as not allowing members to use cash and expecting them to work inside their kibbutz, and the high provision of local public goods such as cultural centers and parks added to kibbutzim's stability by increasing the cost of exit.

The traditional egalitarian kibbutz provided members with full insurance against income, health, and unemployment shocks, and the mutual aid that existed across kibbutzim protected against negative shocks to the individual kibbutz. This full income equality with full insurance was sustained for more than half a century, until the mid-1980s.

And yet, despite kibbutzim's success, the kibbutz population has never accounted for more than 7 percent of the Jewish population in Palestine, suggesting that even under favorable conditions, the vast majority of Israeli Jews prefer not to live communally with full income equality.[1]

---

[1] Nozick's essay (1997) similarly concludes that the case of the kibbutz suggests that when given the choice, very few people would choose to live under socialism.

To be sure, over the years, members became dissatisfied with various aspects of the kibbutz and introduced a number of reforms. For example, parents were not happy with their children sleeping outside of their homes and eventually brought them back to live with their parents. Other reforms included hiring nonmembers from outside the kibbutz, introducing cash allowances, and allowing members to hold jobs outside their kibbutz. However, members who worked outside the kibbutz had to contribute their entire salaries to the kibbutz.

But the kibbutz way of life only truly came under pressure in the mid-1980s when, against a background of improving employment opportunities in cities for skilled workers, a debt crisis struck kibbutzim. The future of kibbutzim became an open question. Many productive members left their kibbutz, willingly giving up their share of kibbutz assets and the insurance kibbutzim provided in exchange for the wage premium their ability could earn them in the cities. By 2000, the percentage of kibbutzniks in the Israeli Jewish population declined to less than 2.5 percent. Only by introducing differential pay, which gave productive members a premium for their ability, could kibbutzim retain some skilled members and remain viable. Many kibbutzim thus departed from full equality and introduced various degrees of pay reforms.

However, the shift away from full equality was not universal. As economic theory predicts, wealthier kibbutzim maintained higher degrees of income equality; some rich kibbutzim are still traditional egalitarian kibbutzim today. Similarly, kibbutzim with stronger socialist ideology were also more likely to maintain income equality.

Although it continues to provide a safety net,[2] the new capitalist kibbutz no longer offers equal earnings; instead, it rewards productivity and effort, with members receiving wages that depend

---

[2] Surveys of Public Opinion conducted in kibbutzim in the period 1990–2002 indicate that although most members support differential reforms, they still want to have some level of equality, and more than 70% object to wages that are as differentiated as in the city. When asked for their most preferable way of life when abstracting from any practical consideration, it appears that most members do not want to live in either a traditional kibbutz or in a city. Most prefer something in the middle.

on their contribution. In linking pay with productivity, kibbutzim provide incentives to members with high earnings potential to stay. The social environment within kibbutzim has also changed. Children and parents eat together at home rather than in the communal dining halls, many of which have closed. Many kibbutzim have turned agricultural land into new neighborhoods for children of kibbutz members, now themselves adult kibbutzniks with children. Many kibbutzim have even opened new capitalist neighborhoods inside the kibbutz, designed for outsiders who want to live in a rural environment and are happy to pay for their land, houses, and services. Kibbutzim have expanded their economic activities, hired outside managers, and have successful tourism and sometimes even high-tech sectors.

The shift away from income equality seems to have led to revival in many kibbutzim. Kibbutz-born people increasingly seek to stay in their kibbutz, either as members or as residents in the new neighborhoods forming at the edges of kibbutzim, and more Israelis are seeking to enter a kibbutz. Incentives to excel in school and in the workplace have improved, providing hope for a well-educated, hard-working membership in the future. Some members, especially older ones, note nostalgically how the kibbutz today is not what it used to be, and how kibbutzniks today care more about themselves and their immediate families and less about the community as a whole. Most agree, however, that the reforms were necessary for retaining the younger generation and ensuring the continued survival of kibbutzim, even if not in the form the founders had envisaged.

SOME BROADER LESSONS

The experience of kibbutzim offers many lessons for economic and social inequality more broadly. Much had previously been written about the failure of socialism and its rejection around the world, and the last decade saw a huge increase in interest in the issue of economic and social equality in the United States and internationally. Social movements led by the middle class to reduce social and economic inequality have increased, with the 2011 social justice protest in Israel and Occupy Wall Street in the United States being just two examples. Thomas Piketty's *Capital in the Twenty-First Century* (2014) provides a further illustration: the book, which was taken by many as evidence that under capitalism the rich become richer and that income inequality should be reduced by means such as inheritance tax, quickly turned into a bestseller and became the highest-selling book ever published by Harvard University Press.

The experience of kibbutzim, a genuine and long-lived social experiment in voluntary socialism and equal sharing, teaches us about equality and inequality, the trade-off between equality and incentives, the sacrifices that living under equal sharing entail, and the conditions under which socialism and income equality can succeed and when they will fail. There are two routes to equality. One is the authoritarian route. Political revolution and a communist government can force equality on the population. History has shown that this method of achieving equality has substantial costs in terms of freedom, and that people would prefer not to give up their freedom to gain equality. The second route is the voluntary route. People enter kibbutzim voluntarily, exit when they wish, and thus do not fully give up their individual freedom of choice. The existence of choice, however, creates problems for the kibbutz in the form of brain drain and adverse selection.

Is it possible to create a voluntary egalitarian society? This book provides an answer that is both optimistic and pessimistic. Yes, it is possible. Equality can work in real life; it did in the kibbutzim for many decades. It is possible to overcome free-riding with social sanctions and rewards, adverse selection with screening and signals for commitment, and brain drain with high communal wealth and training in kibbutz-specific education and skills. Kibbutzim stood for many years as "proof" that socialism and income equality can actually work. This was especially impressive because kibbutz members could leave at will, unlike workers on collective farms in Russia and China. The success of the kibbutz was also impressive because, unlike in the case of many communes in history, kibbutz members were never marginal in Israeli society. However, opponents of socialism gladly point to the recent shift away from income sharing and communal ownership of property as a proof that any socialist society is doomed to fail. They point out that all socialist societies have eventually failed because pioneering idealism is short-lived, and over time equal sharing leads to free-riding, adverse selection, and brain drain.

The study of kibbutzim from an economic perspective yields several additional insights. Income equality provided insurance to kibbutzniks, much as it still does in villages in developing countries and other communities.[3] At the same time, it brought the risks of free-riding and adverse selection. Kibbutzim effectively limited these problems, but at the cost of individual privacy, which helps explain why such societies are so rare.

Developed countries may learn that in a world where skilled citizens have the option to move between countries, being rich helps maintain the welfare state. A rich country can afford a lot of redistribution through high taxes without experiencing brain drain of its most-skilled citizens, whereas a less wealthy country cannot. A rich European country forced by a crisis to reduce living standards might experience emigration of its best workers to a less equal country such as the United States. To retain talent, it may be forced to reduce its redistribution.

Organizations such as partnerships could learn that revenue sharing provides valuable insurance to workers, meaning they may be willing to accept lower wages than they would absent insurance. However, any revenue-sharing or other sharing arrangement comes at the risk of losing the most-talented and hardest-working employees, who might prefer to work for a firm that lets them keep all the financial returns for their ability and effort. Here one lesson from kibbutzim is again that it helps to be rich—Google can pay

---

[3] For a classic reference on insurance in developing countries, see Townsend (1994) and the huge literature that followed. Moreover, some of the rules and norms in kibbutzim are similar to those of micro finance organizations in developing economies such as consumer credit markets for high-risk borrowers (Karlan and Zinman 2009), group lending institutions (Stiglitz 1990; Varian 1990; Besley and Coate 1995; Giné et al. 2010), and rotating savings institutions (e.g., Besley, Coate, and Loury 1993; Calomiris and Rajaraman 1998).

its most talented engineers less than the competition because they offer free meals, many amenities, a comfortable work environment, and a sense of job security. Other lessons for firms worrying about adverse selection and brain drain are to screen workers carefully, ideally on the basis of commitment to the common mission in addition to talent; to introduce noncompete clauses that increase the cost of leaving; and to invest in workers' firm-specific human capital, which is more valuable within the firm than outside it.

Any insurance scheme, including car insurance, health insurance, life insurance, and social security, including Medicaid and Medicare, has to deal with the insurance/incentive trade-off. Insurance is valuable for every risk-averse person, which is why we all want to be insured. At the same time, high insurance levels increase the potential for adverse selection and moral hazard. Kibbutzim again illustrate why insurance companies tend to be very selective and to offer less insurance to people who are perceived to be higher risk, and why more-comprehensive insurance coverage is so much more expensive. The logic of adverse selection that caused kibbutzim to be selective about applicants also helps explain why programs such as Medicaid and Medicare require universal mandatory coverage; otherwise the young and the healthy will opt out and cause the whole insurance scheme to unravel.

Finally, an economic perspective of the kibbutz helps illustrate the fundamental difference between proponents (e.g., Democrats in the United States) and opponents (e.g., Republicans) of high taxation. Each side emphasizes a different side of the equality/incentives trade-off. Proponents of high taxation and high redistribution emphasize the benefits, such as the alleviation of poverty. Opponents of strong redistribution emphasize the costs—that high taxes discourage people from working hard and reduce the wealth of society as a whole. The main difference is that proponents of high taxation believe that the benefits of high taxes exceed the costs, and opponents of high taxes think exactly the reverse. Another difference is that proponents of high taxes, like kibbutz members before the crisis, put higher trust in the government to do a good job with the taxes it collects.

In the end, however, the lesson from kibbutzim is more fundamental than all these examples. Equality is natural and desirable for many people, but it is difficult to manage in light of the forces that undermine it. The kibbutzim as we know them worked in a moment in time in Israeli history; they might (or might not) be gone in fifty years. But the desire to self-organize in supportive societies will remain.

CHAPTER 13

Epilogue

From the outside, Kibbutz Negba today looks very much as it did when my brother and I were children. But the similarities are only superficial. As a result of the major reforms that have taken place in the kibbutz since the late 1990s, Negba is now a very different place. Members pay for everything with their own money, and incomes are no longer shared equally among members. The dining hall has closed, and part of the building it used to occupy has been converted to a children's amusement center that is open (for a fee) to the general public. Another part is used for occasional kibbutz holiday parties. The big kitchen is rented out to a company that bakes gluten-free Kosher cookies for the Jewish Orthodox community.

My brother, born and raised in Jerusalem, chose to live in a kibbutz that went through a similar transformation away from equal sharing. His wife, born and raised in Kibbutz Ramat HaKovesh, works in the city. The kibbutz remains a fantastic place for young children. My nephews go to the high-quality kibbutz daycare and elementary school, which are within three minutes' walk of their apartment. They are all independent, roaming around barefoot in the kibbutz gardens, playing outside with friends, or swimming in the huge water reservoir that has been turned into a beautiful swimming pool.

Some kibbutz traditions are still celebrated. For example, there is still a big celebration of Shavout, the Feast of Weeks, a Jewish holiday—also called the Harvest Holiday, or the First Fruits (*Bikkurim*)

Holiday—just like in the old days. While the holiday is important from a religious perspective, kibbutzniks celebrate its agricultural dimension, and have developed a colorful tradition celebrating the bringing of *bikkurim*. My mother celebrated it when she was a child, my brother and I loved to come visit Negba for the Shavout celebration, his children celebrate it in the same way in Ramat HaKovesh, and my children love to celebrate the holiday with them. The children sing, dance, and bring the *bikkurim*; Ramat HaKovesh also has the tradition of showcasing the children born during the past year, their most precious *bikkurim*. Each economic branch (*anaf*) of the kibbutz presents its products in front of the entire cheering membership, as shown in figures 13.1, 13.2, and 13.3. Only the Pilates branch was a reminder this year that the kibbutz has changed.

In my last visit in 2016, my brother showed me how the trees tell the story of Ramat HaKovesh. The large *Ficus* trees leading to the dining hall were planted in 1938, a few years after the kibbutz was established; the magnolia tree was donated by American Jews to celebrate the perseverance of the kibbutz members who were locked in their residences while their kibbutz was searched by the British during the mandate; the olive trees, which now stand in the middle of the kibbutz next to the children's daycare center, once served as the signpost for the southern border of the kibbutz; eight oak trees were planted in memory of eight kibbutz members who died when their car exploded on a landmine in the early days; and of course there are the *yad lamegenim*, the two halls commemorating the members' families who died during the Holocaust and the kibbutz members who died in wars. These halls are dear to the kibbutz, almost holy. They are surrounded by beautifully landscaped gardens and a sweeping lawn. Nothing is to be built on this grass, because the kibbutz made a decision that the dining hall should always be seen from these halls, to maintain a visual connection between the dead and the living.

Unlike in many kibbutzim, the dining hall in Ramat HaKovesh is still open. Meals are no longer free, but they are subsidized. The dining hall is no longer the place where everyone meets every day. However, members who work in the kibbutz, as well as children in daycare and elementary school, can still enjoy lunch there.

Figures 13.1, 13.2 and 13.3: Shavout celebration in Kibbutz Ramat HaKovesh, June 6, 2016. Source: Photos by author.

Like other kibbutzim, Ramat HaKovesh is building a new neighborhood (*harchava*) for young families with children within the kibbutz, in an area just outside the current residential area, in what used to be kibbutz orchards. Apartments are no longer uniform in size and shape; members with greater resources purchase nicer apartments. The land, however, belongs to the kibbutz, so if they decide to leave at some point they will have to sell their apartment back to the kibbutz.

I wonder what my grandmother would think about these recent reforms. Surely, it would have been tough to see the egalitarian community she and Buzik helped build transformed into a more capitalist society. On the other hand, I think of how she graciously she responded when she learned of my mother's plan to leave the kibbutz. Perhaps she would have supported the reforms, despite her personal preference. After all, the changes represent the wishes of the new generation. Indeed, it is kibbutzim's willingness to implement fundamental reforms to adapt to their economic environment that distinguishes them from other utopian communities. Their remarkable flexibility demonstrates their survival instincts and viability.

My uncle and I still enjoy sitting on the sunny grass of the kibbutz and chatting. The grass is still green, and the crickets still chirp in the trees. We talk about his work at the kibbutz factory, about the directions the kibbutz is taking, about the past, present, and future. Talking about the kibbutz is our way of talking about life. The conversation typically starts with a technical description of an innovation of the kibbutz irrigation system, but before long we are talking about the tension between economic models and human feelings; about community, equity, and sacrifice; and about human nature.

The kibbutz experience shows that the pessimistic and optimistic views that my uncle and I voiced in that earlier debate are both partially right. Income equality and communal living are possible under certain circumstances. The fact that both kibbutzim and kibbutzniks respond to economic incentives does not undermine the importance of the kibbutz movement as a fascinating experiment in voluntary socialism, nor does it undermine the great achievements of this movement. On the contrary, the long persistence of kibbutzim despite facing the economic challenges associated with equality makes the kibbutz communities more interesting for social scientists, and their achievements and lessons more meaningful. On the other hand, kibbutzim did enjoy governmental support throughout their successful period, and they did eventually decline, at least from their traditional form.

It is impossible to know what the future holds for kibbutzim. My best guess is that they will continue to survive into the twenty-first century in an altered form. Most kibbutzim will continue to reform and privatize, while a few wealthy ones will retain a more traditional form, demonstrating that income equality and traditional kibbutz life remain possible despite the changed outside world. If a kibbutz stops being a kibbutz when it abolishes income equality and communal ownership of property, then kibbutzim will continue to decline. However, if a kibbutz stops being a kibbutz only when mutual aid and support of weak members cease to be defining principles, my guess is that kibbutzim will continue to thrive. The revival of kibbutz life will go on, and kibbutzim will attract new members and inspire people around the world. Even if kibbutzim eventually disappear, they have taught us that appropriate incentives can shape human nature to be cooperative, considerate, and socially desirable.

Kibbutz timeline

1882–1903 First Aliyah: Immigration of mostly Eastern European Jews to Ottman Palestine. The new migrants mostly established *moshavot*, Jewish settlements with privately owned land rather than kibbutzim.

1904–1914 Second Aliyah, the pioneers who created kibbutzim: Following rising anti-Semitism and pogroms in Europe, most Eastern European Jews moved to the United States; some moved to Palestine.

1910 First kibbutz: Degania is established near the Sea of Galilee. Over the next few decades, a harsh physical environment and low living standards exist in Ottoman Palestine and in kibbutzim in particular.

1914–1918 World War I

1917 Winds of change: Balfour Decaration indicates Britain's intention to establish a national home for the Jewish people in Palestine; October Revolution in Russia.

1919–1923 Third Aliyah: Triggered by anti-Semitism and increased hopes following the Balfour Declaration; the creation of moshavim, non-collective Zionist settlements; British mandate for Palestine officially confirmed by League of Nations.

1924–1928 Fourth Aliyah: Immigration of mostly Eastern European Jews following increasing anti-Semitism in Europe and the closure of the US borders.

1929–1939 Fifth Aliyah: Immigration of German and Eastern European Jews following rising persecution in Europe and Nazi Germany.

1930s and 1940s Expansion: Dozens of kibbutzim established; kibbutzim population grows substantially.

1936–1939 Tower and stockade: Arab revolt against the British and Zionists; new kibbutzim and moshavim are built under tower-and-stockade enterprise.

1939–1945 World War II: Germany invades Poland; Jews sent to concentration camps.

1941 The Final Solution: Mass murder of six million European Jews by Nazi Germany starts; Palmach, the strike force of Hagannah (the underground fighting force of the Jewish community in Palestine) established and associated with kibbutzim.

1947–1948 Israel's independence: United Nations votes to partition Palestine between the Arabs and the Jews; British mandate ends; State of Israel is declared, its borders often tracing the location of kibbutzim; Arab-Israeli War starts; kibbutzim play a big role in state-buiding; mass migration to Israel of Jews from postholocaust Europe and Arab countries starts.

1950s Industrialization: Kibbutzim's agriculture flourishes; kibbutzim start to industrialize; kibbutzim increasingly hire outside labor, including Jews from Middle Eastern countries.

1951 Ideological divide: Split of Kibbutz Meuhad Federation on ideological grounds regarding whether kibbutzim should support the Soviet Union or the United States in the Cold War.

1952 German reparations: German reparations to Israel and individual Nazi victims brings private money into kibbutzim.

1956 Suez Crisis: Israel invades Egypt and takes the Sinai Penisula; Israel forced to withdraw a year later.

1967 Six-Day War: Between Israel and neighboring states Egypt, Syria, and Jordan.

1970s Elite status: Kibbutzim are thriving economically; kibbutzniks are middle class in terms of their living standards, and considered an elite by many.

1977 Turning point in Israeli politics: A right-wing Likud government is elected for the first time in Israel; the new government doesn't view kibbutzim as favorably as previous Labor governments.

1970s–1980s End of communal sleeping: Kibbutzim start to abolish communal sleeping arrangement of children (*lina meshutefet*), who move to their parents' homes (*lina mishpachtit*).

1985 Financial crisis: A severe financial crisis hits many kibbutzim and leaves them with huge debts and substantially lower living standards.

1989 Haircut: An arrangement to settle debt signed between kibbutzim, the government, and the banks (supplement arrangement signed in 1996 and 1999).

1990s Shift away from equal sharing: Many kibbutzim introduce major reforms and abandon full income equality; the "communal stream" (*hazerem hashitufi*) established by kibbutzim that stick to the founding principles and as a reaction to the differential wage reforms.

2000s Further privatization: Many kibbutzim seek to abolish communal ownership of property and, in particular, to allow members to own their apartments; new neighborhoods are built (*harchava*), mostly for kibbutz children but also some neighborhoods are designed for nonmembers.

Acknowledgments

The research underlying this book started almost twenty years ago when I wrote my PhD dissertation at Northwestern University on kibbutzim. I am eternally grateful to my advisor Joel Mokyr, who supported this project in so many ways from the very beginning. This book would never have been completed without his continuous guidance, boundless energy, contagious enthusiasm, and endless generosity. Joel continues to be an inspiration, both professionally and personally. I cannot think of a more supportive environment than the one I had at Northwestern. I had a terrific dissertation committee in Joel Mokyr, Joe Ferrie, Rob Porter, Bill Rogerson, and Kathy Spier, and my research in those days also greatly benefited from the advice of Igal Hendel, Chiaki Moriguchi, and Aviv Nevo, and from many hours of discussions and conversations with Fabio Braggion, Adeline Delavande, Nir Jaimovich, Nisan Langberg, and Luis Vasconcelos.

Of my fabulous Stanford colleagues, I am especially grateful to my fellow economic historians Avner Greif and Gavin Wright, who read and commented on numerous versions of the manuscript and offered great advice. Their support and encouragement during all these years kept me going. I would also like to thank Mark Granovetter, Jonathan Levav, Jon Levin, and Reviel Netz for their insightful comments and thoughtful advice. The Stanford-wide social science history group has been very supportive of this project, especially Steve Haber, Lisa Blaydes, Tino Cuellar, Jim Fearon, Saumitra Jha, Peter Koudijs, Ian Morris, Norman Naimark, Josh Ober, Jack Rakove, Ken Scheve, and Barry Weingast. Other colleagues who offered great suggestions on various aspects of the book include Ken

Arrow, Doug Bernheim, Nick Bloom, Michael Boskin, Tim Bresnahan, Raj Chetty, Mark Duggan, Pascaline Dupas, Liran Einav, Matt Gentzkow, Amir Goldberg, Nir Halevy, Matt Jackson, Pete Klenow, Muriel Niederle, John Pencavel, Luigi Pistaferri, and John Shoven. Among my many wonderful current and former students who contributed to this project, I should single out Isabelle (Izi) Sin. Izi provided superb research assistance when she was in graduate school, and continued to offer thoughtful suggestions years after she graduated. Izi meticulously and tirelessly edited the entire manuscript, fixing my writing and saving me from embarrassments, but amazingly without ever editing out my voice. While she is a professional economist, her editing skills are second to none. I also want to acknowledge the excellent research assistance and valuable feedback from Guy Kasznik, Helen Kissel, Shirlee Lichtman, Roy Mill, Santiago Perez, Jared Rubin, Gui Woolston, and Tom Zohar.

Outside of Northwestern and Stanford, the project benefited from the comments and suggestions of a long list of scholars. Although this list is incomplete, I must mention Manuel Amador, Josh Angrist, Orazio Attanasio, Sascha Becker, Eli Berman, Lee Benham, Dan Bogart, Dora Costa, Giacomo De Giorgi, Eyal Dvir, Avi Ebenstein, Zvi Eckstein, Amy Finkelstein, Price Fishback, Oded Galor, Nachum Gross, Elhanan Helpman, Phillip Hoffman, Rob Jensen, Seema Jayachandran, Naomi Lamoreaux, Aprajit Mahajan, Bob Margo, Joram Mayshar, Deirdre McCloskey, Jacob Metzer, Kris Mitchener, Kaivan Munshi, Suresh Naidu, Nathan Nunn, Motty Perry, Ben Polak, Christina Romer, Jean-Laurent Rosenthal, Ariel Rubinstein, Emmanuel Saez, Carol Shiue, Nathan Sussman, Peter Temin, Manuel Trajtenberg, Richard Sosis, John Wallis, Yishay Yafeh, Noam Yuchtman, and Yosi Zeira. I am grateful to Barry Eichengreen, Claudia Goldin, and Tim Guinnane, who encouraged me from an early stage to write this book. I also wish to thank my long-time coauthors, Leah Boustan, Katherine Eriksson, and Victor Lavy, for their great support. Some of the research underlying this book was previously published in academic journals. I thank the editors and referees of each of these journals, especially Daron Acemoglu, David Autor, Ed Glaeser, Larry Katz, Rachel McCleary, and Timothy Taylor, for their many insights and suggestions.

Special thanks to Marina Krakovsky who was instrumental in the development stage of this manuscript and who encouraged me to tell my family story, and to Marc Alvidrez, whose thoughtful comments helped me make the book more accessible to the non-economist. Special thanks also to the artist Raphael Perez for allowing me to use his wonderful painting for the cover of this book. I fell in love with this art work as soon as I saw it, but only later, when Raphael explained that he painted the kibbutz with its traditional water tower and tractors inside Rothschild Boulevard (one of the main streets of the city of Tel Aviv), did I realize how appropriate the painting was for the book.

I gratefully acknowledge financial support from the National Science Foundation (SES-0720901), the Falk Institute for Economic Research, the Sapir Center for Development, Sloan Fellowship, the Northwestern Dissertation Dean Fellowship, Northwestern's center of Jewish Studies, and the Economic History Association Dissertation Award. I thank the Census Bureau of Statistics in Israel for making available the linked 1983–1995 population censuses, and the National Insurance Institute (NII) for making available to Victor and me the post-secondary schooling data in their protected research lab with restricted access at NII headquarters in Jerusalem.

At Princeton University Press, I thank Joe Jackson and Seth Ditchik for being such supportive editors, and for their endless patience in waiting for my manuscript. I can only hope they find the final product worth the wait. I thank Ellen Foos for providing great editorial advice, and Molan Goldstein for her sharp-eyed copy editing of the manuscript.

In the kibbutz, I am indebted to Ruthi and Avner Barzilai and to Mashka from Kibbutz Negba, to Sheer Abramitzky from Kibbutz Ramat HaKovesh, and to Aunt Naomi and Uncle Uri from Kibbutz Heftziba. They all went out of their way to help me in every matter about which I consulted them. Most of all, I thank my late grandmother, Breindel, a member of Kibbutz Negba for half a century, whose fascination with the kibbutz must have been contagious. I wish she were here with me on this day.

Finally, this book would not have been possible without the endless love and support of my family. Gil and Tali are not just a brother and sister but also great friends. Bracha and Icho are the world's best parents and they define what it means to be good human beings. It is only for their love and unconditional support that I am who I am. My grandmother, Rachel, whose energy and wisdom I admire, has always been there for me. My late grandfather, Moshe, an impressive man and a real mensch, has always been a great inspiration for me. My biggest debt, however, is to Noya, my wife and best friend. Her patience, sensitivity, strength, and dedication made this book possible. Nothing I have achieved would have been possible, let alone worth achieving, without her. And our boys, Roee, Ido, and Tom who fill our lives with joy and happiness and who make it all worthwhile. This book is dedicated to Noya and to them.

References

Abell, Peter. *The Viability of Industrial Producer Co-operation*. Wiley, 1983.

Abramitzky, Ran. "The Limits of Equality: An Economic Analysis of the Israeli Kibbutz." PhD diss., Northwestern University, 2005.

———. "The Limits of Equality: Insights from the Israeli Kibbutz." *Quarterly Journal of Economics* 123.3 (2008a): 1111–1159.

———. "Testing Self-Selection in Migration: Evidence from the Israeli Kibbutz." 2008b. Available at SSRN, https://papers.ssrn.com/sol3/papers.cfm?abstract_id=1233683.

———. "The effect of redistribution on Migration: Evidence from the Israeli Kibbutz." *Journal of Public Economics* 93.3 (2009): 498–511.

———. "Lessons from the Kibbutz on the Equality-Incentives Trade-off." *Journal of Economic Perspectives* 25.1 (2011a): 185–207.

———. "On the (Lack of) Stability of Communes: An Economic Perspective." In *The Oxford Handbook of the Economics of Religion*, ed. Rachel M. McCleary, 169–189. Oxford University Press, 2011b.

Abramitzky, Ran, and Fabio Braggion. "Migration and Human Capital: Self-Selection of Indentured Servants to the Americas." *Journal of Economic History* 66.04 (2006): 882–905.

Abramitzky, Ran, Zephyr Frank, and Aprajit Mahajan. "Risk, Incentives, and Contracts: Partnerships in Rio de Janeiro, 1870–1891." *Journal of Economic History* 70.03 (2010): 686–715.

Abramitzky, Ran, and Victor Lavy. "How Responsive Is Investment in Schooling to Changes in Redistributive Policies and in Returns?" *Econometrica* 82.4 (2014): 1241–1272.

Abramitzky, Ran, and Isabelle Sin. "Book Translations as Idea Flows: The Effects of the Collapse of Communism on the Diffusion of Knowledge." *Journal of the European Economic Association* 12.6 (2014): 1453–1520.

Ackerberg, Daniel A., and Maristella Botticini. "The Choice of Agrarian Contracts in Early Renaissance Tuscany: Risk Sharing, Moral Hazard, or Capital Market Imperfections?" *Explorations in Economic History* 37.3 (2000): 241–257.

Albarran, Pedro, and Orazio P. Attanasio. "Limited Commitment and Crowding Out of Private Transfers: Evidence from a Randomised Experiment." *Economic Journal* 113.486 (2003): C77–C85.

Alchian, Armen A., and Harold Demsetz. "Production, Information Costs, and Economic Organization." *American Economic Review* 62.5 (1972): 777–795.

Alesina, Alberto, and Nicola Fuchs-Schündeln. "Good-bye Lenin (or Not?): The Effect of Communism on People's Preferences." *American Economic Review* 97.4 (2007): 1507–1528.

Alesina, Alberto F., Edward L. Glaeser, and Bruce Sacerdote. "Work and Leisure in the US and Europe: Why So Different?" In *NBER Macroeconomics Annual 2005*, vol. 20, ed. Mark Gertler and Kenneth Rogoff, 1–100. MIT Press, 2006.

Alesina, Alberto, and Dani Rodrik "Distributive Politics and Economic Growth." *Quarterly Journal of Economics* 109 (1994): 465–490.

Amemiya, Takeshi. *Advanced Econometrics.* Harvard University Press, 1985.

Angrist, Joshua, and Victor Lavy. "The Effects of High Stakes High School Achievement Awards: Evidence from a Randomized Trial." *American Economic Review* 99.4 (2009): 1384–1414.

Angrist, Joshua D., and Jörn-Steffen Pischke. *Mastering Metrics: The Path from Cause to Effect.* Princeton University Press, 2014.

Atkinson, Anthony B., Thomas Piketty, and Emmanuel Saez. "Top Incomes in the Long Run of History." *Journal of Economic Literature* 49.1 (2011): 3–71.

Attanasio, Orazio, and Katja Kaufmann. *Educational Choices, Subjective Expectations, and Credit Constraints.* No. w15087. National Bureau of Economic Research, 2009.

Autor, David, and Lawrence Katz. "Changes in the Wage Structure and Earnings Inequality." In *Handbook of Labor Economics*, ed. O. Ashenfelter and D. Card, 3A:1463–1555. Elsevier, 1999. http://www.sciencedirect.com/science/article/pii/S1573446399030072.

Autor, David H., Lawrence F. Katz, and Melissa S. Kearney. "Trends in US Wage Inequality: Revising the Revisionists." *Review of Economics and Statistics* 90.2 (2008): 300–323.

Autor, David H., Lawrence F. Katz, and Alan B. Krueger. "Computing Inequality: Have Computers Changed the Labor Market?" *Quarterly Journal of Economics* 113.4 (1998): 1169–1213.

Aydemir, Abdurrahman Bekir, and Arthur Sweetman. "First- and Second-Generation Immigrant Educational Attainment and Labor Market Outcomes: A Comparison of the United States and Canada." *Research in Labor Economics/Immigration-Trends, Consequences and Prospects for the United States* 27 (2007): 215–270.

Azarnert Leonid, Dror Goldberg, and Raphael Franck, "Adjustment to Money in the Privatized Kibbutz." Working paper, 2014.

Bandy, Matthew S. "Fissioning, Scalar Stress, and Social Evolution in Early Village Societies." *American Anthropologist* 106.2 (2004): 322–333.

Banerjee, Abhijit V., Timothy Besley, and Timothy W. Guinnane. "The Neighbor's Keeper: The Design of a Credit Cooperative with Theory and a Test." *Quarterly Journal of Economics* 109.2 (1994): 491–515.

Barkai, Haim. *Growth Patterns of the Kibbutz Economy.* North-Holland, 1977.

———. *Incentives, Efficiency, and Social Control: The Case of the Kibbutz.* Maurice Falk Institute for Economic Research in Israel, 1978.

———. *Kibbutz Efficiency and the Incentive Conundrum.* Maurice Falk Institute for Economic Research in Israel, 1986.

Becker, Gary S. "An Economic Analysis of Fertility." In National Bureau of Economic Research, *Demographic and Economic Change in Developed Countries,* 209–240. Columbia University Press, 1960.

———. "Investment in Human Capital: A Theoretical Analysis." *Journal of Political Economy* 70.5.2 (1962): 9–49.

———. *Human Capital and the Personal Distribution of Income: An Analytical Approach.* Institute of Public Administration, University of Michigan, 1967.

Beito, David T. *From Mutual Aid to the Welfare State: Fraternal Societies and Social Services, 1890–1967.* University of North Carolina Press, 2003.

Benham, Lee, and Philip Keefer. "Voting in Firms: The Role of Agenda Control, Size and Voter Homogeneity." *Economic Inquiry* 29.4 (1991): 706–19. doi:10.1111/j.1465-7295.1991.tb00856.x.

Ben-Ner, Avner. "On the Stability of the Cooperative Type of Organization." *Journal of Comparative Economics* 8.3 (1984): 247–260.

———. "Preferences in a Communal Economic System." *Economica,* n.s., 54.214 (1987): 207–221.

Ben-Porath, Yoram. "The Production of Human Capital and the Life Cycle of Earnings." *Journal of Political Economy* 75.4 (1967): 352–365.

———. "Fertility in Israel, an Economists Interpretation: Differentials and Trends, 1950–1970." Rand Corporation, 1970.

———. "Economic Analysis of Fertility in Israel." *Economics of the Family: Marriage, Children, and Human Capital,* ed. Theodore W. Schultz, 189–224. University of Chicago Press, 1974.

Ben-Rafael, Eliezer. *Crisis and Transformation: The Kibbutz at Century's End.* SUNY Press, 1997.

Benabou, Roland. "Inequality and Growth." *NBER Macroeconomics Annual 1996,* 11:11–92. MIT Press, 1996.

Berman, Eli. "Sect, Subsidy, and Sacrifice: An Economist's View of Ultra-Orthodox Jews." *Quarterly Journal of Economics* 115.3 (2000): 905–953.

———. *Hamas, Taliban and the Jewish Underground: An Economist's View of Radical Religious Militias.* No. w10004. National Bureau of Economic Research, 2003.

Besley, Timothy. "Nonmarket Institutions for Credit and risk sharing in Low-Income Countries." *Journal of Economic Perspectives* 9.3 (1995): 115–127.

Besley, Timothy, and Stephen Coate. "Group Lending, Repayment Incentives and Social Collateral." *Journal of Development Economics* 46.1 (1995): 1–18.

Besley, Timothy, Stephen Coate, and Glenn Loury. "The Economics of Rotating Savings and Credit Associations." *American Economic Review* 83.4 (1993): 792–810.

Bettelheim, Bruno. *The Children of the Dream*. Macmillan, 1969.

Betts, Julian R. "What Do Students Know about Wages? Evidence from a Survey of Undergraduates." *Journal of Human Resources* (1996): 27–56.

Billingsley, Sunnee. "The Post-Communist Fertility Puzzle." *Population Research and Policy Review* 29.2 (2010): 193–231.

Blanchard, Olivier. "The Economic Future of Europe." *Journal of Economic Perspectives* 18.4 (2004): 3–26.

Borjas, George J. "Self-Selection and the Earnings of Immigrants." *American Economic Review* 77.4 (1987): 531–53.

———. "Self-Selection and the Earnings of Immigrants: Reply." *American Economic Review* 80.1 (1990): 305–308.

———. "Immigration and Self-Selection." In *Immigration, Trade, and the Labor Market*. University of Chicago Press, 1991. 29–76.

———. "The Economics of Immigration." *Journal of Economic Literature* 32.4 (1994): 1667–1717.

Borjas, George J., Stephen G. Bronars, and Stephen J. Trejo. "Self-Selection and Internal Migration in the United States." *Journal of Urban Economics* 32.2 (1992): 159–185.

Botticini, Maristella, and Zvi Eckstein. "Jewish Occupational Selection: Education, Restrictions, or Minorities?" *Journal of Economic History* 65.4 (2005): 922–48.

———. *The Chosen Few: How Education Shaped Jewish History*. Princeton University Press, 2012.

Brainerd, Elizabeth. "Winners and Losers in Russia's Economic Transition." *American Economic Review* 88.5 (1998): 1094–1116.

Brenner, Dror, and Yona Rubinstein. "The Returns to Education and Family Income." Unpublished manuscript, Department of Economics, Brown University, 2011.

Buber, Martin. *Paths in Utopia*. Syracuse University Press, 1949.

Burdín, Gabriel. "Equality under Threat by the Talented: Evidence from Worker-Managed Firms." *Economic Journal* 126.594 (2016): 1372–1403. doi:10.1111/ecoj.12272.

Burt, Ronald S. *Brokerage and Closure: An Introduction to Social Capital*. Oxford University Press, 2005.

Calomiris, Charles W., and Indira Rajaraman. "The Role of ROSCAs: Lumpy Durables or Event Insurance?" *Journal of Development Economics* 56.1 (1998): 207–216.

Cappelen, Alexander W., John A. List, Anya Samek, and Bertil Tungodden. "The Effect of Early Education on Social Preferences." NBER Working Paper no. 22898 (2016). http://www.nber.org/papers/w22898.

Card, David. "Using Geographic Variation in College Proximity to Estimate the Return to Schooling." NBER Working Paper no. 4483 (1993). http://davidcard.berkeley.edu/papers/geo_var_schooling.pdf.

———. "The Causal Effect of Education on Earnings." In *Handbook of Labor Economics*, vol. 3, ed. Orley Ashenfelter and David Card, 1801–1863. Elsevier, 1999.

———. Estimating the Return to Schooling: Progress on Some Persistent Econometric Problems." *Econometrica* 69.5 (2001): 1127–1160.

———. "Earnings, Schooling, and Ability Revisited." In *35th Anniversary Retrospective*, ed. Solomon W. Polachek and Konstantinos Tatsiramos, 111. Emerald Group, 2012.

Card, David, and John E. DiNardo. "Skill-Biased Technological Change and Rising Wage Inequality: Some Problems and Puzzles." *Journal of Labor Economics* 20.4 (2002): 733–783.

Cardon, James H., and Igal Hendel. "Asymmetric Information in Health Insurance: Evidence from the National Medical Expenditure Survey." *RAND Journal of Economics* 32.3 (2001): 408–427.

Carliner, Geoffrey. "Wages, Earnings and Hours of First, Second, and Third Generation American Males." *Economic Inquiry* 18.1 (1980): 87–102.

Carneiro, Robert L. "On the Relationship between Size of Population and Complexity of Social Organization." *Southwestern Journal of Anthropology* 23.3 (1967): 234–243.

Chetty, Raj, John N. Friedman, Tore Olsen, and Luigi Pistaferri. "Adjustment Costs, Firm Responses, and Micro vs. Macro Labor Supply Elasticities: Evidence from Danish Tax Records." *Quarterly Journal of Economics* 126.2 (2011): 749–804.

Chiappori, Pierre-Andre, and Bernard Salanie. "Testing for Asymmetric Information in Insurance Markets." *Journal of Political Economy* 108.1 (2000): 56–78.

———. "Testing Contract Theory: A Survey of Some Recent Work." CESIFO Working Paper no. 738 (2002).

Chiquiar, Daniel, and Gordon H. Hanson. "International Migration, Self-Selection, and the Distribution of Wages: Evidence from Mexico and the United States." *Journal of Political Economy* 113.2 (2005): 239–281.

Chiswick, Barry R. "The Effect of Americanization on the Earnings of Foreign-Born Men." *Journal of Political Economy* (1978): 897–921.

———. "Are Immigrants Favorably Self-Selected?" *American Economic Review* 89.2 (1999): 181–185.

———. "Are Immigrants Favorably Self-Selected?" *Migration Theory: Talking across Disciplines* (2013): 61.

Choy, James P. "Religion and the Family: The Case of the Amish." University of Warwick, Department of Economics, 2016. http://www.warwick.ac.uk/fac /soc/economics/research/workingpapers/2016/twerp_1114_choy.pdf.

Clark, Colin. The Conditions of Economic Progress. Macmillan, 1940.

Coate, Stephen, and Martin Ravallion. "Reciprocity without Commitment: Characterization and Performance of Informal Insurance Arrangements." Journal of Development Economics 40.1 (1993): 1–24.

Coate, Stephen, and Martin Ravallion. "Reciprocity without Commitment: Characterization and Performance of Informal Insurance Arrangements." Journal of Development Economics 40.1 (1993): 1–24.

Cohen, Alma, Rajeev Dehejia, and Dmitri Romanov. Do Financial Incentives Affect Fertility? NBER Working Paper no. 13700 (2007). http://www.nber.org /papers/w13700.

Cohen, Gerald Allan. Rescuing Justice and Equality. Harvard University Press, 2009.

Coleman, James S. "Social Capital in the Creation of Human Capital." American Journal of Sociology 94 (1988): S95–S120.

———. Foundations of Social Theory. Harvard University Press, 1994.

Corgnet, Brice, Roberto Hernan-Gonzalez, and Stephen Rassenti. "Peer Pressure and Moral Hazard in Teams: Experimental Evidence." Review of Behavioral Economics 2.4 (2015): 379–403.

Coşgel, Metin M., and John E. Murray. "Productivity of a Commune: The Shakers, 1850–1880." Journal of Economic History 58.02 (1998): 494–510.

Craig, Ben, and John Pencavel. "The Behavior of Worker Cooperatives: The Plywood Companies of the Pacific Northwest." American Economic Review 82.5 (1992): 1083–1105.

Cremer, Helmuth, and Pierre Pestieau. "Factor Mobility and Redistribution." In Handbook of Regional and Urban Economics, vol. 4, ed. J. Vernon Henderson and Jacques Thisse, 2529–2560. Elsevier, 2004.

Crocker, Keith J., and John R. Moran. "Contracting with Limited Commitment: Evidence from Employment-Based Health Insurance Contracts." RAND Journal of Economics 34.4 (2003): 694–718.

Danziger, Leif, and Shoshana Neuman. "Equality and Fertility in the Kibbutz." Journal of Population Economics 6.1 (1993): 57–66.

David, H., Lawrence F. Katz, and Alan B. Krueger. "Computing Inequality: Have Computers Changed the Labor Market?" Quarterly Journal of Economics 113.4 (1998).

Davis, Steven J., and Magnus Henrekson. Tax Effects on Work Activity, Industry Mix and Shadow Economy Size: Evidence from Rich-Country Comparisons. No. w10509. National Bureau of Economic Research, 2004.

Demeny, Paul. "Pronatalist Policies in Low-Fertility Countries: Patterns, Performance, and Prospects." Population and Development Review 12 (1986): 335–358.

Diamond, Jared M. *Guns, Germs, and Steel: The Fates of Human Societies.* W. W. Norton, 1999.

DiNardo, John, and David Card. "Skill-Biased Technological Change and Rising Wage Inequality: Some Problems and Puzzles." *Journal of Labor Economics* 20.4 (2002): 733–783.

DiNardo, John, Nicole M. Fortin, and Thomas Lemieux. "Labor Market Institutions and the Distribution of Wages, 1973–1992: A Semiparametric Approach." *Econometrica* 64.5 (1996): 1001–1044.

Don, Yehuda. "Altruism and Cooperative Survival." *Advances in Economic Analysis of Participatory and Labor-Managed Firms* 5 (1995): 185–204.

Dror, Yuval. "The History of Kibbutz Education: Practice into Theory." *Utopian Studies* 13.2 (2002): 129–131.

Dunbar, Robin. *Grooming, Gossip, and the Evolution of Language.* Harvard University Press, 1998.

———. "Gossip in Evolutionary Perspective." *Review of General Psychology* 8.2 (2004): 100.

Eaton, Jonathan, and Harvey S. Rosen. "Optimal Redistributive Taxation and Uncertainty." *Quarterly Journal of Economics* 95.2 (1980): 357–364.

Ebenstein, Avraham, Moshe Hazan , and Avi Simhon. "Changing the Cost of Children and Fertility: Evidence from the Israeli Kibbutz." *Economic Journal* 126.597 (2016): 2038–2063.

Epple, Dennis, and Thomas Romer. "Mobility and Redistribution." *Journal of Political Economy* 99.4 (1991): 828–858.

Farrell, Joseph, and Suzanne Scotchmer. "Partnerships." *Quarterly Journal of Economics,* 103.2 (1988): 279–297.

Feinberg, Matthew, Robb Willer, Jennifer Stellar, and Dacher Keltner. "The Virtues of Gossip: Reputational Information Sharing as Prosocial Behavior." *Journal of Personality and Social Psychology* 102.5 (2012): 1015–1030. doi:10.1037/a0026650.

Feldstein, Martin, and Marian Vaillant Wrobel. "Can State Taxes Redistribute Income?" *Journal of Public Economics* 68.3 (1998): 369–396.

Fehr, Ernst, and Urs Fischbacher. "The Nature of Human Altruism." *Nature* 425.6960 (2003): 785–791.

Fehr, Ernst, and Simon Gächter. "Cooperation and Punishment in Public Goods Experiments." *American Economic Review* 90.4 (2000a): 980–994.

———. "Fairness and Retaliation: The Economics of Reciprocity." *Journal of Economic Perspectives* 14.3 (2000b): 159–181.

———. "Altruistic Punishment in Humans." *Nature* 415.6868 (2002): 137–140.

Fehr, Ernst, and Klaus M. Schmidt. "A Theory of Fairness, Competition, and Cooperation." *Quarterly Journal of Economics* 114.3 (1999): 817–868.

Feinberg, Matthew, Robb Willer, Jennifer Stellar, and Dacher Keltner. "The Virtues of Gossip: Reputational Information Sharing as Prosocial Behavior." *Journal of Personality and Social Psychology* 102.5 (2012): 1015.

Feinberg, Matthew, Robb Willer, and Michael Schultz. "Gossip and Ostracism Promote Cooperation in Groups." *Psychological Science* 25.3 (2014): 656–664.

Ferrie, Joseph P. "How Ya Gonna Keep 'Em Down on the Farm [When They've Seen Schenectady]? Rural to Urban Migration in the US, 1850–70." Working paper (1999a).

———. *Yankeys Now: Immigrants in the Antebellum US, 1840–1860.* Oxford University Press on Demand, 1999b.

———. "History Lessons: The End of American Exceptionalism? Mobility in the United States since 1850." *Journal of Economic Perspectives* 19.3 (2005): 199–215.

Finkelstein, Amy N., and Kathleen M. McGarry. "Private Information and Its Effect on Equilibrium: New Evidence from Long Term Care Insurance." California Center for Population Research, 2003.

———. "Multiple Dimensions of Private Information: Evidence from the Long-Term Care Insurance Market." *American Economic Review* 96.4 (2006): 938–958.

Finkelstein, Amy, and James Poterba. "Testing for Adverse Selection with 'Unused Observables.'" NBER Working Paper no. 12112 (2006).

Fisher, Allan G. B. "Production, Primary, Secondary and Tertiary." *Economic Record* 15.1 (1939): 24–38.

Fishman, Aryei. *Judaism and Modernization on the Religious Kibbutz.* Cambridge University Press, 1992.

———. "Religious Socialism and Economic Success on the Orthodox Kibbutz." *Journal of Institutional and Theoretical Economics (JITE)/Zeitschrift für die gesamte Staatswissenschaft* 150.4 (1994): 763–768.

Foster, Andrew D., and Mark R. Rosenzweig. "Technical Change and Human-Capital Returns and Investments: Evidence from the Green Revolution." *American Economic Review* (1996): 931–953.

Foster, George. "Interpersonal Relations in Peasant Society." *Human Organization* 19.4 (1960): 174–178.

Frank, Robert. *The Darwin Economy.* Princeton University Press, 2011.

Freeman, Richard. "The Overeducated American." Academic Press, 1976.

Friedman, Milton, and L. J. Savage. "The Utility Analysis of Choices Involving Risk." *Journal of Political Economy* 56.4 (1948): 279–304.

Frisch, R. "The Return to Schooling—The Causal Link between Schooling and Earnings." Working Paper 2007.03, Research Department, Bank of Israel, 2007.

Frisch, R., and J. Moalem. "The Rise in the Return to Schooling in Israel in 1976–1997." Working Paper 99.06, Research Department, Bank of Israel, 1999.

Froese, Paul. *The Plot to Kill God: Findings from the Soviet Experiment in Secularization.* University of California Press, 2008.

Gabriel, Paul E., and Susanne Schmitz. "Favorable Self-Selection and the internal migration of Young White Males in the United States." *Journal of Human Resources* 30.3 (1995): 460–471.

Garicano, Luis, and Thomas N. Hubbard. "Specialization, Firms, and Markets: The Division of Labor within and between Law Firms." *Journal of Law, Economics, and Organization* 25.2 (2009): 339–371.

Garicano, Luis, and Tano Santos. "Referrals." *American Economic Review* 94.3 (2004): 499–525.

Gavron, Daniel. *The Kibbutz: Awakening from Utopia*. Rowman and Littlefield, 2000.

Gaynor, Martin, and Paul Gertler. "Moral Hazard and Risk Spreading in Partnerships." *RAND Journal of Economics* 26.4 (1995): 591–613.

Genesove, David. "Adverse Selection in the Wholesale Used Car Market." *Journal of Political Economy* 101.4 (1993): 644–665.

Gerschenkron, Alexander. "Economic Backwardness in Historical Perspective: A Book of Essays." Belknap Press, 1962. http://www.eh.net/?s=Economic+backwardness.

Getz, Shlomo. "Surveys of Changes in Kibbutzim." Institute for Research of the Kibbutz and the Cooperative Idea, University of Haifa, Reports (booklet for various years from 1998–2011).

Giné, Xavier, Pamela Jakiela, Dean Karlan, and Jonathan Morduch. "Microfinance Games." *American Economic Journal: Applied Economics* 2.3 (2010): 60–95.

Golan, Orna. *Kibbutz's Child* [in Hebrew]. Akad Publication, 2012.

Gur, Batya. *Communal Child Rearing* [in Hebrew]. Ketter, (1991).

Gould, Eric D., and Omer Moav. "Israel's Brain Drain." *Israel Economic Review* 5.1 (2007): 1–22.

Gould, Eric, and Omer Moav (2016) "Does High Inequality Attract High Skilled Immigrants?" *Economic Journal* 126.593 (2016): 1055–1091.

Glatzer, Nahum N. (ed.), *The Judaic Tradition: Texts*. Behrman House, 1982.

Granovetter, Mark. "Economic Action and Social Structure: The Problem Of Embeddedness." *American Journal of Sociology* 91.3 (1985): 481–510.

———. "The Impact of Social Structure on Economic Outcomes." *Journal of Economic Perspectives* 19.1 (2005): 33–50.

Greene, William H. *Econometric Analysis*. Pearson Education India, 2003.

Greenwald, Bruce C., and Robert R. Glasspiegel. "Adverse Selection in the Market for Slaves: New Orleans, 1830–1860." *Quarterly Journal of Economics* 98.3 (1983): 479–499.

Greif, Avner. "Reputation and Coalitions in Medieval Trade: Evidence on the Maghribi Traders." *Journal of Economic History* 49.04 (1989): 857–882.

———. "Contract Enforceability and Economic Institutions in Early Trade: The Maghribi Traders' Coalition." *American Economic Review* 83.3 (1993): 525–548.

———. "Cultural Beliefs and the Organization of Society: A Historical and Theoretical Reflection on Collectivist and Individualist Societies." *Journal of Political Economy* 102.5 (1994): 912–950.

———. *Institutions: Theory and History*. Cambridge University Press, 2003.

Greif, Avner, Paul Milgrom, and Barry R. Weingast. "Coordination, Commitment, and Enforcement: The Case of the Merchant Guild." *Journal of Political Economy* 102.4 (1994): 745–776.

Gronau, Reuben. "The Effect of Children on the Housewife's Value of Time." *Journal of Political Economy* 81.2 (1973): S168–199.

———. "Wage Comparisons—A Selectivity Bias." *Journal of Political Economy* 82.6 (1974): 1119–1143.

Guinnane, Timothy W. "Cooperatives as Information Machines: German Rural Credit Cooperatives, 1883–1914." *Journal of Economic History* 61.02 (2001): 366–389.

Gur, Batya. *Murder on a Kibbutz: Communal Case*. Harper Perennial, 1995.

Guttman, Joel M. "Understanding Collective Action: Matching Behavior." *American Economic Review* 68.2 (1978): 251–255.

Guttman, Joel M., and Adi Schnytzer. "Strategic Work Interactions and the Kibbutz-Kolkhoz Paradox." *Economic Journal* 99.397 (1989): 686–699.

Harari, Yuval Noah. *Sapiens: A Brief History of Humankind*. Random House, 2014.

Harel, Yehuda. *The New Kibbutz* [in Hebrew]. Keter, 1993.

———. *Privatized* [in Hebrew]. Carmel, 2010.

Harris, Milton, and Bengt Holmstrom. "A Theory of Wage Dynamics." *Review of Economic Studies* 49.3 (1982): 315–333.

Heckman, James. "Shadow Prices, Market Wages, and Labor Supply." *Econometrica: Journal of the Econometric Society* (1974): 679–694.

———. "Sample Selection Bias as a Specification Error (with an Application to the Estimation of Labor Supply Functions)." NBER Working Paper no. 172 (1977).

———. "Varieties of Selection Bias." *American Economic Review* 80.2 (1990): 313–318.

Heckman, James J., and Bo E. Honore. "The Empirical Content of the Roy Model." *Econometrica: Journal of the Econometric Society* (1990): 1121–1149.

Heckman, James J., and Guilherme L. Sedlacek. "Self-Selection and the Distribution of Hourly Wages." *Journal of Labor Economics* 8.1.2 (1990): S329–S363.

Helman, Amir. "The Economic Factor in Leaving the Kibbutz" [in Hebrew]. Research paper, Rupin College, 1982.

———. "The Israeli Kibbutz as a Socialist Model." *Journal of Institutional and Theoretical Economics (JITE)/Zeitschrift für die gesamte Staatswissenschaft* 148.1 (1992): 168–183.

———. "Privatization, Efficiency and the Kibbutz System." *Economic Quarterly* 40.1 (1993): 48–57.

Hendel, Igal, and Alessandro Lizzeri. "The Role of Commitment in Dynamic Contacts: Evidence from Life Insurance." *Quarterly Journal of Economics* 118.1 (2003).

Henrich, Joseph, Boyd Robert, Bowles Samuel, Camerer Colin, Fehr Ernst, Gintis Herbert and McElreath Richard. "In Search of Homo Economicus: Behavioral Experiments in 15 Small-Scale Societies." *American Economic Review* 91.2 (2001): 73–78.

Hertzberg, A. *The Zionist Idea: A Historical Analysis and Reader.* Jewish Publication Society, 1959.

Hewstone, Miles, Mark Rubin, and Hazel Willis. "Intergroup Bias." *Annual Review of Psychology* 53.1 (2002): 575–604.

Hleihel, Ahmad. "Fertility among Jewish and Muslim Women in Israel, by Level of Religiosity, 1979–2009." Israel Central Bureau of Statistics, Demography and Census Department. Working Paper Series 60 (2011).

Hoffman, Philip T. "The Economic Theory of Sharecropping in Early Modern France." *Journal of Economic History* 44.02 (1984): 309–319.

Holmstrom, Bengt. "Moral Hazard in Teams." *Bell Journal of Economics* 13.2 (1982): 324–340.

Hostetler, John A. *Hutterite Society.* Johns Hopkins University Press (1997).

Hostetler, John A., and Gertrude E. Huntington. *The Hutterites in North America.* Thomson Brooks/Cole, 2002.

Iannaccone, Laurence R. "Sacrifice and Stigma: Reducing Free-Riding in Cults, Communes, and Other Collectives." *Journal of Political Economy* 100.2 (1992): 271–291.

Inbari, Assaf. *Habaitah (Going home)* [in Hebrew]. Yedi'ot Aharonot, 2009.

Israel Ministry of Education. *Statistics of the Matriculation Examination (Bagrut) Test Data.* Ministry of Education Chief Scientist's Office, 2001.

Jaffe, Eliezer. "Manual for Establishing a Moshav Ovdim" [in Hebrew]. N.p., 1919.

Jensen, Robert. "The (Perceived) Returns to Education and the Demand for Schooling." *Quarterly Journal of Economics* 125.2 (2010).

Johnson, Allen W., and Timothy K. Earle. *The Evolution of Human Societies: From Foraging Group to Agrarian State.* Stanford University Press, 2000.

Kandel, Eugene, and Edward P. Lazear. "Peer Pressure and Partnerships." *Journal of Political Economy* 100.4 (1992): 801–817.

Kane, Thomas J. "College Entry by Blacks since 1970: The Role of College Costs, Family Background, and the Returns to Education." *Journal of Political Economy* (1994): 878–911.

Kanter, R. M. *Commitment and Community: Communes and Utopias in Sociological Perspective.* Harvard University Press, 1972.

Kanovsky, Eliyahu. "The Economy of the Israeli Kibbutz." In *The Economy of the Israeli Kibbutz.* Harvard University Press, 1966.

Kanter, Rosabeth Moss. *Commitment and Community: Communes and Utopias in Sociological Perspective.* Harvard University Press, 1972.

Karlan, Dean, and Jonathan Zinman. "Observing Unobservables: Identifying Information Asymmetries with a Consumer Credit Field Experiment." *Econometrica* 77.6 (2009): 1993–2008.

Katz, Lawrence F. "Changes in the Wage Structure and Earnings Inequality." In *Handbook of Labor Economics*, vol. 3, ed. Lawrence Katz and David Autor, 1463–1555. Elsevier, 1999.

Katz, Lawrence F., and Claudia Dale Goldin. *The Race between Education and Technology*. Harvard University Press, 2008.

Katz, Lawrence F., and Alan B. Krueger. "Computing Inequality: Have Computers Changed the Labor Market?" *Quarterly Journal of Economics* 113:4 (1998): 1169–1213.

Kehoe, Timothy J., and David K. Levine. "Debt-Constrained Asset Markets." *Review of Economic Studies* 60.4 (1993): 865–888.

———. "Liquidity Constrained Markets versus Debt Constrained Markets." *Econometrica* 69.3 (2001): 575–598.

Keren, Michael, David Levhari, and Michael Byalsky. "On the Stability and Viability of Co-operatives: The Kibbutz as an Example." *Acta Oeconomica* 56.3 (2006): 301–321.

Klinov, Ruth, and Michal Palgi. *Standard of Living in Kibbutzim—A Comparison with Urban Families*. Working Paper no. A06.05, Falk Research Institute, Jerusalem (2006).

Knez, Marc, and Duncan Simester. "Firm-wide Incentives and Mutual Monitoring at Continental Airlines." *Journal of Labor Economics* 19.4 (2001): 743–772.

Kniffin, Kevin M., and David Sloan Wilson. "Evolutionary Perspectives on Workplace Gossip: Why and How Gossip Can Serve Groups." *Group and Organization Management* 35.2 (2010): 150–176.

Kremer, Michael. *Why Are Worker Cooperatives So Rare?* NBER Working Paper no. 6118 (1997).

Kropotkin, Peter. *Mutual Aid: A Factor of Evolution*. Courier Corp., [1902] 2012.

Lamoreaux, Naomi R. "Constructing Firms: Partnerships and Alternative Contractual Arrangements in Early Nineteenth-Century American Business." *Business and Economic History* 24.2 (1995): 43–71.

Lamdan, Erella. "From Silence to Screaming to Conversation—Three Generations of Motherhood in the Kibbutz." In *Coming from Silence* [in Hebrew]. Yad Ṭabenḳin, 2009.

Lang, Kevin, and Peter-John Gordon. "Partnerships as Insurance Devices: Theory and Evidence." *RAND Journal of Economics* 26.4 (1995): 614–629.

Laroque, Guy, and Bernard Salanié. "Does Fertility Respond to Financial Incentives?" IZA Discussion Paper no. 3575 (2008).

Lazear, Edward P. "Salaries and Piece Rates." *Journal of Business* (1986): 405–431.

———. "Performance Pay and Productivity." *American Economic Review* 90.5 (2000a): 1346–1361.

———. "The Power of Incentives." *American Economic Review* 90.2 (2000b): 410–414.

Lee, Lung-Fei. "Unionism and Wage Rates: A Simultaneous Equations Model with Qualitative and Limited Dependent Variables." *International Economic Review* 19.2 (1978): 415–433.

Leshem, N. *The Song of the Grass: Conversations with Women of the Kibbutz First Generation* [in Hebrew]. Yad Tabenkin, 1991.

Leviatan Uriel. *Factors Connecting Kibbutz Children to Their Kibbutz and Reasons for Their Exodus* [in Hebrew]. Institute for Study and Research of the Kibbutz, University of Haifa, 1975.

———. *Rotation in Central Positions in the Kibbutz—an Update* [in Hebrew]. Institute for Study and Research of the Kibbutz, University of Haifa, 1993.

———. *Negative Selection among Youngsters in the Kibbutz* [in Hebrew]. Institute for Study and Research of the Kibbutz, University of Haifa, 1996.

Leviatan, Uri, Hugh Oliver, and Jack Quarter. *Crisis in the Israeli Kibbutz: Meeting the Challenge of Changing Times.* Greenwood, 1998.

Leviatan, Uri, and Elliette Orchan. "Kibbutz Ex-members and Their Adjustment to Life Outside the Kibbutz." *Interchange* 13.1 (1982): 16–28.

Leviatan, Uriel, and Menachem Rosner. *Belief in Values and Change in Values among Kibbutz Members* [in Hebrew]. Institute for Study and Research of the Kibbutz, University of Haifa, 2000.

Levin, Jonathan, and Steven Tadelis. "Profit Sharing and the Role of Professional Partnerships." *Quarterly Journal of Economics* 120.1 (2005): 131–171.

Liebig, Thomas, and Alfonso Sousa-Poza. "How Does Income Inequality Influence International Migration?" Paper presented at European Regional Science Association, Vienna, 2003.

Lieblich, Amia. *Kibbutz Makom: Report from an Israeli Kibbutz* [in Hebrew]. Shocken, 1981.

Lieblich, Amia, Rivka Tuval-Mashiach, and Tamar Zilber. *Narrative Research: Reading, Analysis, and Interpretation.* Sage, 1998.

Ligon, Ethan. "Risk Sharing under Varying Information Regimes: Theory and Measurement in Village Economies." Working paper no. 727, Dept. of Agricultural and Resource Economics. University of California at Berkeley (1994). http://purl.umn.edu/201473.

———. "Risk Sharing and Information in Village Economies." *Review of Economic Studies* 65.4 (1998): 847–864.

Ligon, Ethan, Jonathan P. Thomas, and Tim Worrall. "Informal Insurance Arrangements with Limited Commitment: Theory and Evidence from Village Economies." *Review of Economic Studies* 69.1 (2002): 209–244.

Lincoln, James R., and Michael L. Gerlach. *Japan's Network Economy: Structure, Persistence, and Change.* Cambridge University Press, 2004.

Luttmer, Erzo FP. "Neighbors as Negatives: Relative Earnings and Well-Being." *Quarterly Journal of Economics* 120.3 (2005): 963–1002.

Maddala, Gangadharrao S. *Limited-Dependent and Qualitative Variables in Econometrics.* Cambridge University Press, 1986.

Manski, Charles F. "Nonparametric Bounds on Treatment Effects." *American Economic Review* 80.2 (1990): 319–323.

Manski, Charles F., and Joram Mayshar. "Private Incentives and Social Interactions: Fertility Puzzles in Israel." *Journal of the European Economic Association* 1.1 (2003): 181–211.

Maron, S. "Recent Developments in the Kibbutz: An Overview." *Journal of Rural Cooperation* 22.1–2 (1994): 5–17.

McCloskey, Donald N. "English Open Fields as Behavior towards Risk." *Research in Economic History* 1.2 (1976): 124–171.

———. "The Prudent Peasant: New Findings on Open Fields." *Journal of Economic History* 51.02 (1991): 343–355.

Mellow, Wesley. "Unionism and Wages: A Longitudinal Analysis." *Review of Economics and Statistics* (1981): 43–52.

Metzer, Jacob. *The Divided Economy of Mandatory Palestine.* Cambridge University Press, 1998.

Milligan, Kevin. "Subsidizing the Stork: New Evidence on Tax Incentives and Fertility." *Review of Economics and Statistics* 87.3 (2005): 539–555.

Mincer, Jacob. "Family Migration Decisions." NBER Working Paper no. 199 (1977).

Mokyr, Joel. *The Gifts of Athena: Historical Origins of the Knowledge Economy.* Princeton University Press, 2002.

Moock, Peter R., Harry A. Patrinos, and Meera Venkataraman. "Education and Earnings in a Transition Economy (Vietnam)." Working paper no. 1920. World Bank Policy Research, 1998.

Mort, J.A., and G. Brenner. *Our Hearts Invented a Place: Can Kibbutzim Survive in Today's Israel?* Cornell University Press, 2003.

Morten, Melanie. "Temporary Migration and Endogenous Risk Sharing in Village India." NBER Working Paper no. 22159 (2016).

Mulder, Laetitia B., Eric van Dijk, David De Cremer, and Henk A. M. Wilke. "Undermining Trust and Cooperation: The Paradox of Sanctioning Systems in Social Dilemmas." *Journal of Experimental Social Psychology* 42.2 (2006): 147–162.

Munshi, Kaivan, and Mark Rosenzweig. *Why Is Mobility in India So Low? Social Insurance, Inequality and Growth.* Working paper, Department of Economics, Brown University, 2009.

Muravchik, Joshua. *Heaven on Earth: The Rise and Fall of Socialism.* Encounter Books, 2003.

Murray, John E. "Human Capital in Religious Communes: Literacy and Selection of Nineteenth Century Shakers." *Explorations in Economic History* 32.2 (1995): 217–235.

Natan, Michael, Aliza Shenbal-Brandes, and Harvi Paskin. "Together and Alone: High School Graduate Kibbutz Children 1969 after 10 Years [in Hebrew]." *Kibbutz* 8 (1982): 105–127.

Near, Henry. *The Kibbutz Movement, A History. Volume I: Origins and Growth, 1909–1939.* Littman Library of Jewish Civilization, 1992.

———. *The Kibbutz Movement: A History. Volume II: Crises and Achievements, 1939–1995.* Littman Library of Jewish Civilization, 1997.

Newey, Whitney K., James L. Powell, and James R. Walker. "Semiparametric Estimation of Selection Models: Some Empirical Results." *American Economic Review* 80.2 (1990): 324–328.

North, Douglass Cecil. *Structure and Change in Economic History.* Norton, 1981.

———. *Institutions, Institutional Change and Economic Performance.* Cambridge University Press, 1990.

North, Douglass C., and Robert Paul Thomas. *The Rise of the Western World: A New Economic History.* Cambridge University Press, 1973.

North, Douglas, and Bary Weingast. "Constitutions and Commitment: The Evolution of Institutional Governing Public Choice in Seventeeth-Century England." *Journal of Economic History* 49.4 (1989): 803–832.

Nozick, Robert. *Socratic Puzzles.* Harvard University Press, 1997.

Olson, Mancur. *The Logic of Collective Action.* Harvard University Press, [1965] 2009.

Oreopoulos, Philip, and Kjell G. Salvanes. "Priceless: The Nonpecuniary Benefits of Schooling." *Journal of Economic Perspectives* 25.1 (2011): 159–84. doi:10.1257/jep.25.1.159.

Ostrom, Elinor. "Collective Action and the Evolution of Social Norms." *Journal of Natural Resources Policy Research* 6.4 (2014): 235–252.

———. *Governing the Commons.* Cambridge University Press, 2015.

Ostrom, Elinor, Roy Gardner, and James Walker. *Rules, Games, and Common-Pool Resources.* University of Michigan Press, 1994.

Oved, Yaácov. *Two Hundred Years of American Communes.* Transaction, 1993.

Oz, Amos, and Nicholas De Lange. *Fima.* New York, NY: Harcourt Brace, 1993.

Palgi, Michal. "Theoretical and Empirical Aspects of Workers' Participation in Decision Making—A Comparison between Kibbutz and Non-kibbutz Industrial Plants in Israel." PhD diss., Hebrew University, Jerusalem, 1984.

Palgi, Michal, and Shaul Sharir. "Survey of Public Opinion in the Kibbutzim" [in Hebrew]. Institute for Research of the Kibbutz and the Cooperative Idea, University of Haifa, 2001.

Palgi, Michal, and Eliat Orchan. "Survey of Public Opinion in the Kibbutzim" [in Hebrew]. Institute for Research of the Kibbutz and the Cooperative Idea, University of Haifa, 2005.

Pavin, Avraham. "The Kibbutz Movement—Facts and Figures 2002." Yad Tabenkin–Research and Documentation Center of the Kibbutz Movement, 2002.

Pencavel, John, and Ben Craig. "The Empirical Performance of Orthodox Models of the Firm: Conventional Firms and Worker Cooperatives." *Journal of Political Economy* 102.4 (1994): 718–744.

Peter, Karl. "The Dynamics of Hutterite Society." University of Alberta Press, 1987.

Pfaff, Steven. "Religion under Communism: State Regulation, Atheist Competition, and the Dynamics of Supply and Demand." In *The Oxford Handbook of the Economics of Religion,* ed. Rachel M. McCleary. Oxford University Press, 2011.

Piketty, Thomas, *Capital in the Twenty-First Century.* Harvard University Press, 2014.

Piketty, Thomas, and Emmanuel Saez. *Income Inequality in the United States, 1913–1998* (series updated to 2000 available). NBER Working Paper no. 8467 (2001).

Pitzer, Donald E., ed. *America's Communal Utopias.* University of North Carolina Press, 1997.

Polanyi, Karl. *The Economy as an Instituted Process.* In *Economic Anthropology: Readings in Theory and Analysis,* ed. Edward E. Leclair and Harold K. Schneider, 122–43. Holt, Rinehart & Winston (1968).

Prendergast, Canice. "The Provision of Incentives in Firms." *Journal of Economic Literature* 37.1 (1999): 7–63.

———. "The Tenuous Trade-off between Risk and Incentives." *Journal of Political Economy* 110.5 (2002): 1071–1102.

Prescott, Edward C. "Why Do Americans Work So Much More Than Europeans?" *Federal Reserve Bank of Minneapolis Quarterly Review* 28.1 (2004): 2–13.

Putterman, Louis. "Incentives and the Kibbutz: Toward an Economics of Communal Work Motivation." *Journal of Economics* 43.2 (1983): 157–188.

Ramos, F. "Out-Migration and Return Migration of Puerto Ricans." In *Immigration and the Work Force,* ed. G. Borjas and R. Freeman, pp. 49–66. NBER and University of Chicago Press, 1992.

Rawls, John. *A Theory of Justice.* Harvard University Press, [1971] 2009.

Richardson, Gary. "The Prudent Village: Risk Pooling Institutions in Medieval English Agriculture." *Journal of Economic History* 65.02 (2005): 386–413.

Ridley, Matt. *The Origins of Virtue.* Penguin UK, 1997.

Robinson, Chris, and Nigel Tomes. "Self-Selection and Interprovincial Migration in Canada." *Canadian Journal of Economics* (1982): 474–502.

Rosenzweig, Mark R. "Risk, Implicit Contracts and the Family in Rural Areas of Low-Income Countries." *Economic Journal* 98.393 (1988): 1148–1170.

Rosner, Menahem. *The Second Generation: Continuity and Change in the Kibbutz.* Greenwood, 1990.

Rosner, Menachem, and Shlomo Getz. "The Kibbutz in the Era of Changes." Hakibbutz Hameuchad and University of Haifa Publishing House, 1996.

Rosner, Menachem, and Arnold S. Tannenbaum. "Organizational Efficiency and Egalitarian Democracy in an Intentional Communal Society: The Kibbutz." *British Journal of Sociology* (1987a): 521–545.

———. "Ownership and Alienation in Kibbutz Factories." *Work and Occupations* 14.2 (1987b): 165–189.

Rosolio, Daniel. *System and Crisis: Crises, Adjustments and Changes in the Kibbutz Movement.* Am Oved, 1999.

Roy, Andrew Donald. "Some Thoughts on the Distribution of Earnings." *Oxford Economic Papers* 3.2 (1951): 135–146.

Ruffle, Bradley J., and Richard Sosis. "Cooperation and the In-group-Out-group Bias: A Field Test on Israeli Kibbutz Members and City Residents." *Journal of Economic Behavior and Organization* 60.2 (2006): 147–163.

———. "Does It Pay to Pray? Costly Ritual and Cooperation." *BE Journal of Economic Analysis and Policy* 7.1 (2007). doi:10.2202/1935-1682.1629.

Russell, Raymond, Robert Hanneman, and Shlomo Getz. *The Renewal of the Kibbutz: From Reform to Transformation.* Rutgers University Press, 2013.

Saez, Emmanuel, Joel Slemrod, and Seth H. Giertz. "The Elasticity of Taxable Income with Respect to Marginal Tax Rates: A Critical Review." *Journal of Economic Literature* 50.1 (2012): 3–50.

Satt, Ehud. "Compensation for Contribution in the Kibbutz: The Lessons of the LMF Model." *Economic Quarterly* no. 147 (1991): 372–386.

———. "Relative Deprivation in the Kibbutz Economy: An Exploration of the Concepts of Equality and Equity." *Economica* 63.250 (1996): S87–S101.

Satt, Ehud, and Haim Ginzburg. "On the Dynamic Effects of Using Hired Labor in the Kibbutz—Theory and Case Studies." *Journal of Comparative Economics* 16.4 (1992): 688–700.

Satt, Ehud, and Z. Sheaffer. "The Anatomy of Using Hired Labor in the Kibbutz: Interdisciplinary Approach and New Data." *Journal of Rural Cooperation* 22 (1994): 131–147.

Schultz, T. Paul. "School Subsidies for the Poor: Evaluating the Mexican Progresa Poverty Program." *Journal of Development Economics* 74.1 (2004): 199–250.

Shatil, I. *The Economy of the Communal Settlement in Israel* [in Hebrew]. Siphriat Poalim, 1955.

Shenker, Barry. *Intentional Communities: Ideology and Alienation in Communal Societies.* Routledge & Kegan Paul, 2011.

Shimony, Uzi, Hannah Goldemberg, Jacob Glick, and Menachem Rosner. *The Kibbutz Industry Motivation* [in Hebrew]. Institute for Study and Research of the Kibbutz, University of Haifa, 1995.

Simons, Tal, and Paul Ingram. "Organization and Ideology: Kibbutzim and Hired Labor, 1951–1965." *Administrative Science Quarterly* (1997): 784–813.

———. "The Kibbutz for Organizational Behavior." *Research in Organizational Behavior* 22 (2000): 283–343.

Skinner, Burrhus Frederic. *Walden Two.* Hackett, 1974.

Sosis, Richard. "Religion and Intragroup Cooperation: Preliminary Results of a Comparative Analysis of Utopian Communities." *Cross-Cultural Research* 34.1 (2000): 70–87.

Sosis, Richard, and Eric R. Bressler. "Cooperation and Commune Longevity: A Test of the Costly Signaling Theory of Religion." *Cross-Cultural Research* 37.2 (2003): 211–239.

Sosis, Richard, and Bradley J. Ruffle. "Ideology, Religion, and the Evolution of Cooperation: Field Experiments on Israeli Kibbutzim." *Research in Economic Anthropology* 23.89 (2004): 117.

Spence, Michael. "Job Market Signaling." *Quarterly Journal of Economics* 87.3 (1973): 355–374.

Spiro, Melford E. *Kibbutz: Venture in Utopia.* Harvard University Press, [1956] 1970.

Spiro, Melford E., and Audrey G. Spiro. *Children of the Kibbutz.* Harvard University Press, 1958.

Stiglitz, Joseph E. "Peer Monitoring and Credit Markets." *World Bank Economic Review* 4.3 (1990): 351–366.

———. *The Price of Inequality: How Today's Divided Society Endangers Our Future.* W. W. Norton, 2012.

Svejnar, Jan. "Labor Markets in the Transitional Central and East European Economies." *Handbook of Labor Economics* 3 (1999): 2809–2857.

Talmon, Yonina. *Family and Community in the Kibbutz.* Harvard University Press, 1972.

Tannenbaum, Arnold Sherwood, Kavcic Bogdan, Rosner Menachem, and G. Weiser. "Hierarchy in Organizations." *Nursing Administration Quarterly* 1.4 (1977): 87–88.

Temin, Peter. "The American Business Elite in Historical Perspective." NBER Historical Paper no. 104 (1997a). https://economics.mit.edu/files/1232.

———. "Is It Kosher to Talk about Culture?" *Journal of Economic History* 57.2 (1997b): 267–87. doi:10.1017/S0022050700018441.

———. "Two Views of the British Industrial Revolution." *Journal of Economic History* 57.1 (1997c): 63–82. doi:10.1017/S0022050700017927.

Tannenbaum, Arnold, Bogan Kavcic, Menachem Rosner, Mino Vianello, and George Wiesner, *Hierarchy in Organizations.* Jossey-Bass, 1974.

Tenbrunsel, Ann E., and David M. Messick. "Sanctioning Systems, Decision Frames, and Cooperation." *Administrative Science Quarterly* 44.4 (1999): 684–707.

Townsend, Robert M. "Risk and Insurance in Village India." *Econometrica: Journal of the Econometric Society* (1994): 539–591.

———. "Financial Systems in Northern Thai Villages." *Quarterly Journal of Economics* (1995): 1011–1046.

Trumper, Ricardo. "Differences in Motivation towards Science Subjects among Kibbutz and Urban High School Students." *Interchange* 28.2–3 (1997): 205–218.

Tzahor, Zeev. *Hayinu Ha'tekuma.* Ha'kibbutz Ha'meauhad, 2015.

Tzur, Zeev. *The Kibbutz Meuchad in the Settlement of Eretz-Israel. Volume III: 1949–1960* [in Hebrew]. Yad Tabenkin, 1984.

Udry, Christopher. "Risk and Insurance in a Rural Credit Market: An Empirical Investigation in Northern Nigeria." *Review of Economic Studies* 61.3 (1994): 495–526.

Uriel, Leviatan. *Factors Connecting Kibbutz Children to Their Kibbutz and Reasons for Their Exodus.* Institute for Study and Research of the Kibbutz, University of Haifa, 1975.

———. *Negative Selection among Youngsters in the Kibbutz.* Institute for Study and Research of the Kibbutz, University of Haifa, 1996.

Uriel, Leviatan, and Menachem Rosner. "Belief in Values and Change in Values among Kibbutz Members." Institute for Study and Research of the Kibbutz, University of Haifa, 2000.

Varian, Hal R. "Monitoring Agents with Other Agents." *Journal of Institutional and Theoretical Economics (JITE)/Zeitschrift für die gesamte Staatswissenschaft* 146.1 (1990): 153–174.

Visler, Uri. *Twenty after Ten* [in Hebrew]. Oranit, 2001.

Ward, Benjamin. "The Firm in Illyria: Market Syndicalism." *American Economic Review* 48.4 (1958): 566–589.

Weiss, Andrew. "Human Capital vs. Signalling Explanations of Wages." *Journal of Economic Perspectives* 9.4 (1995): 133–154.

Weiss, Yoram. "The Formation and Dissolution of Families: Why Marry? Who Marries Whom? And What Happens upon Divorce." In *Handbook of Population and Family Economics*, ed. Mark Rosenzweig and Oded Stark, 1:81–123. Elsevier, 1997. http://public.econ.duke.edu/~vjh3/e195S/readings/Weiss.pdf.

Werwatz, Axel. "Semiparametric Analysis of German East-West Migration Intentions: Facts and Theory." *Journal of Applied Economics* 13 (1998): 525–541.

Willis, Robert J., and Sherwin Rosen. "Education and Self-Selection." *Journal of Political Economy* 87.5.2 (1979): S7–S36.

Wooldridge, Jeffrey M. *Introductory Econometrics: A Modern Approach.* Nelson Education, 2015.

Yamagishi, Toshio. "Exit from the Group as an Individualistic Solution to the Free Rider Problem in the United States and Japan." *Journal of Experimental Social Psychology* 24.6 (1988): 530–542.

Yanay, A. "The Moshav and Sharing [in Hebrew]." *Davar*, January 9, 1940: 10–20.

Yariv, Leeat. "The Israeli Kibbutz—An Industrial Revolution with Ideology." Working paper (2004).

Index

THE PRINCETON ECONOMIC HISTORY OF THE WESTERN WORLD
JOEL MOKYR, SERIES EDITOR

Lending to the Borrower from Hell: Debt, Taxes, and Default in the Age of Philip II by Mauricio Drelichman and Hans-Joachim Voth

Power to the People: Energy in Europe over the Last Five Centuries by Astrid Kander, Paolo Malanima, and Paul Warde

Fragile by Design: The Political Origins of Banking Crises and Scarce Credit by Charles W. Calomiris and Stephen H. Haber

The Son Also Rises: Surnames and the History of Social Mobility by Gregory Clark

Why Did Europe Conquer the World? by Philip T. Hoffman

The Rise and Fall of American Growth: The U.S. Standard of Living since the Civil War by Robert J. Gordon

Unequal Gains: American Growth and Inequality since the 1600s by Peter H. Lindert and Jeffrey G. Williamson

Brazil in Transition: Beliefs, Leadership, and Institutional Change by Lee J. Alston, Marcus André Melo, Bernardo Mueller, and Carlos Pereira

The Great Leveler: Violence and the History of Inequality from the Stone Age to the Twenty-First Century by Walter Scheidel

The Mystery of the Kibbutz: Egalitarian Principles in a Capitalist World by Ran Abramitzky